Ayurvedic Cooking for Health and Consciousness

Dr. Nibodhi Haas

Mata Amritanandamayi Center
San Ramon, California, United States

Ayurvedic Cooking for Health and Consciousness
by Dr. Nibodhi Haas

Published by:
Mata Amritanandamayi Center
P.O. Box 613
San Ramon, CA 94583
United States

Second edition January 2024

In India:
www.amritapuri.org
inform@amritapuri.org

In USA:
www.amma.org

In Europe:
www.amma-europe.org

The information in this book is for educational purposes only. It is not intended to diagnose, prevent or treat any disease or disorder.

Dedication

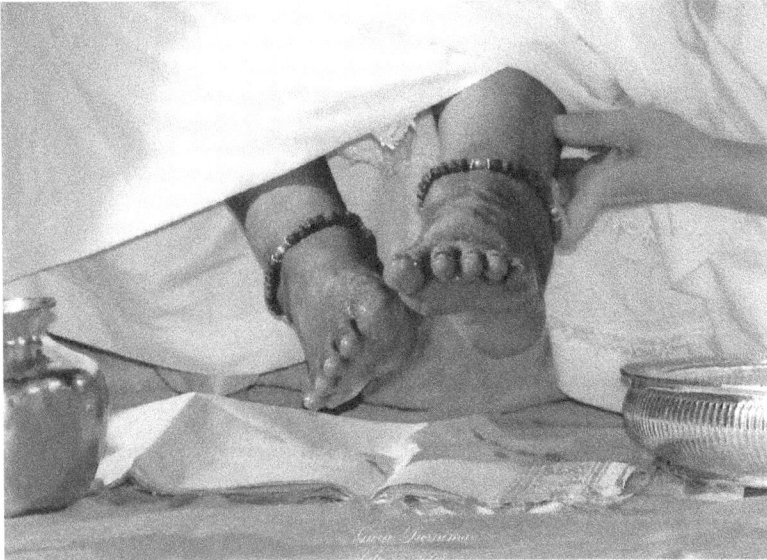

*May the tree of our life be firmly rooted in the soil of love.
Let good deeds be the leaves on that tree, may words of kindness
form its flowers and may peace be its fruits. – Amma*

With love and devotion I offer this book at the Lotus Feet of my
Beloved Sat Guru Sri Sri Mata Amritanandamayi Devi, the living
embodiment of Annapurna Devi.

Amma Amma taye
Akhilandesvari niye
Annapurnnesvari taye
Adi Parashakti niye

"O Mother, Mother, Divine Mother
Goddess of the Universe
Giver of food to all creatures
Thou art the Primal Supreme Power"

Contents

Contents

Sri Mata Amritanandamayi

The world should know that a life dedicated to selfless love and service is possible. Love is our true essence. Love has no limitations of caste, religion, race or nationality. We are all beads strung together on the same thread of love.

– Amma

Through Her extraordinary acts of love and self-sacrifice, Mata Amritanandamayi, or Amma (Mother) as She is known, has endeared Herself to millions of people around the world. Tenderly caressing everyone who comes to Her, holding them close to Her heart in a loving embrace, Amma shares boundless love with all - regardless of their beliefs, who they are or why they have come to Her. In this simple yet powerful way, Amma is transforming the lives of countless people, helping their hearts to blossom, one embrace at a time. In the past 37 years, Amma has physically hugged more than 30 million people from all parts of the world.

Her tireless spirit of dedication to uplifting others has inspired a vast network of charitable activities through which people are discovering the sense of peace that comes from selflessly serving others.

Amma's teachings are universal. Whenever She is asked about her religion, She replies that Her religion is love. She does not ask anyone to believe in God or to change their faith, but only to inquire into their own real nature, and to believe in themselves.

Among the wide array of charitable projects that have been inspired by Amma are free homes for the poor, disaster relief work, an orphanage, free food, medicine and pensions for destitute women, sponsored weddings for the poor, free legal aide, prisoner's welfare programs, extensive healthcare programs that include multi-specialty hospitals and medical camps which offer free healthcare to the poor, and many schools, colleges and educational programs.

For more information on Amma's charitable activities please visit,
www.amritapuri.org
www.amma.org
www.embracingtheworld.org

PART ONE

Ayurveda and Food

Chapter 1

Annapurna's Prasad

Panchabhuta Palini Annapurna
Pratyaksadevata Annapurna

"O, Goddess Annapurna, you rule the five elements:
space, air, fire, water and earth.
You are the visible deity in the manifestation of food."

The food that we eat, the water that we drink, the air that
we breathe, the land that we live on, who has given these?
The Mother who has no beginning or end has given these. The
eternally blissful Mother has given these.
O Mother Kali, immortal Goddess, Mother of the world.
Wisdom and art for the soul and mind, the notes of all music
sung by the tongue, who has given these?
The Mother seated on a lotus, the eternally blissful Mother,
She has given these. The sunrise and the shining moon which
illuminate the sky, the riches of harvest which are nourished by
the rain who has given these?
The Mother holding the sword and the trident in Her
hands, the eternally blissful one, She has given all of these.

– Unnum Sorum (English Translation),
Bhajanamritam Vol. 4

Who is Annapurna Devi?

The resolve of the Supreme Being is behind everything—
behind the blossoming of a flower, the chirping of a bird,
the movement of the wind, and the flames of a fire. It is the
power by which everything grows, the power that sustains
everything. That divine resolve is the underlying cause of the
birth, growth, and death of all living beings. It is the cause of
the entire creation. The Power of the Supreme Being sustains
the world. Without this Power, the world would cease to exist.

– Amma

Annapurna Devi is the Goddess of food and nourishment. She is the sustainer of life on Earth. Annapurna bestows the blessings of food and all forms of nourishment and love to all the beings in creation. In Sanskrit *'anna'* means food and *'purna'* means complete; together Annapurna signifies complete nourishment and love for all creation. In India it is believed that if those who worship and pray to Annapurna Devi, will never go hungry, and their lives will be filled with wholeness and love.

Annapurna is considered an incarnation of the Goddess Parvati, the wife of Shiva. In India, Lord Shiva (Divine Consciousness) is shown with his begging bowl (signifying humility), asking Annapurna to bless Him with *prasad* (blessed food or a blessed object) that gives the shakti (energy) to achieve knowledge and enlightenment. Annapurna is the Divine Mother aspect of nourishment and unconditional love. When food is cooked with a spirit of love, gratitude and sacredness, it becomes *prasad*.

What is Prasad?

Not a grain of the food we eat is made purely by our own
effort. What comes to us in the form of food is the toil of our

sisters and brothers, and the bounty of nature and God's compassion. Even if we have a million dollars, we still need food to satisfy our hunger. After all, we cannot eat dollars. So we should never eat anything without first praying with a feeling of humbleness and gratitude. Consider your food to be the Goddess Lakshmi (the Goddess of Prosperity), and receive it with devotion and reverence. Food is Brahman (the Supreme Being). Eat the food as God's prasad (blessed gift).

– Amma

Prasad is the grace of the deity given to the worshipper in the form of food after worship. *Prasad* is considered to be the grace given by God, a Sat Guru, a Saint or a Deity in the form of food. It is the food or any gift that has been first offered in worship or prayer or to a saint or deity. It also translates to that which is given by a holy person. The literal meaning is "grace." The *prasad* is permeated with the Guru's or Deity's blessing and grace.

Prasad is considered to be simultaneously a mental condition of generosity, giving and kindness as well as the food that is offered in love to God or the Guru and then consumed. One of the most vital components of all the world's religions and spiritual traditions is the perception of food as being sacred. All of the world religions and traditions have some sort of guidelines regarding the sacredness of food and the proper methods of preparation, cooking and offering the food to the divine.

The food we consume is the primary and most vital and tangible exchange we make with the environment. Food is in itself Mother Earth's *prasad*, Her communion. She toils tirelessly to provide for all Her children. Food is an affirmation of interconnection and unity with Mother Nature.

Amma says, "Nature is our first mother. She nurtures us throughout our lives. Our birth mother may allow us to sit on her lap for a couple of years, but Mother Nature patiently bears our weight our

19

entire life. Just as a child is obligated to his birth mother, we should feel an obligation and responsibility towards Mother Nature. If we forget this responsibility, it is equal to forgetting our own self. If we forget Nature, we will cease to exist, for to do so is to walk towards death. "

Growing and preparing food mindfully and with an attitude of gratitude and love is one step towards re- establishing our harmony with nature.

By praying before meals, we surrender and open to the grace of the universe that allows us to exist. Having gratitude for what we have also opens us up to the interconnectedness and sacredness of all life. Amma often says, "While enjoying creation, remember the Creator." Traditionally, mealtime is the time when the family or community comes together to pray and celebrate the creation.

Aum brahmarpanam brahma havir brahmagnau
brahmana hutam brahmaiva tena gantavyam
brahma karma samadhina

Brahman is the oblation. *Brahman* is the food offering.
By *Brahman* it is offered into the fire of *Brahman*.
Brahman is that which is to be attained.
By complete absorption (*samadhi*) in the action of *Brahman*.

Bhagavad Gita, 4:24

Chapter 2

What is Ayurveda?

Ayurveda is a holistic system of medicine originating from India. It has been practiced for over 6,000 years. It is the ancient wisdom of living in harmony with our Self and our environment. The knowledge of ayurveda offers spiritual insights for living happy, healthy and peaceful lives while seeking the ultimate goal of Self-Realization. It describes the nature of the universe with all its manifestations and how to bring ourselves into harmony with it. It is based on the understanding that the whole universe is interconnected and interdependent.

Ayurveda means "knowledge of life" as it is composed of the two words *"ayus"*, meaning life, and *"veda"*, meaning knowledge. In Ayurveda the process of *"ayus"* (life) is considered to be a combined state of body, senses, emotions, psyche/mind and soul. *"Ayus"* refers to all stages of life, including birth, childhood, adulthood, and the process of dying and going beyond death. Thus, Ayurveda has individualized applications for all stages in the journey of life.

Overall, Ayurveda aims to provide guidance regarding diet and lifestyle so that healthy people can stay healthy and those with health challenges can improve their health. Ayurveda is a set of practical, simple guidelines for creating long life and well-being. By applying these guidelines, one can remain in harmony with the environment, ward off disease and lead a balanced life.

There are several aspects to Ayurveda that make it a unique system of healing. It is based on a constitutional model and recommendations will often be different for each person. Ayurveda understands that there are energetic forces that influence nature and human beings. These forces are called the *tridoshas*. The universe is made up of five elements; ether, air, fire, water and earth. All of creation is a dance or a play of these five elements. They interact together to make up the three *doshas* (the bodily humors- *vata*, *pitta* and *kapha*). The word dosha actually means "impurity" or "imbalance". The doshas are responsible for biological, psychological and physiological processes in our body, mind and consciousness. When in harmony, they sustain balance within us.

Ayurveda has many branches of healing methods. Among these are the practice of herbal medicine and natural body care. Ayurvedic formulas and body care products are traditionally prepared without the use of chemicals, pesticides or herbicides. Using natural products is particularly valuable in the modern age where imbalance and sickness often arise due to an onslaught of chemicals and artificial ingredients. The main aims of Ayurveda are the prevention, treatment and cure of disease as well as the promotion of health on four levels: physical, mental, emotional and spiritual.

Today, Ayurveda is at the forefront of body- mind- spirit medicines. It has spread far beyond its traditional base and is gaining attention throughout the world. Ayurveda, with its understanding of life and consciousness, has much to offer individuals, communities and our Mother Earth as a whole. In the age in which we are living, there is a major decline of harmony. The environment and Mother Nature are in serious need of help. The planet and humanity are in a state of great imbalance. Resources are quickly diminishing while war and sickness are on the constant rise. Ayurveda offers a realistic and practical solution to many of these problems. By learning more about the principles of Ayurveda, and embracing Ayurvedic lifestyle and health care, we can support a more harmonious earth, while improving the health of our bodies and developing more positive relationships.

Ayurveda teaches us how to create balance in order to attain perfect health. As we better understand our body- mind- soul union we are able to extend the span of life and create longevity. The deeper purpose of this science, however, is to provide the opportunity for Self- Realization, to know the true Self, *Sat Cid Ananda* (truth consciousness bliss). We must recognize that our bodies and minds are constantly changing and that we live in a world of duality. Our task is to discover the veiled part of us that is always there – the knower, the seer, the infinite unchanging Source. With diligence, perseverance and patience we can wake up from *maya* (the dream/illusion) and become free of suffering. And as we awaken to our true Self, we create freedom in our body- mind- spirit. Ayurveda recognizes that we came to this earth to remember who we are and to follow that dharma. It advises us to learn to take care of this physical existence while seeking *moksha* (liberation). When harmony of body- mind-spirit is established we become free.

The Doshas

In the cave of the body is eternally set the one unborn. The earth is His body. (Though) moving within the earth, the earth knows Him not. The water is His body. (Though) moving within the water, the water knows Him not. The fire is His body. (Though) moving within the fire, the fire knows Him not. The air is His body. (Though) moving within the air, the air knows Him not. The ether is His body. (Though) moving within the ether, the ether knows Him not. The mind is His body. (Though) moving within the mind, the mind knows Him not. The intellect is His body. (Though) moving within the intellect, the intellect knows Him not. The ego is His body. (Though) moving within the ego, the ego knows Him not. The mind- stuff is His body. (Though) moving within the mind-stuff, the mind- stuff knows Him not. The unmanifest is His body. (Though) moving within the unmanifest, the unmanifest knows Him not. The imperishable is His body. (Though) moving within the imperishable, the imperishable knows Him not. The Death is His body. (Though) moving within Death,

*Death knows Him not. He, then, is the inner- self of all beings,
sinless, heaven- born, luminous, the Supreme Purusha.*

– Adhyatma Upanishad 1.1

The most fundamental principle of Ayurveda is the concept of *tridosha*, literally meaning the three humors/imbalances. All matter is composed of the *panchamahabhutas* (the five elements) that exhibit the properties of *prithvi* (earth), *jala* (water), *tejas* (fire), *vayu* (wind) and *akasha* (space).

The structural aspect of our body is made up of these five elements, but the functional aspect of the body is governed by three *doshas*. Ether and air constitute *vata*; fire, *pitta*; and water and earth, *kapha*. *Vata- pitta- kapha* is present in every cell, tissue and organ.

Vata regulates movement and governs the nervous system. *Pitta* is the principle of biotransformation and governs the metabolic processes in the body. *Kapha* is the principle of cohesion and functions through the body fluids. In each individual the three doshas manifest in different combinations and thereby determine the *prakriti* (the physiologic constitution) of an individual. *Vata, pitta and kapha* are present in each individual and express in each human being differently according to predominance of their *gunas* (different qualities.)

All of creation is a dance or a play of these five elements. The word *dosha* also means vitiated or out of balance. Such an imbalance occurs as a result of improper diet, seasonal changes, physical or mental stress, etc. Actually, imbalance in the *doshas* occur to protect the body from physiological harm. The *doshas* are responsible for biological, psychological and physio- pathological processes in our body, mind and consciousness. They can maintain homeostasis or wreak havoc in our lives when they are disturbed. Each individual in creation is a unique blend of the three *doshas*. No two beings identical. From the three doshas come the seven constitutional types; the three mono *dosha* types; (*vata, pitta* and *kapha)*; the three dual *dosha* types consisting of (*vata- pitta, vata- kapha* and *pitta- kapha*) and the *tridosha type*, meaning that they have a balance of all three (*vata- pitta- kapha*). When the *tridoshas* are balanced, the individual experiences health on all levels: mental, physical and spiritual. This balance means much more to creating harmony than the mere absence of disease.

There are generally two types of imbalances; natural and unnatural. Natural imbalances are due to time and age. *Vata, pitta*, and *kapha* increase and become predominant during different stages of one's life, during seasonal changes and during certain times of day. For example, *vata* is predominant during the latter part of one's life, during the fall season and during late afternoon, as well as during the last part of night and the last part of digestion. *Pitta* is predominant during middle age, during the summer season, at midday, at midnight and during the middle part of digestion. *Kapha* is predominant during childhood, during the spring season, in late morning, at the first part of evening and during the early part of digestion. These types of imbalances can be rectified through lifestyle adjustments.

Unnatural imbalances of the *doshas* can be caused by inappropriate diet and inappropriate lifestyle, physical, mental or emotional trauma, viruses, parasites, etc. While some of these circumstances are beyond our control, the type of lifestyle we live, the foods we eat, and our actions are within our control. By following the correct lifestyle regime for our *dosha* we can minimize unnatural disturbances. To learn to balance the *doshas*, one must first understand what causes the *doshas* to increase. The reason, according to the principles in Ayurveda, is: like increases like. Herein lays one of the true beauties of Ayurveda- its principles are so simple, basic, and natural.

The primary method of maintaining *doshic* balance is through diet. Food and diet play a vital role in our lives. May we learn to eat and live in harmony with nature and our Self.

Nature is a huge flower garden. The animals, birds, trees, plants and people are the garden's fully blossomed flowers of diverse colors. The beauty of this garden is complete only when all of these exist as a unity, thereby spreading the vibrations of love and oneness. Let us work together to prevent these diverse flowers from withering away, so that the garden may remain eternally beautiful.

– Amma

Chapter 3

The Ayurvedic Diet

The Ayurvedic physician begins the cure of disease
by arranging the diet that is to be followed by the patient.
Ayurvedic physicians rely so much on diet that it is declared
that all diseases can be cured by following dietary rules
carefully along with the proper herbal supplements;
but if a patient does not attend to his diet, a
hundred good medicines will not cure him.

– Charaka Samhita, 1.41

The Ayurvedic diet not only nourishes the body, but also restores balance of the *doshas*, which is essential for maintaining health. An Ayurvedic diet is based on the individual constitution. Medicine for one person may be poison for another. Each individual has unique dietary requirements; depending on one's *dosha*, or constitutional type, some foods can be beneficial and others should be avoided. When choosing what to eat, one must consider the season, weather, time of day and quality of food, as well as one's mental and emotional attitudes at the time of hunger.

When we ingest food, we participate in the creative process of Nature. Healthy food rejuvenates the cells for our stomach lining, skin, etc. How we eat also determines the effect of the food on our body. If we feel emotionally imbalanced when we eat, the food may disrupt the body's natural order. If we overeat or eat too quickly, the poorly digested end product predisposes us to ill health. Food intake should contribute to order and coherence in the body. It should help us stay balanced and boost our overall immunity. Ayurveda teaches that right diet is the foundation of healing. For maximum health and vitality, the ideal diet is one that balances the *doshas*.

Every food contains the five elements and the three *doshas* in different proportions. Consumption of each food will affect our elemental *doshic* balance in a positive or a negative way. If a person already has an element in sufficient quantity by inheritance, they must be careful not to ingest too much of that element, or an imbalance may manifest. Following an Ayurvedic diet is not difficult. For every food that will aggravate the *doshas,* there are plenty of alternative, beneficial and tasty foods. Wrong or destructive eating habits are a result of past conditioning by family, friends and society. By creating new dietary patterns, we can enhance all levels of wellbeing.

Dharmic Dining

Diet has a great deal of influence on our character. Children, you should take care to eat only simple, fresh, vegetarian food (sattvic food). The nature of the mind is determined by the subtle essence of the food we eat. Pure food creates a pure mind. Without forsaking the taste of the tongue, the taste of the heart cannot be enjoyed.

– Amma

Saving the lives of animals may save your own life. Extensive evidence shows that vegetarian and/or vegan diets are by far the healthiest diets. Scientific research is now proving that over- consumption of cholesterol and saturated fats found in animal products leads to heart disease and the numerous forms of cancers. The consumption of animal products also leads to obesity, diabetes, hypertension, arthritis, gout, kidney stones and a vast number of other diseases. In addition, modern- day factory farming methods use excessive amounts of hormones, antibiotics, chemical fertilizers and drugs to increase their output and profits. Commercial animal products contain high levels of herbicides and pesticides. When humans consume animal products, their bodies receive these poisons and become toxic.

Since the 1960s, scientists have suspected that a meat- based diet is related to the development of arteriosclerosis and heart disease. As early as 1961, a study published in the *Journal of the American Medical Association* reported, "Ninety to ninety- seven percent of heart disease can be prevented by a vegetarian diet." Since that time, several well- organized studies have scientifically shown that, after tobacco and alcohol, the consumption of meat is the greatest single cause of mortality in Europe, the United States, Australia and other affluent areas of the world.

The human body is unable to process and utilize excessive amounts of animal fat and cholesterol, which accumulate on the inner walls of the arteries, constrict the flow of blood to the heart resulting in high blood pressure, heart disease and strokes. Research during the past twenty years also strongly suggests a link between meat- eating and cancer of the colon, rectum, breast and uterus.

An article in *The Lancet*, a UK- based medical journal, reported, "People living in the areas with a high- recorded incidence of carcinoma of the colon tend to live on diets containing large amounts of fat and animal protein; whereas those who live in areas with a low incidence live on largely vegetarian diets with little fat or animal matter." Why do meat- eaters seem more prone to these diseases? Biologists and nutritionists have discovered that the human intestinal tract is simply not suited for digesting meat. Flesh- eating animals have short intestinal tracts, only three times the length of the body, to rapidly pass decaying toxin- producing meat out of the body. Since plant foods decay more slowly than meat, plant- eaters have intestines at least six times the length of the body. Humans have the long intestinal tract of a herbivore.

Another major concern with meat is that of chemical contamination. As soon as an animal is slaughtered, its flesh begins to putrefy, and after several days it turns a sickly gray- green. The meat industry masks this discoloration by adding nitrites, nitrates and other preservatives to give the meat a bright red color. But research now shows that most of these preservatives are carcinogenic. Further exacerbating the problem is the massive amount of chemicals fed to livestock[1].

Gary and Steven Null, in their book *Poisons in Your Body*, reveal to us something that ought to make anyone think twice before buying another steak or ham: "The animals are kept alive and fattened by continuous administration of tranquilizers, hormones, antibiotics and 2,700 other drugs. The process starts even before birth and continues long after death. Although these drugs will still be present in the meat when you eat it, the law does not require that they be listed on the package."

Many people feel concerned that they will not meet daily requirements for protein on a diet that excludes animal products. Dr. Paavo Airo, a leading authority on nutrition and natural biology, answers: "The official daily recommendation for protein has gone down from the 150 grams recommended 20 years ago to only 45 grams today. Why? Because reliable worldwide research has shown that we do not need so much protein, that the actual daily need is only 35 to 45 grams. Protein consumed in excess of the daily need is not only wasted, but actually can cause harm to the body, as it strains to digest it. In order to obtain 45 grams of protein a day from your diet you do not have to eat meat; you can get it easily from a 100 percent vegetarian diet of a variety of grains, lentils, nuts, vegetables and fruits."

Ahimsa Ahara (Non- Violent Diet)

Our task must be to free ourselves. By widening our circle of compassion to embrace all living creatures and

---

[1] The term "livestock" refers to all farmed animals, including pigs, birds raised for meat, egg- laying hens and dairy cows.

the whole of nature and its beauty. Nothing will benefit human health and increase our chances of survival for life on earth as much as the evolution to a vegetarian diet.

— Albert Einstein

Generally, Ayurveda encourages one to follow a *sattvic* diet. A Yogic diet promotes *sattva* (purity) and *ahimsa* (non- violence). Killing animals for food is not only violence to the animal, but is also harmful to the environment and all the hungry people in the world. It promotes ongoing suffering. A surprising amount of people don't consider fish to be meat. Fish are, in fact, animals and can feel suffering as they are being killed. When an animal is killed, it releases fear hormones and other toxins into its body, which the meat- eater later ingests and is absorbed into his or her body. That negative emotional vibration then enters the person's consciousness. In addition, meat is dead. It is completely void of *prana* (life force). As such, according to Ayurveda, meat creates *tamas* (dullness/dark-ness) in the mind and body.

In the ancient Indian epic *Mahabharata*, there are numerous statements against killing animals. "Who can be more cruel and selfish than he who augments his flesh by eating the flesh of innocent animals? Those who desire to possess good memory, beauty, long life with perfect health and physical, moral and spiritual strength should abstain from animal food." In addition to the concerns of health and ethics, the vegetarian and vegan lifestyle has a higher spiritual dimension that can help us develop our natural apprecia-tion and love of God.

To Be Vegan or Not to Be

A single commercial dairy cow produces about 120 pounds of wet manure per day, which is equivalent to the waste produced by 20–40 people. That means California's 1.4 million dairy cows produce as much waste as 28–56 million people.

– US Environmental Protection Agency Fall 2001

Traditional Ayurveda uses dairy products as both food and medicine. Unfortunately, in the current state of the world, the commercial dairy industry is a major contributor to planetary destruction and worldwide hunger. Unless needed for personal health requirements, it is becoming necessary to seriously consider minimizing or eliminating dairy consumption.

If commercialized factory farming and the use of meat were to be eliminated, humanity could restore the traditional methods of agriculture. In such systems, cows and goats are a vital part of the ecosystem and are honored with the love and respect they deserve. In this case, organic dairy farms could serve a vital role in preservation of the ecosystem.

The term vegan was coined by Donald Watson in 1944 and was defined as follows: "Veganism is a way of eating and living, which excludes all forms of exploitation of, and cruelty to, the animal kingdom, and includes a reverence for life. It applies to the practice of living on the products of the plant kingdom to the exclusion of flesh, fish, fowl, eggs, honey, animal milk and its derivatives, and encourages the use of alternatives for all commodities derived wholly or in part from animals."

Veganism is not necessarily about personal purity or separating oneself from society, but rather about applying an awareness of compassion and justice to our often unseen and ignored relationships with animals and Mother Nature.

Dietary Ecological Footprint

If anyone wants to save the planet, all they have to do is stop eating meat. That's the single most important thing you can do. It's staggering when you think about it. Vegetarianism takes care of so many things in one shot: ecology, famine, cruelty.

– *Paul McCartney*

Eating vegan is the most economically and environmentally sound diet. It is a method of preserving the human race. It is far more environmentally efficient than feeding the animals that are farmed for a meat- based diet. Veganism substantially reduces the wastes, pollution and deforestation caused by commercial animal farming.

The following findings were compiled from the executive summary of *Livestock's Long Shadow: Environmental Issues and Options*, a 2006 report published by the United Nations Food and Agriculture Organization:

"**Climate change:** With rising temperatures, rising sea levels, melting icecaps and glaciers, shifting ocean currents and weather patterns, climate change is the most serious challenge facing the human race. The livestock sector is a major player, responsible for 18 percent of greenhouse gas emissions measured in CO_2 equivalent. This is a higher share than transport. Livestock are also responsible for almost two- thirds (64 percent) of anthropogenic ammonia emissions, which contribute significantly to acid rain and acidification of ecosystems.

"**Water:** The livestock sector is a key player in increasing water use, accounting for over 8 percent of global human water use, mostly for the irrigation of feed crops. It is probably the largest sectoral source of water pollution, contributing to eutrophication, 'dead' zones in coastal areas, degradation of coral reefs, human health problems, emergence of antibiotic resistance and many others. The major sources of pollution are from animal wastes, antibiotics and hormones, chemicals from tanneries, fertilizers and pesticides used for feed crops and sediments from eroded pastures.

"**Environmental degradation:** Expansion of livestock production is a key factor in deforestation, especially in Latin America where the greatest amount of deforestation is occurring – 70 percent of previous forested land in the Amazon is now occupied by pastures, and feed crops cover a large part of the remainder.

"**Biodiversity:** Indeed, the livestock sector may well be the leading player in the reduction of biodiversity, since it is the major driver of deforestation, as well as one of the leading drivers of land degradation, pollution, climate change, overfishing, sedimentation of coastal areas and facilitation of invasions by alien species."

Global meat consumption remains on the rise. The United States and China, which contain 25 percent of the world's population, combine to consume 35 percent of the world's beef, over half of the world's poultry and 65 percent of the world's pork. Brazil and the European Union included, this group, roughly 33 percent of the world's population consumes more than 60 percent of the world's beef, more than 70 percent of the world's poultry and more than 80 percent of the world's pork.

Currently the planet is home to nearly 1 billion pigs, 1.3 billion cows, 1.8 billion sheep and goats and 13.5 billion chickens – more than two chickens for each man, woman and child on the planet. We have severely altered vast ecosystems and devoted massive amounts of resources to support the world's burgeoning livestock. These animals need to be fed. They need water to survive. If they are ranged, they need land. And these animals produce enormous quantities of waste.

The enormous ecological footprint of meat production is alarming. It ranges from forest destruction in Central and South America for ranching, to suppression of native predators and competitors in the United States. Nearly one- quarter of the world's meat, primarily beef and mutton, depends on a natural ecosystem – rangelands. As overgrazing becomes the norm in much of the world, rangelands are being pushed beyond their limits.

Seven kilograms of grain are required to produce one kilogram of beef; the conversion is 4- to- 1 for pork and 2- to- 1 for poultry. Each kilogram of meat represents several kilograms of grain that could be consumed directly by humans, not to mention the water and farmland required growing the grain. To put this in simplified terms, the beef in a hamburger represents enough wheat to produce five loaves of bread.

Huge amounts of food – not to mention the water and farmland required growing the food – can be freed up by modest reduction in meat production. For example, if the 670 million tons of the world's grain that is fed to livestock were reduced by 10 percent, the resulting grain could feed 225 million people or keep up with growth in the human population over the next three years.

If each American reduced his or her meat consumption by just 10 percent, roughly equivalent to eating one less dish of meat each week, enough grain would be saved to feed 50 million people – the number of people estimated to go hungry in the United States each day.

The massive waste produced by livestock threatens waterways worldwide. In the United States, where 130 times more animal manure is produced than human waste annually– 5 tons for every US citizen – animal waste is the principal source of water pollution. And livestock farms are getting larger throughout the world. Iowa Senator Tom Harkin's recent bill to reform livestock waste management estimates that one 50,000- acre hog farm under construction in Utah will produce more waste than the city of Los Angeles.

According to the Environmental Protection Agency, the world's livestock herds are the largest source of human- induced emissions of methane – a potent greenhouse gas contributing to climate change. For those concerned about our environment and the future of humanity, eliminating meat consumption is a fundamental necessity. Reducing and even better, eliminating consumption is a fundamental necessity.

Peter Singer stated, "Those who claim to care about the well-being of human beings and the preservation of our environment should become vegetarians. They would thereby increase the amount of grain available to feed people elsewhere, reduce pollution, save water and energy, and cease contributing to the clearing of forests... When non- vegetarians say that 'human problems come first,' I cannot help wondering what exactly it is that they are doing for human beings that compels them to continue to support the wasteful, ruthless exploitation of farm animals."

Environmental Facts About Eating Meat and Dairy

Humankind has not woven the web of life.
We are but one thread within it.
Whatever we do to the web, we do to ourselves.
All things are bound together.
All things connect.

– Chief Seattle, 1854

- Human population of United States: 243,000,000
- Number of human beings who could be fed by the grain and soybeans eaten by US livestock: 1,300,000,000
- Sacred food of Native Americans: Corn
- Percentage of corn grown in United States eaten by human beings: 20
- Percentage of corn grown in United States eaten by livestock: 80

- Percentage of oats grown in United States eaten by livestock: 95
- Percentage of protein wasted by cycling grain through livestock: 90
- Percentage of carbohydrate wasted by cycling grain through livestock: 99
- Percentage of dietary fiber wasted by cycling grain through livestock: 100
- How frequently a child dies of starvation: Every 2 seconds
- Pounds of potatoes that can be grown on 1 acre of land: 20,000
- Pounds of beef that can be produced on 1 acre of land: 165
- Percentage of US agricultural land used to produce beef: 56
- Pounds of grain and soybeans needed to produce 1 pound of feedlot beef: 16
- Pounds of protein (grain and vegetable) fed to chickens to produce 1 pound of protein as chicken flesh: 5 pounds
- Pounds of protein (grain and vegetable) fed to hogs to produce 1 pound of protein as hog flesh: 7.5 pounds
- Number of children who starve to death every day: 40,000
- Number of pure vegetarians who can be fed on the amount of land needed to feed 1 person consuming meat- based diet: 20
- Number of people who will starve to death this year: 60,000,000
- Number of people who could be adequately fed by the grain saved if Americans reduced their intake of meat by 10 percent: 60,000,000
- Historic cause of demise of many great civilizations: Topsoil depletion
- Percentage of original US topsoil lost to date: 75
- Amount of US cropland lost each year to soil erosion: 4,000,000 acres (size of Connecticut)
- Percentage of US topsoil loss directly associated with raising livestock: 85

- Number of acres of US forest which have been cleared to create cropland to produce a meat- centered diet: 260,000,000
- How often an acre of US trees disappears: Every 8 seconds
- Amount of trees spared per year by each individual who switches to a pure vegetarian diet: 1 acre
- A driving force behind the destruction of the tropical rainforests: Industrialized nations' dependency on meat
- Current rate of plant and animal species extinction due to destruction of tropical rainforests and related habitats: One thousand per year
- User of more than half of all water used for all purposes in Europe and North America: Livestock production
- Water needed to produce 1 pound of wheat: 25 gallons
- Water needed to produce 1 pound of meat: 2,500 gallons
- Cost of common hamburger meat if water used by meat industry was not subsidized by US taxpayers: $35/pound
- Current cost for pound of protein from wheat: $1.50
- Current cost for pound of protein from beefsteak: $15.40
- Cost for pound of protein from beefsteak if US taxpayers ceased subsidizing meat industry's use of water: $89
- Length of time world's petroleum reserves would last if all human beings ate meat- centered diet: 13 years
- Length of time world's petroleum reserves would last if all human beings ate vegetarian diet: 260 years
- Principal reason for US military intervention in Persian Gulf: Dependence on foreign oil
- Barrels of oil imported daily by US: 6,800,000
- Percentages of energy return (as food energy per fossil energy expended) of the most energy efficient farming of meat: 34.5%

- Percentages of energy return (as food energy per fossil energy expended) of the least energy efficient plant food: 328%
- Pounds of soybeans produced by the amount of fossil fuel needed to produce 1 pound of feedlot beef: 40
- Percentage of raw materials consumed in US for all current purposes for production used to produce current meat- centered diet: 33
- Percentage of raw materials consumed in US for all purposes needed to produce fully vegetarian diet: 2
- How frequently a heart attack strikes in US: Every 25 seconds
- How frequently a heart attack kills in US: Every 45 seconds
- Most common cause of death in US: Heart attack
- Risk of death from heart attack by average man: 50%
- Risk of death from heart attack by average vegetarian man: 15%
- Risk of death from heart attack by average pure vegan: 4%

Organic Food

Treat the earth well.
It was not given to you by your parents,
it was loaned to you by your children.
We do not inherit the Earth from our Ancestors,
we borrow it from our children.

– Native American Proverb

Many years ago, traditional agriculture used methods that respected nature's rhythms and utilized only substances that nature provided. The widespread use of chemical fertilizers, pesticides and herbicides in farming has upset nature's balance, threatening the wellbeing of not only of our external environment but also the internal environment of our bodies.

Many farmers, having noticed these detrimental effects, have returned to using systems of organic agriculture that increase soil fertility and restore harmony in nature. These systems include the addition of natural inputs such as compost, animal manures and biodynamic preparations, as well as appropriate crop rotations. Plants grown in well- balanced, fertile soils are strong and healthy. They resist disease and pests in the same way that healthy, happy humans resist disease.

Pesticides and chemical fertilizers are not necessary for farming. They are very destructive to soil life and to the health of plants. Residues of toxic pesticides and herbicides, when consumed through our food, accumulate in human body tissue. They also end up in waterways where their impact spreads widely throughout nature. Globally, more than five billion pounds of pesticides are used every year.

In addition to being completely free from all chemicals, certified organic food is never irradiated after harvest. To become certified organic, produce must be grown in soil that is tested to be free from heavy- metal contamination. There is scientific evidence showing that the accumulation of the above- mentioned toxic substances in our bodies can lead to a wide variety of health problems, including impaired immune function, cancer, allergies, auto- immune diseases, impaired fertility and birth defects. Annually, close to five million people worldwide suffer from symptoms of pesticide poisoning. Furthermore, 10,000 people actually die each year from these poisons. Studies have shown that the lifespan of conventional commercial farmers is significantly shorter than that of organic farmers.

Currently many non- organic, commercial foods are being genetically modified. Genetically Modified Organisms (GMO's) present a profound danger to humans as well as to the ecosystem. Many species of animals, such as the monarch butterfly, are becoming extinct due to GMO's. For vegetarians, GMO's pose another problem, as they are frequently spliced from animal DNA. It is hypothesized by many experts that GMO food will eventually even alter human DNA. As GMO's are a recent creation, their long- term effects are unknown.

In India and other developing nations, western-based GMO and pesticide companies are aggressively promoting extremely heavy use of chemicals for farming. This is leading to serious soil depletion and water contamination. Many insects are developing stronger resistance to pesticides, and sometimes even huge amounts of chemicals are ineffective. For this reason, many farmers have little or no yield, year after year. Having gone deeply in debt to these chemical companies, the farmers begin to feel hopeless. Unfortunately, large numbers of Indian farmers are committing suicide by drinking their pesticides. The societal reproductions of this are vast. Entire families die on a daily basis. Amma is deeply concerned about this issue and is working to help the farmers and their families. When we choose organic, non- GMO foods, we are doing our part to try to end this tragic situation.

Certified organic food has much higher nutritional content than non- organic food, so the consumer gets more for their money. Many people also find that organic food tastes better. Organic food has higher life force (*prana*) than commercial food. Thus, it is clear that eating organic food is a primary step towards personal and global health.

"Nature gives all of Her wealth to human beings. Just as Nature is dedicated to helping us, we too should be dedicated to helping Nature. Only then can the harmony between Nature and humanity be preserved." - Amma

Food as Prayer

*Not a grain of the food we eat is made purely by our own
effort. What comes to us in the form of food is the toil of our
sisters and brothers, and the bounty of Nature and God's
compassion. Even if we have a million dollars, we still need
food to satisfy our hunger. After all, we cannot eat dollars.
So we should never eat anything without first praying with
a feeling of humility and gratitude. Consider your food to
be the Goddess Lakshmi (the Goddess of Prosperity), and
receive it with devotion and reverence. Food is Brahman (the
Supreme Being). Eat the food as God's prasad (blessed gift).*

– Amma

We hear Amma constantly reminding us that we are not the body;
we are the *Atma* (the Supreme Self). So why bother to eat health-
fully? These bodies are vehicles for transporting the soul. Just as we
would not put gasoline mixed with dirt into our cars, we should
consider what type of fuel we put into our soul's vehicle.

At the same time, we should be careful not to take our diets
so seriously that we lose a sense of gratitude for whatever food we
receive. Our thoughts and attitude during meals affect our digestion and assimilation as much as the food itself. We are blessed if
we have enough food to provide energy and nutrition. Millions of
people do not have this.

We have infinite potential to heal ourselves and the planet by
making some simple changes to our dietary habits. Amma again and
again reflects to us that Mother Nature is very much out of balance.
She constantly encourages us to help restore that balance. By Her
Grace, may we each find that balance internally and externally.

Chapter 4

Food as Medicine

Ayurvedic Eating Principles

The following are general principles that should be followed when eating. They will assure optimum digestion, assimilation and elimination. Never overeat. Half the stomach should be for food, a quarter for liquid, and the remaining portion for the movement of air. The less food you eat, the more mental control you will have. Do not sleep or meditate immediately after eating; if you do, you won't be able to digest the food properly. Always mentally repeat your mantra while you eat. This will purify the food and your mind at the same time.

– Amma

- Eat to about three quarters of your capacity. Do not leave the table very hungry or very full.

- Avoid taking a meal until the previous meal has been digested. Allow approximately 3- 6 hours between meals.

- Eat in a settled and quiet atmosphere. Do not work, read or watch TV during meal times. Avoid talking, if possible. Eat slowly with awareness.

- Choose foods by balancing physical attributes. In general, the diet should be balanced to include all six tastes. Specific recommendations may be found in this book about eating according to your constitutional type. In Ayurveda, foods are classified into six

43

tastes: sweet, sour, salty, bitter, pungent and astringent. Ayurvedic practitioners recommend including all of these six tastes in each meal. Each taste has a balancing ability; including some of each minimizes cravings and balances the appetite and digestion. The average North American and European diet tends to have too much of the sweet, sour and salty tastes and not enough of the bitter, pungent and astringent tastes.

- Choose foods that are *sattvic*.
- Choose whole, fresh, in- season, local foods.
- Yogurt, cheese, cottage cheese and buttermilk should be avoided at night.
- Follow food- combining laws (listed later in this chapter).
- It is best not to cook with honey, as it becomes *ama* (toxic) when cooked.
- Take a few minutes to sit quietly after a meal before returning to activity.
- Follow proper eating rules: have breakfast between 7- 9 am, lunch 10- 2 pm and dinner at 4- 6 pm.
- Wash face, hands and feet before meals. Dine in an isolated, neat and clean place. The environment should be pleasant. The eater should be in a comfortable seated position.
- Eat only food prepared by loving hands in a loving way. This method of food preparation increases the vitality- giving quality of the food.
- Chew food until it is an even consistency before swallowing.
- Hard items should be consumed in the beginning of the meal, followed by soft foods and subsequently liquids.
- Do not drink cold drinks just prior to or while eating. Also do not drink large quantities of liquids during meals, for this habit weakens digestion. A few sips of warm water are alright with meals.

- Heavy substances, such as rich desserts, after meals are contra-indicated and should be avoided.
- Consumption of excessively hot food leads to weakness. Cold and dry foods lead to delayed digestion.
- No traveling, vigorous exercising or sexual intercourse within one hour after a meal. This will impede digestion. Walking (10- 20 min.) after a meal can help digestion.
- Avoid meals when thirsty and water while hungry.
- Avoid meals immediately after exertion.
- Avoid meals when there is not an appetite.
- Don't suppress the appetite as it leads to body pain, anorexia, lassitude, vertigo and general debility.
- Don't suppress thirst as it leads to general debility, giddiness and heart diseases.

Eating Habits That Decrease Health

- Overeating
- Eating when not hungry
- Emotional eating
- Drinking juice or excess water during food
- Drinking chilled water at any time
- Eating when constipated or emotionally imbalanced
- Eating at the wrong time of day
- Eating too many heavy foods or too few light foods
- Snacking on anything except fruit in between meals
- Eating incompatible food combinations

6 Types of Nutritional Imbalances

1. <u>Quantitative Deficiency</u>: under- nutrition due to insufficient food

2. <u>Quantitative Excess</u>: excessive amounts of any food or water; taken at the wrong time; food not appropriate for constitution

3. <u>Qualitative Deficiency</u>: wrong food combining, which results in malnutrition; toxic conditions and lack of essential nutrients.

4. <u>Qualitative Excess</u>: emotional overeating; eating rich and high fatty foods, fried foods, wrong foods for constitution

5. <u>*Ama-* Producing</u>: eating foods and improper food combining that leads to toxemia and other digestive disorders. This also means eating foods with toxins such as pesticides, herbacides, hormones and antibiotics.

6. <u>*Prakruti* Disturbing</u>: eating foods not appropriate for one's constitution, which may lead to reduced *agni* (digestive fire), immunity and disease

These six factors lead to depletion of *agni* (digestive fire) and the build up of *ama* (toxins).

Sattvic Eating

*The person who always eats (sattvic) wholesome food enjoys a
regular lifestyle, remains unattached to the objects of the senses,
gives and forgives,
loves truth and serves others without disease.*

— Vagbhata Sutrasthana

*When food is pure, the mind is pure; this creates an
oasis for awakening and provides an awakening that
affects every level of our health (body- mind- spirit).*

— Chandogya Upanishad

Ayurveda encourages eating a *sattvic* diet. The *rishis* gave criteria for eating a *sattvic* diet. It includes:

1. Foods grown in healthy fertile soil

2. Foods that are attractive in appearance (ripe and bountiful)

3. Foods that are protected from animals (insects, parasites, worms and harmful bacteria)

   Modern Day Additions:

1. Foods grown without pesticides, herbicides, fungicides, chemical fertilizers, hormones, antibiotics, irradiation, gmo's, etc. This includes foods grown without harming the earth or its inhabitants (*ahimsa*).

2. Food should be whole, fresh and unprocessed/unrefined, not canned, preserved, etc. No chemical additives.

3. Animal food is dead, it is *tamasic* and there is no life force. *Sattvic* foods contains between 75- 90 percent water content. It nourishes life. It is filled with *prana*, with energy.

Sattvic foods prevent free- radicals because they are rich amounts in anti- oxidants. Free radicals destroy enzymes, amino acids and impede other cellular elements and activities. Free radicals are electron-deficient molecules that are produced from oxygen and heated fats or oils in the body. This destroys health. Health and longevity are dependent on hydration and anti- oxidant- rich foods.

Food Combining Principles

Don't Eat:	with:
Beans:	fruit, cheese, eggs, fish, milk, meat, yogurt
Eggs:	fruit, beans, cheese, fish, kichari, **milk**, meat, yogurt
Grains:	fruit
Fruit:	**any other food**, except dates/almonds are okay
Honey & ghee:	by equal weight: avoid 1tsp honey/3tsp ghee (1tsp.each is okay)
Hot Drinks:	mangoes, cheese, fish, meat, starch, yogurt
Lemon:	cucumbers, milk, tomatoes, yogurt
Melons:	**any other food, including other melons**
Milk:	**bananas**, cherries, melons, sour fruit, bread, fish, kichari, meat
Nightshades:	cucumbes, dairy products
Radishes:	bananas, raisins, milk
Tapioca/Yogurt:	fruit, cheese, eggs, fish, hot drinks, meat, **milk**, nightshades

Foods in **Bold** are the most difficult combinations and cause ama (toxins) to build within the body.

Ayurveda recommends that honey should not be cooked. When cooked, honey becomes sticky glue that adheres to mucous membranes and clogs the gross and subtle channels, producing toxins. Raw honey is considered to be *amrita* (nectar).

Ayurveda also finds that pasteurized and/or homogenized dairy causes *ama* (toxins), and is not recommended. Additionally, Ayurveda recommends consuming raw dairy and avoiding dairy produced in factory farms that use hormones, antibiotics and steroids.

The Six Tastes

The six tastes are based on the actual taste in the mouth. Each taste has unique therapeutic properties. This applies to food, herbs and minerals. Balancing the tastes according to *dosha* is the key to health. Each of the tastes is governed by two of the five elements and either increases or decreases the *doshas*.

1. **Sweet:** made of earth and water, decreases *vata* and *pitta* and increases *kapha*

   • Sweet fruits: figs, grapes, oranges, dates, pears

   • Most legumes: beans, lentils, peas

   • Most grains: wheat, rice, corn, barley, most bread

   • Milk and sweet milk products: cream, ghee, butter

   • Sugar in any form: white, refined sugars, all natural sugars, honey

   • Certain cooked vegetables: starchy tubers like potato, carrot, sweet potato, beet root

2. **Sour:** made of earth and fire, decreases *vata* and increases *pitta* and *kapha*.

   • Sour milk products: yogurt, cheese, whey, sour cream.

   • Sour fruits: lemon, sour oranges

   • Fermented substances: soy sauce, vinegar, wine, sour cabbage.

3. **Salty:** made of water and fire, decreases *vata* while increasing *pitta* and *kapha*

   • Salt: sea salt, rock salt

   • Salty food: seaweed, pickles, chips

4. **Pungent:** made of fire and air, decreases *kapha* and increases *pitta* and *vata*

- Few vegetables: radish, onion
- Spices: ginger, cumin, garlic, chili, mustard seeds, black pepper

5. **Bitter:** made of air and ether, decreases *pitta* and *kapha* and increases *vata*

   - Certain fruits: olives, grapefruits
   - Vegetables: eggplant, chicory, bitter gourd, zucchini
   - Green leafy vegetables: spinach, green cabbage, brussel sprouts
   - Certain spices: fenugreek, turmeric

6. **Astringent:** made of air and earth, decreases *pitta and kapha*

   - Sweetener: honey
   - Nuts: walnuts, hazelnuts, cashews
   - Legumes: beans, lentils
   - Vegetables: sprouts, lettuce, rhubarb, green leafy vegetables, most raw vegetables.
   - Fruits: persimmons, berries, pomegranates, apple (to some degree) and unripe fruits.

Vata is decreased by sweet, sour and salty tastes. It is also decreased by foods that are heavy, oily and hot. *Vata* is increased by pungent, bitter and astringent tastes, as well as foods that are light, dry and cold. *Pitta* is decreased by sweet, bitter and astringent tastes in cold, heavy and oily foods. *Pitta* is increased by pungent, sour and salty tastes as well as foods that are hot, light and dry. *Kapha* is decreased by pungent, bitter and astringent tastes in foods that are light, dry and warm. *Kapha* is increased by sweet, sour and salty tastes, as well as foods that are heavy, oily and cold.

Chapter 5

Eating According to Your Constitution

The benefits of eating according to your constitution

- better health, youthfulness and memory
- more energy, endurance and strength
- a gradual decrease in existing imbalances
- prevention of imbalances
- greater ability to handle stress and anxiety
- saves money in the long run improved sleep and concentration
- better digestion, metabolism and elimination healthier skin, complexion and slowed down aging
- healthier progeny
- stronger immune system
- weight loss or gain (depending on what you need) and better sense of control
- improved meditation and yoga practice
- overall happy life

Vata- Pacifying Diet

Usually *vata* season lasts from November through February (the cold, windy and dry season). This will vary depending on location.

51

During this time of year, the qualities of *vata* increase naturally. Thus, one should take extra care during this time to take lots of warm food and drinks, including heavier and oilier foods. Eat more of the sweet, sour and salty tastes. Avoid dry or cold food or drinks. Eat less pungent, bitter and astringent tastes overall.

General Guidelines:

- Sip hot water (with lemon or lime) during the meal to aid digestion
- Favor cooked, warm, unctuous foods
- Favor fresh, organic, locally grown foods
- Eat a variety of foods having all six tastes; vary the foods you eat
- Eat more sweet fruit; even eat fruit as a whole meal

Favor foods that are:

- Oily, heavy, warm, sweet, sour and salty
- Beverages: almond milk, aloe vera juice, apple cider, apricot, berry (not cranberry), carrot, cherry, grain beverages, grape, lemonade, mango, miso broth, orange, papaya, peach, pineapple, rice milk, sour juices, vegetable bouillon
- Herbal teas: ajwain, bancha, chamomile, clove, comfrey, elderflower, eucalyptus, fennel, fenugreek, ginger (fresh), hawthorne, juniper berry, lavender, lemon grass, licorice, marshmallow, oat straw, orange peel, pennyroyal, peppermint, rosehips, saffron, sage, sarsaparilla, sassafras, spearmint
- Condiments: mango chutney, dulse, gomasio, hijiki, kelp, ketchup, lemon, lime, lime pickle, mango pickle, mayonnaise, mustard, pickles, scallions, seaweed, vinegar
- Dairy: raw butter, ghee, whole milk – (cow and goat) avoid homogenized dairy products, lassi, cheese (cow and goat), fresh homemade paneer, cottage cheese, sour cream, yogurt

- Food Supplements: aloe vera juice, bee pollen, amino acids, calcium, copper, iron, magnesium, royal jelly, spirulina, blue- green algae, vitamins A, B, B_{12}, C, D, E, and EFAs (essential fatty acids found in cold pressed oils from hemp seed, evening primrose, black currant seed, flax seed, borage oils)
- Fruits: ripe, sweet cooked apples, applesauce, avocado, banana, berries, cherries, coconut, dates, figs, grapefruit, grapes, kiwi, lemon, lime, mango, melons, oranges, papaya, peaches, pineapple, plums, raisins and prunes (soaked in water), pomegranate, rhubarb, strawberries, tamarind
- Grains: whole amaranth, cooked oats, quinoa, seitan (wheat meat), sprouted wheat bread (Essene style), white basmati rice
- Legumes: mung beans, mung dal, tur dal, urad dal. NOTE: all legumes should be well-cooked
- Nuts: almonds (soaked and peeled, without skins are best), black walnuts, brazil nuts, cashews, charole, coconut, filberts, hazelnuts, macadamia nuts, peanuts, pecans, pine nuts, pistachios, walnuts
- Oils: ghee, olive oil, sunflower oil are especially good and most other oils are generally okay; use coconut, sesame and avocado oils externally only
- Seeds: hemp, chia, flax, halva, pumpkin, sesame, sunflower
- Spices: ajwain, allspice, almond extract, anise, asafoetida (hing), basil, bay leaf, cardamom, cayenne, cinnamon, clove, green coriander leaf, cumin, dill, fennel, fenugreek, garlic, ginger (especially fresh), marjoram, mint, mustard seeds, nutmeg, orange peel, oregano, paprika, parsley, peppermint, pippali, poppy seed, rosemary, saffron, savory, spearmint, star anise, tarragon, thyme, turmeric, vanilla, wintergreen
- Sweeteners: stevia, barley malt, fructose, fruit juice concentrates, honey, jaggery, molasses, rice syrup, raw sugar or sucanat, turbinado sugar
- Vegetables: daikon radish, red cabbage and dark leafy greens

(cooked, in moderation), asparagus, beets, carrots, cilantro, cucumber, fennel (anise), garlic, green beans, green chilies, leeks, mustard greens, okra, olives (black), onions (cooked), parsnips, peas (cooked), sweet potato, pumpkin, radish (cooked), rutabaga, summer squash, taro root, watercress, zucchini

Reduce foods that are

- Dry, light, cold, spicy, bitter, astringent
- Beans: reduce intake of beans; all of which increase *vata*, except mung dal
- Vegetables: raw vegetables, cruciferous vegetables, frozen, canned, fried foods, leftovers
- Spices: minimize use of chilies and red pepper
- Grains: reduce intake of rye, oats, corn, millet, barley
- Fruits: dry, light, or astringent fruits such as apples, pears, berries and dried fruits
- Dairy: homogenized dairy, milk (also yogurt) with fruits, vegetables
- Also avoid all iced/cold foods and drinks

Pitta- Pacifying Diet

Pitta season lasts from July through October (hot and dry). Again, this will vary depending on location. During this time favor foods and drinks that are cooling. Eat foods of sweet, bitter and astringent tastes. Also include fresh, sweet fruits and vegetables that grow during the *pitta* season. Eat less pungent, sour and salty foods. Avoid yogurt, cheese, tomatoes, vinegars and hot spices, as they all greatly increase *pitta*.

Favor foods that are

- Oily, heavy, cold, bitter, sweet and astringent
- Beverages: almond milk in moderation, aloe vera juice, apple, apricot, berry, cherry, grain beverages, grape, mango, mixed vegetable, peach, pear, pomegranate, prune, rice milk
- Herbal Beverages: alfalfa, bancha, barley, blackberry, borage, burdock, catnip, chamomile, chicory, comfrey, dandelion, fennel, ginger (fresh), hibiscus, hops, jasmine, kukicha, lavender, lemon balm, lemon grass, licorice, marshmallow, nettle, oat straw, passion flower, peppermint, raspberry, red clover, sarsaparilla, spearmint, strawberry, violet, wintergreen yarrow
- Condiments: chutney, coriander leaves, sprouts
- Dairy: raw is best, butter (unsalted), cow or goat cheese (soft/unsalted), ghee, whole cow and goat milk (avoid homogenized), lassi
- Food Supplements: aloe vera juice, barley green brewer's yeast, calcium, magnesium, zinc, spirulina, blue- green algae, vitamins D, E and EFAs (essential fatty acids found in cold pressed oils from hemp seed, evening primrose, black currant seed, flax seed, borage), whey protein powder as a protein supplement (isolate only, do not use concentrates or hydrolyzed as the protein have been denatured)
- Fruits (ripe and sweet): apples, applesauce, apricots, avocado, berries (sweet), cherries, coconut, dates, figs, grapes (red and purple), mango, melons, oranges, papaya, pears, pineapple, plums, pomegranate, prunes, raisins, watermelon
- Grains: whole amaranth and barley, cereals, oat bran, oats, whole grain pasta, spelt, sprouted wheat bread (Essene style), tapioca, white basmati rice
- Legumes: adzuki beans, black beans, black- eyed peas, chickpeas (garbanzo beans), kidney beans, lentils (brown and red), lima beans, mung beans, mung dal, navy beans, peas (dried), pinto

beans, cheese, flour, split peas, white beans. *NOTE*: All legumes should be well- cooked
- Nuts: almonds (soaked and peeled), coconut
- Oils: ghee, olive, coconut
- Seeds: hemp, flax, pumpkin, sunflower
- Spices: basil (fresh), black pepper and fresh ginger (in moderation), cardamom, cinnamon, coriander, cumin, dill, fennel, mint, peppermint, spearmint, saffron, turmeric, rock salt
- Sweeteners: stevia, barley malt, agave, fruit juice, maple syrup, rice syrup, raw sugar or sucanat, rock crystal sugar, honey
- Vegetables: artichoke, asparagus, beets, bitter melon, broccoli, brussels sprouts, cabbage, carrots, cauliflower, celery, cilantro, cucumber, dandelion greens, fennel, green beans, kale, dark leafy greens, leeks, okra, olives (black), onion (cooked), parsley, parsnip, peas, sweet potatoes, prickly pear leaves, pumpkin, rutabaga, spaghetti squash, sprouts, squash (winter and summer), taro root, wheat grass sprouts, zucchini

Reduce foods that are

- Dry, light, warm, salty, spicy and sour
- Oils: Reduce the use of almond, corn and sesame oils
- Spices: Avoid chili and cayenne
- Grains: Brown rice, corn, millet and rye intake should be reduced
- Fruits: Reduce intake of sour fruits, such as olives, under- ripe pineapples or persimmons, sour oranges and unripe bananas
- Sweeteners: Large quantities of honey should be avoided
- Dairy: Reduce use of cheese, yogurt, sour cream and cultured buttermilk

Kapha Pacifying Diet

Kapha season lasts from March through June (wet and cool/rainy season) depending on location. During *kapha* season eat foods that are light and oily. Take warm food and drinks. Eat foods that are pungent, bitter and astringent in taste. Avoid foods that are sweet, salty and sour flavored.

Favor foods that are

- Dry, warm, light, spicy, bitter, astringent
- Beverages: Aloe vera juice, apple cider, apricot, berry, black tea (spiced), carrot, cherry, cranberry, grain beverages, grape, mango, peach, pear, pomegranate, prune
- Herbal Teas: Alfalfa, bancha, barley, blackberry, burdock, chamomile, chicory, clove, cinnamon, dandelion, fenugreek, ginger, hibiscus, jasmine, juniper berry, kukicha, lavender, lemon balm lemon grass, nettle, passion flower, peppermint, raspberry, red clover, sassafras, spearmint, strawberry, wintergreen, yarrow, yerba mate
- Condiments: Black pepper, chili peppers, chutney, coriander leaves, dulse, hijiki, horseradish, lemon, mustard (without vinegar), scallions, seaweed, sprouts
- Dairy: (Raw and organic) cottage cheese (from skimmed goat milk), lassi, non- fat goat milk. Avoid homogenized dairy
- Food Supplements: Aloe vera juice, amino acids, barley green, bee pollen, brewer's yeast, copper, calcium, iron, magnesium, zinc, royal jelly, spirulina, blue- green algae, vitamins A, B, B_{12}, C, D, E, EFAs (essential fatty acids found in cold- pressed oils from hemp seed, evening primrose, black currant seed, flax seed and borage oils), whey protein powder (isolate only/ not concentrated or hydrolyzed)
- Fruits: Apples, applesauce, apricots, berries, cherries, cranberries,

dried fruit, guava, peaches, pears, persimmon, pomegranate, prunes, raisins

- Grains: (whole) barley, buckwheat, cereals (dry or puffed), corn (organic, non- GMO), couscous, granola, millet, muesli, oat bran, oats, polenta, quinoa, rye, basmati rice, spelt, sprouted wheat bread (Essene style), tapioca, wheat bran

- Legumes: adzuki beans, black beans, black- eyed peas, chick peas, lentils (red and brown), lima beans, mung beans, mung dal, navy beans, peas (dried), pinto beans, split peas, tur dal, white beans. All should be well- cooked with spices

- Oils: ghee, mustard oil

- Seeds: hemp, chia, flax, popcorn, pumpkin seeds, sunflower seeds

- Spices: all spices except salt, especially fresh ginger

- Sweeteners: stevia, fruit juice, honey

- Vegetables: artichoke, asparagus, beet greens, beets, bitter melon, broccoli, cabbage, carrots, cauliflower, celery, cilantro, corn, daikon radish, dandelion greens, eggplant, fennel (anise), garlic, green beans, green chilies, horseradish, kale, kohlrabi, leafy greens (lettuces), leeks, mushrooms, mustard greens, okra, onions, parsley, peas, hot peppers, prickly pear, rutabaga, spinach, sprouts, summer squash, cooked tomatoes, turnip greens, turnips, watercress, wheat grass

Reduce foods that are

- Oily, cold, heavy, sweet, sour
- Nuts: avoid nuts
- Oils: Avoid large amounts of any oil
- Vegetables: Cucumbers, sweet potatoes, okra, tomatoes
- Spices: Avoid salt, salty foods (pickles, chips)
- Grains: Wheat, rice

- Fruits: Avoid grapes, bananas, figs, oranges, limes, coconuts, mangoes, pineapples, dates, melons
- Sweeteners: Avoid sugar products
- Dairy: Yogurt, cream, ice cream, sour cream, cheese, butter, any excess of whole milk are not recommend

Chapter 6

Healing Properties of Food

All the world seeks food. It is the life source of all beings.
Clarity, longevity, intelligence, happiness, contentment,
strength and knowledge are all rooted in food.

— *Charaka Samhita*

Vitamins and Minerals

Traditionally, Ayurveda encourages that we receive our vitamins and minerals through whole foods as they are the easiest to digest, absorb and assimilate. Each of the *doshas* has specific requirements for different vitamins and minerals. Likewise, each of the *doshas* can have different types of deficiencies. Our food has become greatly depleted due to GMOs, chemicals, artificial fertilizers and pesticides. Sometimes it becomes necessary to supplement our diet with additional vitamins and minerals. *Vata dosha* tends to be deficient in vitamins A, B, C, D and E and lacks the minerals zinc and calcium. *Pitta* tends to lack vitamins A, B and K and the minerals calcium and iron. *Kapha* tend to be deficient in vitamins B6 and D. This section takes a deeper look at the different vitamins and minerals and explains their effects on our bodies. Additionally, it explores where in the diet one can naturally find these different vitamins and minerals.

Vitamins and minerals are organic substances that are found in foods. The human body needs them to work properly, so it can grow and develop properly. They assist in maintaining the natural balance in the body. Each vitamin and mineral has a unique role to play, and creates a different effect on the *doshas*.

There are essentially two types of vitamins: fat soluble and water soluble. When we consume foods that contain fat- soluble vitamins, the vitamins are stored in the fat tissues of the body and in the liver. They are stored in the body fat until they are required. They may stay in the body for a few days to up to six months. When they are needed, special carriers in the body take them to where they are needed. Vitamins A, D, E and K are all fat- soluble vitamins.

Water-soluble vitamins don't get stored in the body. They travel through the bloodstream for immediate use. Whatever the body doesn't need or use comes out through urination.

Water soluble vitamins need regular replacement. These vitamins includes vitamin C, B vitamins — B1 (thiamin), B2 (riboflavin), niacin, B6 (pyridoxine), folic acid, B12 (cobalamine), biotin and pantothenic acid. The body is capable of numerous functions. However, one thing it can't do is produce vitamins. That's where food is necessary. The body gets the vitamins and minerals it needs from the foods we eat. Different foods contain different vitamins and minerals. This is why it is so important to eat a wide variety of foods.

Vitamins

Vitamin A (Retinol/Beta Carotene): Vitamin A can be found in dark green vegetables, especially dark leafy greens (kale, collards, spinach), orange and yellow fruit and vegetables (oranges, mango, squash, zucchini, carrots, pumpkin, sweet potatoes and yams, corn) soy, lentils, garbanzo beans and milk. If there is a vitamin A deficiency, there may be dry, rough, itchy or flaky skin; wrinkles, pimples, premature ageing, dandruff, splitting of the nails, poor vision, burning and itchy eyes and thickening of the cornea. Vitmain A is necessary for vision, skin, bone and tooth growth, immunity and reproduction. Deficiency is usually found in *vata* and *pitta* doshas.

Vitamin B1 (Thiamin): B1 can be found in rice, most whole grains, blackstrap molasses, most green vegetables, beans, soy and nuts. B1 is necessary for proper nerve function and energy through carbohydrate metabolism. Deficiencies may lead to poor memory and weak digestion, fatigue, edema, ear problems, irritability, heart weakness and nervous system disorders. B1 deficiencies can affect all three *doshas*.

Vitamin B2 (Riboflavin): B2 is usually found in millet, rye, corn, soy, whole wheat, wheat germ, beans, milk, avocado, legumes, nuts, blackstrap molasses and dark leafy greens. B2 is necessary for the digestion and assimilation of protein, carbohydrates and fats. It also helps to maintain healthy and vibrant skin. Deficiencies can lead to itchy, burning and bloodshot eyes, sensitivity to light, premature hair loss or graying and liver disorders. Deficiency of B2 is more common in *pitta* but can affect *vata* and *kapha* as well.

Vitamin B3 (Niacin): B3 is found in wheat, buckwheat, barley, rice, black beans, sesame seeds, nuts, all dark leafy greens and milk. B3 assists the body processing protein and fats, helps to maintain a strong nervous system, skin and digestion. Deficiencies often lead to fatigue and a lack of mental energy and clarity, nervous system weaknesses, poor digestion and low circulation. Deficiencies usually affect *vata* and *pitta*, but as with all B vitamins, *kapha* can be affected as well.

Vitamin B5 (Pantothenic acid): B5 is found in all whole grains, corn, beans, and cruciferous vegetables such as broccoli, cabbage and cauliflower. B5 is necessary for digestion of nutrients and making new red blood cells. A lack of B5 can lead to weakened immunity, an increase in colds and infections, poor digestion and malabsorption, nerve and heart disease, muscle cramping, allergies and hair loss. Deficiencies mostly affect *vata*, secondarily *pitta*.

Vitamin B6 (Pyridoxine): B6 is found in dark leafy greens, seaweeds, peas, sunflower seeds, walnuts, nutritional yeast, brown rice, buckwheat, beans, carrots and bananas. B6 assists with the assimilation and use of protein and fats; supports the nervous and immune systems; helps blood carry oxygen to the bodily tissues; helps break down copper and iron; prevents one type of anemia and helps maintain normal blood sugar levels. A lack of B6 may contribute to weakened digestion and immunity, hormonal imbalances, eczema, anemia, edema, PMS and a dry, itchy and flaky scalp (dandruff). B6 deficiencies primarily affect *kapha* and secondarily *pitta*.

Vitamin B 7 (Biotin): Biotin is mostly found in fruits and helps with the synthesis of fats, glycogen and amino acids. Biotin is also found in whole grains, nuts, seeds, soy beans, legumes and cauliflower. A lack of biotin in the diet can lead to anemia, depression, weak metabolism, premature balding, adrenal weakness, testosterone disorders and dermatitis. However, deficiencies are rare. It mostly affects *vata* and *pitta*.

Vitamin B9 (Folic acid): B9 is found mostly in seaweeds, microalgae, whole grains, green and root vegetables, sprouted grains, soy, yogurt, wheat and nutritional yeast. Deficiency leads to anemia, gastrointestinal disorders and premature hair loss. It mostly affects *pitta*.

Vitamin B12 (Cyanocobalamin): B12 is found in asparagus, spirulina, chlorella, blue- green algae, miso, tempeh, nutritional yeast, seaweeds (hiziki, wakame, arame, kombu, dulse, etc.), alfalfa sprouts, unpasteurized fermented foods, peas, okra, potatoes, carrots, parsley, cabbage, kale, chard, mustard greens, beans, mung dhal, tomatoes, bell peppers, all berries, citrus fruit, melons, mangos, papaya, pineapple, all grains and dairy products. B12 is needed for the production and maintenance of red blood cells, healthy nervous system, DNA, RNA and general immunity. A deficiency can lead to nervous system disorders, emotional disorders, depression, lethargy, premature ageing, fatigue, insomnia, stress, immune weakness, weak memory and a lack of concentration. B12 deficiencies tend to manifest in *vata*.

Vitamin C (Ascorbic acid): Vitamin C is in all citrus fruits, berries, sprouts, tomatoes, bell peppers, cabbage, broccoli, kiwi, parsley, potatoes and amaranth. Vitamin C is necessary for proper immune function, digestion and assimilation. It aids in the assimilation of iron. It contains antioxidants that protect against cell damage, boost the immune system and form collagen in the body. Deficiency can lead to adrenal weakness, bleeding gums, poor immunity, heavy metal poisoning and obesity. A lack of Vitamin C generally affects *vata doshas*.

Vitamin D (Calciferol): The best source of vitamin D is sunshine! In food, vitamin D is found in flax, dark leafy greens, super greens and chlorophyll-rich foods, sunflower sprouts and whole grains. Vitamin D deficiencies can lead to weakened bones, teeth, hair and nails. A lack of vitamin D is usually associated with *vata* and *kapha dosha*.

Vitamin E (Alpha- tocopherol): Vitamin E is in whole grains, dark leafy greens, nuts, seeds, dairy products (especially butter and milk), blackstrap molasses, sprouted wheat, sprouts, asparagus and wheat germ. A lack of vitamin E can lead to weakness of the muscles, heart and nerves, weak adrenals and dry skin. A deficiency in vitamin E mostly affects *vata dosha*.

Vitamin F: Vitamin F is mostly found in oils such as linseed, olive oil, flaxseed, soy and safflower oils. Most vegetable and seed oils contain vitamin F. A deficiency can lead to all types of heart disorders, cholesterol imbalance, female reproductive disorders, skin problems, candidiasis, hypertension, cystic fibrosis, liver disorders, malformed *dhatus* (seven layers of bodily tissue) and various intestinal disorders. A lack of vitamin F can affect any *dosha*.

Vitamin K: Vitamin K is found in milk products, blackstrap molasses, green vegetables and eggs. A lack of vitamin K may contribute to, balding, bleeding, lack of energy, general weakness and premature ageing. A deficiency usually affects *pitta* but *vata* and *kapha* can be affected as well.

Vitamin P (Bioflavonoid): Found in the white inner skin of citrus fruits, as well as in peppers, buckwheat and black currants. It has excellent immune enhancing properties. Deficiencies of vitamin P are extremely rare.

Minerals

Note: All mineral deficiencies tend to be related to the *vata dosha*, secondarily to *pitta*.

Calcium: Calcium is found in dairy products, seaweeds, dark leafy greens, nuts and seeds, dried fruit, asparagus, artichokes, avocados, broccoli, tofu and oats. Deficiencies can lead to weakened hair, bones, and nails, PMS, insomnia, muscle cramping, rickets in children and osteoporosis. An excess of calcium can lead to kidney stones, calcium deposits and constipation. Exess calcium can also hinder the assimilation of iron.

Chromium: Chromium primarily is found in whole grains and cereals. It is also prevalent in red grapes, bananas, apples, potatoes, green beans and oranges. While humans only require trace amounts, it is necessary for regulating blood sugar levels. A deficiency can lead to hypoglycemia, arteriosclerosis, memory loss and lack of mental concentration, physical and mental fatigue and retarded or delayed growth (especially within the muscles).

Copper: Copper is found in seaweeds (especially kelp), legumes, grains, avocados, raisins, seeds and nuts. It is necessary to help assimilate iron and other minerals. It is required for skin and hair pigmentation. It is also required to make new red blood cells, connective tissue and nerve fibers. A deficiency can lead to loss of hair color and poor skin tone. A deficiency contributes to osteoporosis, osteoarthritis and rheumatoid arthritis, cardiovascular disease, colon cancer and chronic conditions involving bone, connective tissue, heart and blood vessels.

Iodine: Iodine is found in iodized salt, seaweeds and beans. It is necessary for the production of the thyroid hormone and regulation of the thyroid glands. A weakness can lead to thyroid disorders, temperature fluctuation, weight fluctuation and dryness of the skin.

Iron: Iron is found in dark leafy greens, seaweeds, parsley, whole grains, potatoes, fruit, raisins, beans and legumes, seeds, nuts and milk. It is essential for red blood cell production and the production of enzymes. A lack of iron can lead to numerous weaknesses such as anemia, low vitality, mental lethargy, weak hair and nails, headaches, low immunity, dry and itchy skin and shortness of breath.

Magnesium: Magnesium is found in whole grains, corn, soy, nuts, seeds, lentils, dried fruits, seaweeds, dark leafy greens, apples, celery, citrus fruits, dairy products and apricots. It helps regulate the heart rhythm, muscle and nerve function, and bone growth and development. A deficiency may lead to weak bones and muscles, low vitality, stress, muscle twitching, cramping and cardiac arrhythmia.

Manganese: Manganese is found in whole grains, green vegetables, seaweeds, nuts and seeds, avocados and blueberries. It plays an important role in the formation of bones. It also helps with enzyme production and proper brain function. A deficiency can lead to bone loss, pain or weakness, poor memory and diabetes.

Molybdenum: Molybdenum is found in legumes, grains and dark leafy greens. It primarily helps with enzyme production and digestion. It helps to regulate the storage and use of iron. Deficiencies are extremely rare.

Phosphorus: Phosphorus is found in whole grains, beans, nuts, seeds, berries, oranges, peaches, lime, cantaloupe, kiwi, dairy and all vegetables. Along with calcium, it helps build bones, teeth and hair. It is also required for proper muscle and nerve function. A deficiency can lead to bone loss, muscle weakness, fatigue and anorexia. Deficiencies are rare. Taking too much can prevent calcium absorption.

Potassium: Potassium is found in bananas, all vegetables, sesame seeds, sunflower and pumpkin seeds, dairy products, dried fruits and oranges. Potassium helps regulate proper nerve and muscle functioning. It is important in maintaining normal fluid balances. It also helps to control blood pressure and reduces risk of kidney stones. A deficiency can lead to depression, arrhythmia, indigestion, dry skin and general weakness.

Selenium: Selenium is found in whole grains, beans, tomatoes, broccoli and brazil nuts. It is required for proper thyroid function and acts aa an antioxidant by protecting the cells from being damaged.

While deficiency is very rare, if this occurs, it can lead to premature aging, loss of skin elasticity and dry, flaky hair.

Silica: Silica is found in horsetail herb, whole grains, sea salt, apricots, strawberries, celery, cucumbers, carrots and seaweeds. It is a vital part of bone production and youthfulness due to its anti- ageing properties. Silica is also one of the most important constituents of the body's connective tissue, including cartilage, vascular lining, tendons and ligaments. It is found in the thymus gland, the adrenal glands, the liver, the spleen and pancreas, and in considerable quantity in the hair. It functions as a cross- linker, providing strength, flexibility, and resilience to collagen and elastic connective tissues. It also plays a vital part in the integrity of the bones, arterial walls, skin, teeth, gums, hair and nails, and has been used to alleviate eczema and psoriasis. While deficiency is rare, it can lead to weak bones, nails and hair.

Sodium Chloride (salt): Sodium chloride is found primarily in salt and seaweeds. The body needs sodium chloride for metabolism. It also helps to maintain the body's pH balance. The amount of salt in the blood is carefully controlled by the kidneys. While deficiencies are rare, they do happen. A sodium chloride deficiency can occur due to diarrhea, vomiting or excessive sweating. It can lead to metabolic alkalosis (body fluids becoming too alkaline), low fluid volume and urinary potassium loss. This can cause further problems in ph balance.

Sulphur: Sulphur is found in nuts, cabbages, apples, cranberries, legumes, onions and beans. Sulphur is in every cell of the human body, with its greatest concentration in hair, skin and nails. It is often referred to as the "beauty mineral" or the "healing mineral" because of its ability to promote circulation and decrease inflammation. Bathing in sulphur pools has been practiced since the beginning of humanity and is linked to longevity. Deficiencies may lead to weak nails and skin problems, like eczema and scaly skin.

Zinc: Zinc is found in pumpkin and sunflower seeds, whole grains, soybeans and most vegetables. Zinc supports the immune and nervous systems. It plays a vital role in digestion, as it is in over 100 different enzymes. A deficiency can lead to delayed sexual development, retardation in growth and development, loss of smell and taste and slow healing capabilities. Additionally it can contribute to night blindness and other eye weaknesses, regular colds and infections, hair loss and bone weakness.

Fruit

In general, most fruit is sweet or sour. The overall *virya* (energy) of fruit is cooling with a sweet *vipaka* (post- digestive effect). Most fruit decreases *vata* and *pitta* while increasing *kapha*, though there are some exceptions. Fruit is one of the most *sattvic* of all foods. Its *prabhava* (special actions) are: relieves thirst, refrigerant, alterative, laxative, mildly cleansing and nurturing. It is mostly made up of the water element and secondarily ether. It helps to build *rasa* (plasma) and creates a lightness and purity in the body. It is best not to combine fruits with any other type of food. It is also best to eat fruit that is local to the area and in season. Here is a detailed list of fruits and their properties.

Apples

Dosha: reduce *pitta* and *kapha*, increase *vata*
Rasa (Taste): sweet, astringent, sour
Virya (Energy): cooling
Vipaka (Post-digestive effect): sweet
Prabhava (Special actions): astringent, alterative, refrigerant

Nutritional Information:

- Provide good amounts of soluble and insoluble fiber, potassium, boron, and some vitamin C and beta- carotene (contained in the peel)
- Make a good tooth cleaner and a gum stimulator because are fibrous, juicy and non- sticky

- Alkalizing
- Contain high amounts of pectin, which promotes healthy intestinal flora and cleanses the liver and gall bladder
- Have nutritive effect on spleen, pancreas and stomach
- Reduce blood cholesterol levels, especially "bad" LDL type cholesterol
- Counter constipation and diarrhoea. The specific combination of fibre types and fruit acids in apples is probably responsible for their well-known ability to prevent and treat constipation. The liquid- gelling pectin and the natural antiviral properties in apples explain their traditional use for diarrhea
- Traditionally used for arthritis, rheumatism and gout. Apples improve digestion and help remove unwanted substances from the body, and these benefits help counter joint problems. The fruit acids in apples are what improve digestion. The antioxidant effect of the flavonoid quercetin also aids in the relief of joint problems
- Defends against other problems such as diarrhea, intestinal bleeding, ulcers, bleeding gums, gall bladder illnesses, inflammations, high cholesterol, auto- intoxication, enteritis, *pitta* and *kapha* types of arthritis, herpes, acidity, heavy metal toxicity, radiation exposure, gastritis, colitis, blood pressure irregularities, viruses and other forms of infections

Apricots

Dosha: reduce *vata* and *kapha*, mildly increase *pitta* in excess, relatively *tridoshic*
Rasa (Taste): sweet, sour
Virya (Energy): warming
Vipaka (Post-digestive effect): sweet
Prabhava (Special actions): relieve thirst, alleviate cough

Nutritional Information:

- Exceptionally high in beta- carotene. Fresh, dark orange apricots are one of the fruits highest in beta- carotene
- Help lower risk of heart disease, stroke, cataracts and some forms of cancer (due to their high beta- carotene content)
- Dried apricots are high in iron and potassium and prevent and treat constipation
- Help prevent and treat high blood pressure (due to high potassium content)
- High in soluble fibre
- Regulate blood sugar levels. Studies have shown that a high intake of soluble fibre regulates blood sugar and energy levels by slowing digestion. Thus apricots also increase stamina
- Prevent iron deficiency and lower cholesterol levels
- Alleviate fever and cough, and counter muscle and nerve disorders

Avocado

Dosha: reduce *vata* and *pitta*, increase *kapha*
Rasa (Taste): astringent
Virya (Energy): cooling
Vipaka (Post-digestive effect): sweet
Prabhava (Special actions): tonic, nutritive, demulcent, emollient

Nutritional Information:

- One of the most important foods in combating cancer
- High in vitamin E, monounsaturated fat, and calories
- Excellent source of protein, vitamin A, C, B- complex, chlorophyll, carbohydrates, calcium, phosphorus, copper and cobalt
- Have inositol in trace amounts
- Contain fourteen minerals that regulate body functions and stimulate growth

- Their fatty substances have a beneficial effect on the body, while animal fats have a harmful effect
- Combat the negative effects of a meat- based diet
- Help with digestive issues, general debility, rheumatism, skin infections, and kidney problems
- Normalize liver and pancreas functions
- Aid in red blood cell regeneration and prevent anemia

Bananas

Dosha: ripe bananas reduce *vata*, increase *pitta* and *kapha*; unripe bananas decrease *pitta* and *kapha* and increase *vata*
Rasa (Taste): sweet, sour (ripe), astringent (unripe)
Virya (Energy): heating
Vipaka (Post-digestive effect): sour
Prabhava (Special actions): astringent, refrigerant, laxative, nutritive, tonic, strengthening, aphrodisiac

Nutritional Information:
- Excellent source of potassium, ripe or unripe
- Very ripe bananas are high in sugars
- The sugars in bananas are easily assimilated and contain numerous vitamins and minerals
- Rich in starch and soluble fibre
- Easy to digest for young children and infants
- Bananas are good in reduction diets because they satisfy the appetite and have minimal fat content
- Regulate high blood pressure
- Good source of natural energy. The starch in less ripe bananas resists digestion. This effect, coupled with the soluble fibre in bananas, provides for longer- lasting energy than most sweet foods, and thus increases stamina

- Strengthen the *mamsa dhatu* (muscle tissue)
- Less ripe bananas counter constipation, ripe bananas relieve diarrhea
- Ripe bananas may raise mood and alleviate insomnia. Bananas are known to have a soothing effect by stimulating serotonin levels. Also known to stimulate serotonin's precursor, tryptophan and vitamin B6
- Ripe bananas are a quickly absorbable carbohydrate
- Treat anaemia and hypertension. Protect against stroke
- Bananas feed the natural acidophilus bacteria in the bowel
- Help treat the following problems: nervous system disorders, alcoholism, heart disorders, hypoglycaemia and reproductive system weaknesses

Berries (applicable to all berries)

Dosha: decrease *pitta* and *kapha*, slightly increase *vata* (especially dry)
Rasa (Taste): sweet, astringent (unripe), sour
Virya (Energy): cooling
Vipaka (Post-digestive effect): pungent
Prabhava (Special actions): refrigerant, astringent, alterative, hemostatic

Nutritional Information:

- Contain significant amounts of iron, copper, manganese, zinc, molybdenum, cobalt, nickel, chromium, fluorine, selenium, silicon, rubidium, aluminium, boron, bromine and others trace minerals
- Have ellagic acid, a substance that greatly reduces the risk of cancer
- Are excellent sources of antioxidants
- Unripe berries counter excessive urination, nocturnal emissions, sexual debility and diarrhea. Berries also act as a liver tonic
- **Blueberries** are *tridoshic* in moderation. They regulate sugar

metabolism and reduce fevers. They are great for the liver and gallbladder, and support eye function. Their antibacterial properties treat urinary tract infections. They are an excellent source of elastagen and collagen. They help with elasticity, thus assisting in joint and tissue repair. They contain a large source of immune enhancing antioxidants. The tannins contained in blueberries are anti- viral.

- **Blackberries** are excellent for building the blood and help treat diarrhea and dysentery. They are excellent against goiter, cholera, hemorrhoids, and insect bites or stings. They can be applied topically to stop burning or stinging. Blackberry bark is especially great when applied topically. The seeds can be used to treat diabetes, sugar in the urine, dehydration or excessive thirst.

- **Raspberries** are relatively *tridoshic*. They can be used during pregnancy to prevent morning sickness. They are excellent for bleeding gums and excess menstruation. Ripe, they are a great blood and liver cleanser. Rasperry leaves make a great tea for women. Raspberries ease the pain of childbirth by increasing the muscle tone of the uterine wall. They are a great source of vitamins A and C, and contain some minerals and B vitamins. Raspberries are very good for obesity, gout, arthritis, diabetes, constipation, hypertension, kidney stones and gallstones. However, eating more than a couple of handfuls of raspberries in one sitting can cause nausea or vomiting. They should never be eaten with dairy products.

Cranberries

Dosha: reduce *pitta*, increase *vata* and *kapha*
Rasa (Taste): sour, astringent
Virya (Energy): heating
Vipaka (Post-digestive effect): pungent
Prabhava (Special actions): diuretic, alterative, hemostatic

Nutritional Information:

- Help prevent and treat urinary tract infections and cystitis in women. The most common type of bacteria that causes urinary tract infections, *Escherichia coli (E.Coli)*, grows and multiplies by attaching itself to the walls of the intestines and bladder. An unidentified substance in cranberries blocks this adhesion
- Contain high amounts of vitamin C
- Assist the body's natural immune defenses
- Have antifungal and antiviral properties
- Prevent kidney stones; small amounts of cranberries lower calcium levels in the urine, preventing stone formation
- Combat *pitta* disorders such as skin rashes, toxic blood, burning urination and edema

Strawberries

Dosha: decrease *vata* and *pitta*, increase *kapha* in excess
Rasa (Taste): sweet, sour
Virya (Energy): cooling, heating (sour)
Vipaka (Post-digestive effect): sweet, pungent (sour)
Prabhava (Special actions): refrigerant, mild astringent, alterative, antacid (tea), relieves thirst.

Nutritional Information:

- One of the richest sources of potassium and vitamins A and C. Have a high content of sodium and easily assimilated iron. Contain some B- vitamins, minerals and fiber
- Alkalize the body due to their high sodium content
- Possess potent anti- oxidant and anti- viral properties
- Breakdown liver toxins and have a tonic effect on the spleen and pancreas
- Are a traditional diuretic and have an excellent healing effect on the kidneys

- Also used to relieve rheumatism, gout, hypertension, constipation and numerous other *vata-* related disorders
- Like raspberries, strawberries protect against viruses
- Fight and prevent cancer, protect against damage to the DNA, treat herpes simplex, counter skin disorders and relieve many other *pitta-* related disorders
- Best to eat alone (can be eaten with other fruit, but still best on their own)

Cherries

Dosha: reduce *vata*, increase *kapha*, increase *pitta* in excess. Sour cherries decrease *vata* and *kapha* while increasing *pitta*
Rasa (Taste): sweet, sour
Virya (Energy): heating
Vipaka (Post-digestive effect): sweet, sour
Prabhava (Special actions): alterative

Nutritional Information:

- High in iron. Also contain vitamin A, phosphorus, potassium and calcium
- Alkalize and mineralize the blood
- Known for their ability to neutralize acids
- Alleviate gout by reducing acid levels (especially uric acid)
- Due to their very high iron content, black cherry varieties are an excellent treatment for anemia
- Act as a great heart tonic, blood builder, and general detoxifier. Combat mental fatigue, insomnia, stress, liver disorders, eye problems, paralysis, arthritis, rheumatism and obesity. Regulate menstrual flow and the causes of PMS
- Tonic for the spleen, pancreas, liver and kidneys

Dates

Dosha: reduce *vata* and *pitta*, increase *kapha*. Dry dates slightly increase *vata*
Rasa (Taste): sweet
Virya (Energy): cooling
Vipaka (Post-digestive effect): sweet
Prabhava (Special actions): nutritive tonic, aphrodisiac, strengthens *dhatus* (tissues), demulcent, laxative, refrigerant, febrifuge

Nutritional Information:

* Rich in calcium, magnesium, phosphorous and potassium
* Provide a useful amount of fibre and iron
* Combined with almonds, they make a superb *ojas* tonic
* With ghee or milk, they are an excellent restorative, especially for the nervous system
* Combat febrile disease
* Rejuvenate the reproductive system and strengthen *ojas*
* Fight all types of injuries and *vata* diseases, especially wasting disorders
* Clean and unclog both the liver and digestive system. Dates are a very effective laxative. They also fight infections and intestinal fevers
* Due to their high phosphorous content, they are excellent in treating cerebral debility

Figs

Dosha: reduce *vata* and *pitta*, increase *kapha*. Dry figs increase *vata*
Rasa (Taste): sweet, astringent
Virya (Energy): cooling
Vipaka (Post-digestive effect): sweet
Prabhava (Special actions): nutritive, demulcent, laxative, antibacterial

Nutritional Information:

- Are very nutritious; the high mineral content of figs closely resembles that of human breast milk
- Dried figs are also highly nutritious as they are high in fibre, potassium, calcium, magnesium and iron
- Contain rich amounts of protein, calcium, iron, phosphorus, manganese, sodium, potassium and vitamins A, B1 and B2. Black figs are exceptionally high in potassium
- Possess a high content of glucose, one of the most easily assimilated fruit sugars
- Have high levels of pectin
- Help maintain intestinal regularity due to laxative and diuretic properties
- Are anti- oxidizing, highly digestible and blood cleansing
- Strengthen the gums, teeth, and tongue
- Have more calcium than milk and more potassium than bananas
- Stimulate the immune system
- Excellent for the liver and provide a large amount of energy to the body
- Counter urinary tract infections, gallstones, chronic coughs and lung, liver and kidney weaknesses. Effective against hemorrhoids and bowel cancer. Help eliminate roundworms
- Medical research shows that eating figs shrinks cancerous tumours

Grapefruit

Dosha: decrease *vata*, increase *pitta*, balanced for *kapha*
Rasa (Taste): sour
Virya (Energy): hot
Vipaka (Post-digestive effect): sour
Prabhava (Special actions): stimulant, expectorant, astringent

Nutritional Information:

- Are low in calories and an excellent source of flavinoids, water-soluble fibres, potassium, vitamin C and folic acid. Rich in citric acid
- Like other citrus fruit, they have anticancer properties
- Grapefruit pectin helps to lower cholesterol
- Eating a grapefruit one to two hours before sleep counteracts insomnia
- Help prevent constipation and stone formation
- Excellent aid in reducing fevers from colds and flu
- Good for any hardening of the body tissue, such as that of the liver and arteries
- Reduce phlegm in the morning time
- Help with weight loss as they aid in the digestion of fats and sugars
- Stimulate liver and pancreatic enzyme secretions
- Assist with numerous cardiovascular disorders
- The seeds are a natural antibiotic and help destroy candida

Grape (red, purple and black varieties)

Dosha: reduce *vata*, increase *pitta* and *kapha*
Rasa (Taste): sweet
Virya (Energy): cooling
Vipaka (Post-digestive effect): sweet

Grapes (green varieties)

Dosha: reduce *vata*, increase *pitta* and *kapha*
Rasa (Taste): sour
Virya (Energy): hot
Vipaka (Post-digestive effect): pungent
Prabhava (Special actions): refrigerant, thirst alleviation, nutritive, demulcent, diuretic, haemostatic, laxative, aphrodisiac

Nutritional Infrmation:

- Have large amounts of vitamins A, C and P (bioflavonoid), and contain the trace element selenium
- High water and magnesium content
- Dark grapes are very high in iron
- In Ayurvedic medicine, grapes are considered one of the most medicinal fruits and are used in hundreds of herbal remedies
- Reduce tumours because they purify the blood and invigorate the immune system
- Rejuvenative for *vata* type diseases and bodies that have become severely wasted and weakened by cancer or immune deficiencies
- Grape sugar is easily digested and assimilated by the blood
- Serve as a tonic by mineralizing and rejuvenating all the *dhatus* (tissues)
- Promote the action of the bowel, cleanse the liver and aid kidney function
- Due to high water content, they help eliminate hardened deposits throughout the body
- Soothe the nervous system
- Excellent blood builders due to their high content of iron
- Provide immediate relief from dehydration, fever, burning and painful breathing
- Excellent for *vata* type wasting disease and *pitta* type inflammatory diseases
- Excellent restorative for eyesight
- Counteract acidity, gout, and edema
- Prevent gum disease and tooth decay
- Cleanse all the *dhatus* and glands
- Raisins have similar effects and are less aggravating to *kapha*, but do aggravate *vata* in excess

Lemons

Dosha: decrease *vata* and *kapha*, increase *pitta.*
Rasa (Taste): sour, astringent
Virya (Energy): hot
Vipaka (Post-digestive effect): sour
Prabhava (Special actions): laxative, expectorant, astringent, refrigerant, relieves thirst, digestive stimulant

Nutritional Information:

- One of the most alkaline foods available
- Very rich in citric acid and vitamin C
- Contain phosphorus, magnesium, potassium, sodium and calcium
- Are antiseptic and protect against stomach and intestinal fermentation
- Can destroy all microbes and create germ invulnerability
- Excellent for fevers and flus as well as in the cleansing processes of the body
- Assist in assimilating and retaining calcium in the body
- Great for all types of lung illnesses
- With salt, lemons counteract sunstroke
- Stop bleeding of the lungs, kidneys, uterus and GI tract
- As an immune stimulant, they are great for scurvy, fevers, and infections
- Wonderful against all types of *vata* diseases such as rheumatism, arthritis, gout, neuralgia
- Can treat many *pitta* disorders such as toxic blood, skin troubles, inflammation, liver and pancreas problems, gallstones

Mangos

Dosha: decrease *vata* and *pitta*, increase *kapha*

Rasa (Taste): sweet
Virya (Energy): hot
Vipaka (Post-digestive effect): sweet
Prabhava (Special actions): demulcent, diuretic, astringent, refrigerant
Unripe mangos are sour and astringent and will decrease *kapha* while increasing *pitta*.
Unripe, the *virya* becomes cooling and the *vipaka* becomes pungent. If they are made into chutney, then the *virya* remains the same as with a ripe mango, due to the sugar.

Nutritional Information:

- Rich in vitamins A and C
- Good source of vitamin E and iron
- Ripe mangoes are rich in beta- carotene
- Have excellent nutritive qualities
- Help to combat stomach acidity
- Counteract nervous or weak digestion, constipation, and general weakness
- Excellent for increasing vitality, strength, *shukra dhatu* (semen), and skin lustre
- Mango skin helps with digestive disorders such as dysentery, diarrhea and hemorrhoids
- Great to eat during pregnancy. They also increase lactation
- Drinking a cup of hot milk with a teaspoon of ghee one hour after eating a ripe mango greatly improves strength, vitality and immunity
- Unripe, sour mangos made into chutney and taken with meals greatly increase digestive power

Melons

Dosha: decrease *pitta*, increase *vata* and *kapha*

Rasa (Taste): sweet
Virya (Energy): cold
Vipaka (Post-digestive effect): sweet
Prabhava (Special actions): refrigerant, febrifuge, diuretic, aphrodisiac

Nutritional Information:

- Should always be eaten alone as they do not combine well with other foods (including other fruits). Do not eat at night
- Good source of potassium and vitamins A, B and C
- The orange varieties have exceptional amounts of beta- carotene
- Very high in silicone, especially when the rind is eaten
- Ripe melons are refreshing, alkalizing, mineralizing, anti- oxidant and diuretic
- Have an anti- clotting action on the blood
- Melons are an excellent supply of distilled water containing the finest mineral elements
- Great against overheating and sunstroke, fevers, thirst, dehydration, irritability due to heat, burning urination and any *pitta* type disorder
- Excellent blood and tissue purifier
- Excellent against typhoid type fevers

Oranges

Dosha: decrease *vata*, increase *kapha* and *pitta* (the sour variety, or if taken in excess)
Rasa (Taste): sweet, sour
Virya (Energy): heating
Vipaka (Post-digestive effect): sweet
Prabhava (Special actions): stimulant, expectorant, appetizer, refrigerant, carminative (peel)

Nutritional Information:

- Oranges are one of the highest sources of vitamin C and bio-flavanoids
- Help the body's natural immune defenses. Vitamin C is vital for resistance to infection, both as an anti- oxidant and in its role in improving iron absorption
- Anti- cancer: In numerous clinical studies, people who eat more oranges and other citrus fruit have lower rates of many types of cancers. Beneficial for both prevention and treatment
- The pectin in oranges helps to lower cholesterol
- The flavanoids and vitamin C in oranges help maintain cell wall strength, aiding capillary circulation
- Excellent for treating over acidity, constipation or a sluggish intestinal tract
- Counteract cough, diabetes, bronchitis, liver and heart disorders and vomiting
- Harmonize the stomach
- Excellent blood purifier

Papayas

Dosha: decrease *vata*, increase *kapha* and *pitta*
Rasa (Taste): sweet, sour
Virya (Energy): heating
Vipaka (Post-digestive effect): sweet
Prabhava (Special actions): stimulant, digestive aid, tonic, demulcent, stimulant, laxative

Nutritional Information:

- Rich in vitamins A, B, C and D
- Rich in calcium, phosphorous and iron
- Excellent to eat in the morning, for they have high nutritional value and are easy to digest

- Excellent food for children as they promote growth
- The papaya is high in digestive properties and has a toning effect on the stomach
- Papayas assist in cleansing the digestive system
- Help to maintain the acid/alkaline balance in the body
- Used in the treatment of stomach ulcers and fevers
- Excellent against convalescence
- Great for the treatment of the pancreas and other digestive difficulties as they regulate sugar metabolism
- Good for liver and spleen disorders
- Stimulate digestive enzymes
- Good for cough and lung disorders
- Topically, they can treat skin disorders like inflammation, eczema and heat rashes

Peaches

Dosha: decrease *vata*, increase *kapha* and *pitta*
Rasa (Taste): sweet, astringent, sour
Virya (Energy): heating
Vipaka (Post-digestive effect): sweet, pungent
Prabhava (Special actions): demulcent, laxative, refrigerant

Nutritional Information:

- A good source of vitamin C and A, potassium and fiber
- Beneficial for lung debility, liver infections, cancer, ulcers, herpes, rheumatic pain, arterial hypertension and anaemia
- Excellent for menstruation, the development of children and convalescence
- Help heal damaged tissue

Pears

Dosha: decrease *pitta* and *kapha*, increase *vata* and *kapha* (sweet variety).
Rasa (Taste): sweet, astringent
Virya (Energy): cooling
Vipaka (Post-digestive effect): sweet, pungent
Prabhava (Special actions): nutritive, demulcent, laxative, tonic, febrifuge, cough suprresant

Nutritional Information:

- Good source of fiber
- Rich in vitamin C. Provide calcium, potassium, phosphorus and many other minerals
- Fight lung disease and are an excellent lung tonic
- Treat diarrhea
- Good for convalescence
- Increase appetite
- Reduce fever, biliousness, hyperacidity, enlarged liver, gall bladder disorders, excessive thirst and dehydration
- Excellent as a laxative and counter stomach disorders, gout and hemorrhoids

Pineapples

Dosha: decrease *vata*, increase *pitta* and *kapha* (sweet variety)
Rasa (Taste): sweet, sour
Virya (Energy): cooling (sweet), warming (sour)
Vipaka (Post-digestive effect): sweet, pungent
Prabhava (Special actions): diuretic, refrigerant, laxative, digestive stimulant, diaphoretic

Nutritional Information:
- One of the most immune enhancing fruits known. They have excellent anti- cancer properties as well as great nutritive value
- Contain carbohydrates, proteins, fats, and water. Also have a substantial amount of calcium, phosphorous, iron, magnesium, potassium, sodium, sulphur and manganese
- Are an excellent source of vitamin C and also have vitamins A, B1 and B2
- Have anti- inflammatory properties
- Pineapple enzymes have been used to treat rheumatoid arthritis and to speed up the repair of injured tissue due to physical injuries, diabetic ulcers and general surgery
- Bromelain, a digestive enzyme, is present in raw pineapple and freshly squeezed juice
- Pineapple enzymes act specifically to break down proteins, reduce blood clotting and remove plaque from arterial walls. Studies suggest that pineapple enzymes may improve circulation in those with narrowed arteries, like angina
- Used to help cure bronchitis and throat infections. They have a laxative effect, and help to clear digestive inflammations and intestinal fevers
- They are efficient in the treatment of arteriosclerosis and anemia
- Are an excellent cerebral tonic, known for combating memory loss, sadness and melancholy
- Counteract the effects of alcohol
- Reduce the toxic effects of cigarette smoke and nicotine

Plums

Dosha: decrease *vata* and *pitta*, increase *kapha*
Rasa (Taste): sweet
Virya (Energy): cooling

Vipaka (Post-digestive effect): sweet
Prabhava (Special actions): refrigerant, laxative, alterative, alleviate thirst

The chinese black plum (umeboshi) is sour and astringent, and has a more heating (*virya*) property with pungent (*vipaka*) post- digestive effect. This variety increases *pitta*. They are a digestive stimulant, as well as anti- bacterial, anti- parasitical and cough supressant.

Nutritional Information:

- Rich in magnesium, sodium, phosphorous and potassium. Also have a good amount of vitamin C
- Provide a useful amount of iron
- Have an excellent laxative effect
- They help clean and unclog the liver and the digestive system. Also help to overcome infections and intestinal fevers
- Due to their high phosphorus content, they provide excellent results when treating cerebral debility
- Beneficial against immune deficiency, fevers and dry coughs

Pomegranates

Dosha: decrease *pitta* and *kapha*, increase *vata*. The sour varieties increase *pitta*
Rasa (Taste): sweet, astringent, sour
Virya (Energy): cooling (sweet), warming (sour)
Vipaka (Post-digestive effect): sweet, pungent
Prabhava (Special actions): astringent, alterative, haemostatic, anti-parasitical (rind)

Nutritional Information:

- Build new red blood cells
- Have a good amount of vitamin C
- Help to cleanse toxic bile and the bile duct

- Cleanse the liver and blood
- Help with indigestion, hyperacidity, gallstones, fever, intermittent or malaria- type fevers, diarrhea, amoebic dysentery, excessive perspiration and numerous other *pitta* type disorders
- Pomegranates have also been known to treat leukorrhea and tapeworm
- Also excellent for the heart, mind and digestive system. Excellent cardiac tonic

Tangerines

Dosha: decrease *vata* and *pitta*, increase *kapha* when eaten in excess.
Rasa (Taste): sweet, sour
Virya (Energy): cooling
Vipaka (Post-digestive effect): sweet
Prabhava (Special actions): refrigerant, expectorant, stimulant, relieve thirst

Nutritional Information:

- High content of phosphorous, magnesium, calcium, vitamin C and numerous other vitamins
- Due to their high content in phosphorus and calcium they benefit the development of *asthi dhatu* (bone and skeletal tissue)
- Their high magnesium content tonifies articulations and muscles, and benefits the intestines and nervous system
- The high vitamin content combats infections
- Tangerines stimulate the appetite and settle the stomach
- Are an excellent treatment for cough, vomiting and phlegm- like discharge

Vegetables

Vegetables are of many different tastes, but the most common is sweet. There is a whole category of bitter vegetables as well. Generally, vegetables are *sattvic* in nature (though not as *sattvic* as fruit), but there are a number of *rajasic* vegetables. Root vegetables tend to be heavy and nutritive, and generally they decrease *vata*, increase *kapha* and are relatively neutral on *pitta*. There are many vegetables such as cabbage, cauliflower, broccoli and celery that aggravate *vata*. Due to their lighter nature, dark leafy greens decrease *kapha* and *pitta* while increasing *vata*. Dark leafy greens are excellent blood cleansers, and while they are filled with vitamins and minerals they are not nutritive in nature. In general, people who have *vata* constitutions need cooked or steamed vegetables with oils and spices. *Pitta* constitutions need a balance of raw and steamed vegetables that are not too spicy. *Pitta* also benefits from freshly squeezed vegetables juices. *Kapha* people do best with cooked or steamed vegetables that are spicy. *Kapha* individuals need *sattvic* foods, so locally grown, organic and in- season vegetables are best.

Artichokes

Dosha: decrease *pitta* and *kapha*, large amounts increase *vata*
Rasa (Taste): sweet, astringent
Virya (Energy): heating
Vipaka (Post-digestive effect): sweet
Prabhava (Special actions): alterative, haemostatic, diuretic

Nutritional Information:

* High amounts of calcium, magnesium, manganese, phosphorus, iron and niacin
* Contain a large amount of vitamin C and are therefore beneficial to immunity
* Excellent for cleansing the liver and gall bladder

- Reduce excess bleeding during menstruation
- Lower cholesterol levels
- Good source of fibre

Asparagus

Dosha: balanced for all three *doshas*
Rasa (Taste): sweet, bitter, astringent
Virya (Energy): cooling
Vipaka (Post-digestive effect): sweet
Prabhava (Special actions): alterative, mild laxative, demulcent, tonic, aphrodisiac, mild sedative, diuretic

Nutritional Information:

- Have plentiful amounts of potassium, zinc, and vitamins A, B-complex, C and E
- Excellent for the liver and high *pitta* conditions
- Alleviate constipation
- As they are high in glutathione, they have excellent anti- carcinogenic properties
- Good for bleeding disorders and infections of the urinary tract and reproductive system (including venereal diseases, herpes, etc)
- Beneficial for dissolving urinary stones
- Reduce fever, edema, gout, and arthritis. The water from boiled asparagus is beneficial for rheumatism

Beets

Dosha: decrease *vata*, increase *pitta* and *kapha* (if taken in excess)
Rasa (Taste): sweet
Virya (Energy): heating
Vipaka (Post-digestive effect): sweet
Prabhava (Special actions): alterative, demulcent, laxative, tonic

Nutritional Information:

- Have some of the vitamins A, B and C
- A good source of calcium, iron, magnesium and phosphorus
- Excellent blood builder/tonic
- Good for healthy menstruation
- Wonderful for the heart and circulatory system
- Beet juice is even more medicinal than beets, and excellent for all *vata-* type weakness
- Beet greens help to cleanse the lymphatic system, liver and gall bladder
- Beneficial for digestive disorders and anemia, as they build new red blood cells

Bitter Melons

Dosha: decrease *pitta* and *kapha*, increase *vata*
Rasa (Taste): bitter
Virya (Energy): cold
Vipaka (Post-digestive effect): pungent
Prabhava (Special actions): alterative, antipyretic, antacid, anti-parasitic

Nutritional Information:

- Have a very high vitamin C content
- As with most bitters, excellent for cleansing the liver, bile, blood and lymph
- One of the best foods for diabetes and all types of kidney disorders, as they improve glucose tolerance without increasing blood insulin levels
- Helpful against intestinal worms
- Have excellent immune boosting properties and combat immune disorders

- Beneficial for weight loss Reduce tumors
- Counteract fever, diarrhea and anemia

Broccoli

Dosha: reduces *pitta* and *kapha*, increases *vata* especially if raw
Rasa (Taste): sweet, pungent, slightly bitter
Virya (Energy): cooling
Vipaka (Post-digestive effect): pungent
Prabhava (Special actions): anti- cancer, immune- stimulant

Nutritional Information:

- Excellent source of vitamins A, C and E, as well as calcium and numerous other minerals
- Anti- cancer
- Strengthens immunity
- Great for all eye- related disorders
- Cleanses and rejuvenates the liver and gall bladder
- Good source of chlorophyll
- Counteracts excess heat disorders (*pitta*)
- Detoxifies blood and skin

Cabbage

Dosha: decreases *pitta* and *kapha*, increases *vata*
Rasa (Taste): sweet, astringent
Virya (Energy): cooling
Vipaka (Post-digestive effect): pungent
Prabhava (Special actions): alterative, anti- cancer

Nutritional Information:

- High amounts of calcium, sulphur, vitamins A and C, as well as numerous other minerals

- Excellent for bleeding stomach ulcers. Studies are showing that cabbage has an excellent ability to treat and prevent colon cancer
- Regulates the spleen, pancreas, and stomach, and treats abdominal spasms, pain and ulcers
- Helps alleviate constipation and remove toxins from the colon
- Counters depression and irritability
- In ancient Rome, it was used as a cure for hangovers
- Good for skin disorders such as eczema, rashes and prickly heat
- Helps to heal infections and strengthen immune system
- Antibacterial and antiviral
- Beneficial for rheumatism, pyorrhea, eye disorders, asthma, TB and immune deficiencies

Carrots

Dosha: decrease *vata* and *kapha*, increase *pitta*
Rasa (Taste): sweet, astringent
Virya (Energy): the root is heating, the juice is cooling
Vipaka (Post-digestive effect): sweet, pungent
Prabhava (Special actions): demulcent, nutritive, digestive stimulant, diuretic, alterative, antiseptic

Nutritional Information:

- Excellent source of calcium and vitamins A, C and D
- Increase blood flow and help to build new blood
- Wonderful for all conditions related to the liver
- Excellent for numerous ailments including rickets, gout, colitis, constipation, arthritis, edema, jaundice, hepatitis, heart disease and skin and colon disorders
- Excellent for cancer, especially of the lung or colon
- Help strengthen bones and make for healthy teeth, eyes and hair
- Carrot juice is great for hemorrhoids and all types of cancers

Cauliflower

Dosha: decreases *pitta* and *kapha*, increases *vata*
Rasa (Taste): sweet, astringent
Virya (Energy): cooling
Vipaka (Post-digestive effect): pungent
Prabhava (Special actions): demulcent, nutritive

Nutritional Information:

- High in vitamins and minerals
- Excellent for weight loss
- Cleanses liver, gall bladder and GI tract
- Reduces the risk of cancer, especially of the colon and stomach
- Excellent for diabetes and kidney weakness
- Strengthens immunity

Celery

Dosha: decreases *pitta* and *kapha*, increases *vata*
Rasa (Taste): sweet, salty, astringent
Virya (Energy): cooling
Vipaka (Post-digestive effect): pungent
Prabhava (Special actions): astringent, nervine, diuretic

Nutritional Information:

- Celery helps cleanse the mind and emotions, sharpens mental perception and aids in meditation. It is a relative of both *brahmi* and *gotu kola* (two Ayurvedic herbs that are beneficial for the mind and meditation)
- Excellent source of minerals that are needed by all *doshas*
- Helps with dizziness, headaches, arthritis, rheumatism, gout, adrenal weakness, diabetes, kidney stones, weight loss and many types of cancer. Also helps to lower blood pressure and alleviate stress
- It is an excellent blood purifier and promotes digestion

- Used to treat hangovers and headaches
- Helps to heal liver and kidney disorders, and is great for urogenital infections
- Good for the nervous system

Cucumbers

Dosha: decrease *vata* and *pitta*, increase *kapha*
Rasa (Taste): sweet, astringent
Virya (Energy): cooling
Vipaka (Post-digestive effect): sweet
Prabhava (Special actions): refrigerant, diuretic

Nutritional Information:

- Enable the body to absorb vitamins, especially when mixed with lemon juice, pepper and salt
- Alleviate thirst and counter urinary tract infections, scanty urination and spleen and stomach disorders
- Contain erepsin, a digestive enzyme that helps digest proteins and rids the intestines of toxins and parasites such as tapeworm
- Externally they are wonderful for the skin and help treat rashes and burns
- Purify the blood, clear acne, and reduce skin inflammations
- Dispel phlegm and heat from the lungs

Eggplant

(Note: In the Ayurveda text, *Charaka Samhita*, eggplant is listed as a fruit, not a vegetable. However, due to modern usage, it is being included in the vegetable section)
Dosha: round variety decreases *vata* and *kapha*, increases *pitta*; long, skinny variety increases *vata* and *kapha*
Rasa (Taste): pungent, astringent, bitter
Virya (Energy): heating

Vipaka (Post-digestive effect): pungent
Prabhava (Special actions): demulcent, nutritive, mild laxative, diuretic, anti- cancer, anti- convulsant

Nutritional Information:

- Helps treat heart and febrile diseases
- Helps with weak or dull eyesight, high cholesterol, arteriosclerosis, convulsions and epilepsy
- Assists in arterial renewal
- Treats dysentery
- Stimulates the immune system
- As it belongs to the nightshade family, it can aggravate allergies, *pitta-* type conditions and arthritis. Causes inflammation and is acid forming.

Kale

Dosha: decreases *pitta* and *kapha*, increases *vata* (especially raw)
Rasa (Taste): astringent
Virya (Energy): cooling
Vipaka (Post-digestive effect): pungent
Prabhava (Special actions): alterative, anti- cancer

Nutritional Information:

- One of the best blood- cleansing and cancer- fighting vegetables. Fights against all types of cancer: lung, stomach, colon, breast, esophagal, mouth, GI tract, bladder, prostate, etc.
- Excellent for the liver and gall bladder
- Contains lutein and zeaxanthin, which help to strengthen the eyes, prevent macular degeneration and decreases risk of colon cancer
- High in chlorophyll, vitamins A and C, riboflavin, niacin, calcium, magnesium, iron, sulphur, sodium, potassium, phosphorus and chlorophyll

- Compared to other vegetables, the calcium in kale is the easiest to assimilate

Lettuce

Dosha: decreases *pitta*, increases *vata* and *kapha*
Rasa (Taste): sweet, astringent
Virya (Energy): cooling
Vipaka (Post-digestive effect): sweet, pungent
Prabhava (Special actions): astringent, diuretic, alterative

Nutritional Information:

- Lettuce is cooling, calming, and cleansing to the mind and emotions
- Helps reduce internal and external burning sensations
- Excellent nervine
- Assists to cleanse the blood and lymph

Mushrooms

Dosha: decrease *pitta* and *kapha*, increase *vata*
Rasa (Taste): sweet, astringent
Virya (Energy): heating
Vipaka (Post-digestive effect): pungent
Prabhava (Special actions): diuretic, astringent, hemostatic

Nutritional Information:

- Mushrooms have no chlorophyll like other vegetables and are *tamasic* in nature
- In general, they are not recommended in a Yogic or Ayurvedic diet
- It is reported that mushrooms absorb toxins, and then eliminate them
- They do provide benefits against edema, obesity, and high cholesterol

- Recent research shows that medicinal mushrooms may assist in fighting cancer. Traditional Chinese medicine has used mushrooms to fight cancer for thousands of years
- History also shows that they have anti- tumor properties and may promote longevity (especially the reishi varieties)
- Mushrooms are high protein, zinc and vitamin B2

Mustard Greens

Dosha: decrease *vata* (cooked) and *kapha,* increase *pitta* slightly
Rasa (Taste): bitter, pungent
Virya (Energy): heating
Vipaka (Post-digestive effect): pungent
Prabhava (Special actions): stimulant, expectorant

Nutritional Information:

- Contain high amounts of calcium, iron, niacin and vitamin A
- Help regulate the function of the colon
- Like kale, mustard greens have great anti- cancer properties
- Good for bones, teeth and hair
- The seeds help eliminate phlegm and excess *kapha* in the body

Okra (Gumbo/Lady's Finger)

Dosha: tridoshic
Rasa (Taste): sweet, astringent
Virya (Energy): cooling
Vipaka (Post-digestive effect): sweet
Prabhava (Special actions): diuretic, demulcent, emollient, alterative, aphrodisiac, tonic

Nutritional Information:

- Excellent for difficult, painful or burning urination

- Contains a high amount of beta- carotene, vitamins B- complex and C
- Treats fevers, stomach ulcers, diarrhea, dysentery, and numerous other intestinal disorders such as spastic colon, diverticulitis and constipation
- Good for treatment of spermatorrhea, leucorrhea, gonorrhea, etc.

Onions

Dosha: cooked decrease *vata* and *kapha*, increase *pitta*; raw decrease *kapha*, increase *vata* and *pitta*
Rasa (Taste): (cooked) sweet; (raw) pungent
Virya (Energy): heating
Vipaka (Post-digestive effect): (cooked) sweet; (raw) pungent
Prabhava (Special actions): stimulant, diaphoretic, aphrodisiac, expectorant

Nutritional Information:
- Increase immunity, and combat colds, flu and general debility
- Counter sexual weakness or debility
- Alleviate blood and lymph stagnation
- Help remove heavy metal toxins
- Eliminate parasites
- Increase amino acid/protein metabolism

Peas: Green

Dosha: decrease *pitta* and *kapha*, increase *vata*
Rasa (Taste): astringent
Virya (Energy): cooling
Vipaka (Post-digestive effect): pungent
Prabhava (Special actions): alterative, astringent

Nutritional Information:

- Good source of fibre, protein, calcium, phosphorus and vitamins A and B- complex
- Excellent for cleansing the blood and regulating blood sugar levels
- Have beneficial effects on the liver, spleen, pancreas and stomach
- Help to prevent colon inflammation, appendicitis and ulcers
- Lower cholesterol and blood pressure
- Have anti- carcinogenic properties and are a protein low in calories

Potatoes

Dosha: decreases *pitta* and *kapha*, increases *vata*
(Note: Curried potatoes with ghee help reduce *vata*; however, they are in the nightshade family of vegetables and in excess will aggravate *vata* and *pitta* to some degree)
Rasa (Taste): astringent, sweet
Virya (Energy): cooling
Vipaka (Post-digestive effect): sweet
Prabhava (Special actions): nutritive, tonic, diuretic

Nutritional Information:

- Have a good amount of potassium and help to lower blood pressure
- Reduce acidity, balance the body's alkalinity and alleviate stomach and duodenal ulcers
- Good anti- cancer and strength- building food
- Reduce inflammation except when there is an arthritic condition
- Help increase the flow of breast milk
- The juice is anti- bacterial
- Help to stop diarrhea
- Potatoes are in the nightshade family and may aggravate anyone with food allergies

Radishes

Dosha: decrease *vata* and *kapha*, increase *pitta*
Rasa (Taste): pungent, astringent
Virya (Energy): heating
Vipaka (Post-digestive effect): pungent
Prabhava (Special actions): appetite and digestive stimulant, expectorant, anti- cough, diuretic, anti- parasitical

Nutritional Information:

- Contain a substantial amount of trace minerals, potassium and vitamins A, B- complex and C
- Help digest heavy foods or large meals
- Excellent for treating colds, flu, respiratory infections, laryngitis, sinusitis and immune deficiencies
- Anti- bacterial, anti- fungal
- Help cleanse the liver and gall bladder and dissolve gallstones
- Help expel intestinal worms

Seaweeds (arame, agar, alaria, bladderwrack, dulse, hijiki, Irish moss, kelp, kombu, nori, sea palm, wakame)

Dosha: decrease *vata* and *pitta*, increase *kapha* if taken in excess
Rasa (Taste): salty, astringent
Virya (Energy): cooling
Vipaka (Post-digestive effect): sweet
Prabhava (Special actions): alterative

Nutritional Information:

- Contain large amounts of all essential trace and ionic minerals; seaweeds have more vitamins and minerals than all other food types
- Seaweeds are very high in protein (up to 38%) and iron
- Nourish blood and plasma

- Counteract edema
- Decongest the body and dissolve tumors and cysts
- Have numerous anti- aging properties
- Reduce cholesterol
- Strengthen digestion and counteract obesity
- Eliminate heavy metals and radioactive toxins from the body
- Act as an antibiotic
- Excellent for reducing enlarged thyroids (hypothyroidism)
- Agar seaweed removes toxins and radioactive waste from the body; it is also an excellent source of vitamin K
- Hiziki and wakame have the highest amount of calcium of any seaweed. One cup of hiziki has more calcium and iron than one cup of milk, and is loaded with protein and vitamins A and B-complex
- Arame is excellent for the female reproductive system due to its very high content of vitamins A and B complex, as well as iodine, calcium and iron
- Kelp and Irish moss are excellent sources of calcium, potassium, magnesium and iron, and are great for thyroid disorders
- Nori is high in protein and vitamins B1, B2, B6, B12, C and E It is helpful for prostate and thyroid disorders

Spinach

Dosha: decreases *kapha*, increases *vata* and *pitta*
Rasa (Taste): sweet, astringent, bitter and pungent depending on variety and method of preparation
Virya (Energy): cooling
Vipaka (Post-digestive effect): sweet or pungent
Prabhava (Special actions): alterative, demulcent, laxative, refrigerant

Nutritional Information:

- Spinach should not be eaten if there is prostate enlargement, gallstones or kidney stones, liver disorders or arthritic conditions
- Contains high amounts of vitamin C, beta- carotene, calcium and phosphorus
- Contrary to popular belief, spinach is not higher in iron than other dark leafy greens
- Excellent for the lungs and treats chronic cough
- Spinach helps soothe the mucus membranes and helps alleviate fevers, burning sensations in the lungs and dry coughs
- Spinach is an excellent blood cleanser. It is beneficial to the stomach and liver
- Helps with vitamin, mineral and blood deficiencies like anemia
- Treats intestinal tract disorders

Squash

Acorn and Butternut

Dosha: balances all three *doshas*
Rasa (Taste): sweet, astringent
Virya (Energy): cooling
Vipaka (Post-digestive effect): pungent
Prabhava (Special actions): nutritive, expectorant, demulcent

Nutritional Information:

- High in vitamin A
- A nutritive tonic beneficial for general debility and weakness
- Good for dry coughs and laryngitis
- Help regulate blood sugar levels

Winter Squash

Dosha: decreases *vata* and *pitta*, increases *kapha*
Rasa (Taste): sweet, astringent
Virya (Energy): heating
Vipaka (Post-digestive effect): pungent
Prabhava (Special actions): demulcent, expectorant

Nutritional Information:

• Provides the same nutritional benefits as all other types of squash
• Is a nutritive tonic that helps strengthen and build the body

Yellow Squash/Zucchini

Dosha: decreases *vata* and *pitta*, increases *kapha*
Rasa (Taste): sweet, astringent
Virya (Energy): cooling
Vipaka (Post-digestive effect): pungent
Prabhava (Special actions): diuretic, alterative, refrigerant, expectorant

Nutritional Information:

• Excellent food to counteract external and internal heat in the body
• Strengthens the bodily tissues
• Good for treating general weakness

Sweet Potatoes and Yams

Dosha: decrease *vata* and *pitta*, increase *kapha*
Rasa (Taste): sweet, astringent
Virya (Energy): cooling
Vipaka (Post-digestive effect): sweet
Prabhava (Special actions): nutritive

Nutritional Information:

Sweet Potatoes

- Contain large amounts of beta- carotene and vitamins A and C
- Excellent food for general weakness and debility, convalescence and immune weakness
- High in anti- oxidants
- Good for the spleen, pancreas, kidneys and stomach. Especially good for lungs
- Excellent for preventing all types of cancer

Yams

- Rejuvenate the female reproductive system
- Help to balance estrogen levels
- Regulate menstruation and help to prevent miscarriages
- Excellent against arthritis and asthma
- Assist in detoxing from heavy metals
- Combat fatigue, stress and stress- related disorders

Tomatoes

Yellow:

Dosha: increases all *doshas*
Rasa (Taste): sweet, sour
Virya (Energy): heating
Vipaka (Post-digestive effect): pungent
Prabhava (Special actions): refrigerant

Red:

Dosha: (raw) increases all *doshas*, (cooked) okay for *vata* and *kapha*
Rasa (Taste): sour, astringent

Virya (Energy): heating
Vipaka (Post-digestive effect): pungent
Prabhava (Special actions): refrigerant

Nutritional Information:

All tomatoes:

- Raw tomatoes heat the stomach and intestines
- Steamed or stewed tomatoes reduce *vata* and *kapha* while increasing *pitta*
- High lycopene content. Lycopene is good for the blood, heart and circulation. It also helps treat high and low cholesterol, hypertension and other stress related disorders
- Cooked tomatoes clear heat from the body and help detoxify the blood
- Contain good amounts of potassium and vitamins A, B- complex and C
- Good in fighting cancer and appendicitis
- Tomatoes are heating in nature and are a nightshade. They should be avoided if there is pre-existing acidity, sciatica, arthritis, inflammation, kidney stones, gallstones, enlarged prostate and toxins in the blood

Turnips

Dosha: decrease *kapha*, increase *vata* and *pitta*
Rasa (Taste): pungent, astringent
Virya (Energy): heating
Vipaka (Post-digestive effect): pungent
Prabhava (Special actions): alterative

Nutritional Information:

- High in vitamin C

- Contain vitamin B- complex, potassium, calcium and several other trace minerals
- Excellent for cleansing the liver, gall bladder, lymph and blood
- Stop bleeding
- Reduce *pitta*-type and *kapha*-type type arthritis
- Have a beneficial effect on kidney stones, obesity, gout and excess mucous
- Have anti- carcinogenic properties

Grains

Grains, in general, balance the *doshas*. They are mostly *sattvic* in nature. Their taste and *vipaka* is sweet. They are neutral in temperature. They can be heating or cooling depending on how they are prepared. Overall, grains are good for all constitutions and all climates. They are an easy to digest bulking agent and help give form to the stool. Grains are of the earth element and have a high nutritive content; therefore they nourish all the *dhatus*. Grains along with legumes contain all the nutrient groups; carbohydrates, proteins, fats, vitamins, minerals and fiber. This is what makes *kichari* (mung dahl and basmati rice) the staple of an Ayurvedic diet.

Amaranth

Dosha: decreases *pitta* and *kapha*, increases *vata* if taken in excess
Rasa (Taste): sweet, bitter
Virya (Energy): cooling
Vipaka (Post-digestive effect): sweet
Prabhava (Special actions): diuretic, demulcent

Nutritional Information:

- Contains vitamin C and is up to 18% protein
- Excellent source of calcium (has more than milk)

- Has the amino acids lysine and methionine
- Great for convalescence and treating lung disorders

Barley

Dosha: decreases *pitta* and *kapha*, increases *vata* if taken in excess
Rasa (Taste): sweet, astringent
Virya (Energy): cooling
Vipaka (Post-digestive effect): sweet
Prabhava (Special actions): diuretic, demulcent

Nutritional Information:

- Good source of protein and contains calcium, phosphorus and iron
- Excellent for convalescence and treating lung disorders
- Alleviates cough, thirst, fever, edema and arthritis
- Stops bleeding
- Excellent for the liver and strengthens the kidneys
- Has a beneficial effect against diarrhea and regulates cholesterol
- Helps with nutrient absorption
- Eliminates toxins, mucous, and excess body fat

Buckwheat

Dosha: decreases *kapha*, increases *vata* and *pitta*
Rasa (Taste): astringent
Virya (Energy): heating
Vipaka (Post-digestive effect): sweet
Prabhava (Special actions): diuretic, demulcent

Nutritional Information:

- Has up to 100% more calcium than other grains
- Contains large amounts of vitamins B- complex and E
- Source of eight essential amino acids

- Good for people with gluten sensitivity
- Helps build blood and nourish the tissues
- Neutralizes acidity and toxins, but may aggravate *pitta* inflammations (especially of the skin)
- Contains rutin, a bioflavanoid, which is excellent for the blood and circulation. Rutin counteracts the effects of radiation
- In Japan, buckwheat is used as a kidney tonic

Corn

Dosha: decreases *kapha*, in excess increases *vata* and greatly increases *pitta*
Rasa (Taste): sweet, astringent
Virya (Energy): heating
Vipaka (Post-digestive effect): sweet, pungent
Prabhava (Special actions): diuretic

Nutritional Information:

- Excellent source of potassium, phosphorus, iron, zinc, magnesium, fibre and vitamins A, B- complex, and C
- Corn is beneficial against jaundice, hepatitis, gallstones, kidney stones, urinary tract infections and edema
- Increases blood Qi or *prana* Used in treatments for heart disease, sexual weakness and appetite loss
- Promotes bile flow
- Helps gain weight and build muscle and bone
- Good nervous system tonic
- Most corn today is genetically modified (GMO); one must take care to only get organic, non- GMO corn whenever possible.
- Corn needs to be avoided if there are digestive disorders, allergies or obesity

Millet

Dosha: decreases *kapha*, slightly increases *vata* and *pitta*
Rasa (Taste): sweet
Virya (Energy): heating
Vipaka (Post-digestive effect): sweet
Prabhava (Special actions): diuretic, demulcent

Nutritional Information:

• High in potassium and vitamin B- complex. High protein content. Has the highest amino acid protein profile compared to any other grain.

• Contains a good amount of iron, lecithin and choline. Has more iron than other grains.

• Excellent nutritive tonic and helps greatly with convalescence

• Prevents gallstones and is useful treating colitis, ulcers and urinary tract disorders

• Tonic for the spleen, pancreas and stomach

• Helps to regulate blood sugar imbalances

• It is the easiest of the grains to digest

Oats

Dosha: decrease *pitta* and *vata*, increase *kapha*
Rasa (Taste): sweet
Virya (Energy): cooling
Vipaka (Post-digestive effect): sweet
Prabhava (Special actions): emollient, demulcent, laxative

Nutritional Information:

• Excellent source of iron, vitamin B- complex and vitamin E

• Nutritive tonic for convalescence

• Calming to the mind and nervous system

• As an adaptogen, oats alleviate stress and tension

- Strengthen all the tissues, especially those of the reproductive system
- Assist in normalizing glucose levels in the blood in diabetic patients
- Slow thyroid conditions
- Help regulate cholesterol levels
- Contain very digestible protein
- Help to stop tobacco addiction

Quinoa

Dosha: decreases *kapha*, increases *vata* and *pitta* if taken in excess, okay in moderation
Rasa (Taste): sweet
Virya (Energy): warming
Vipaka (Post-digestive effect): sweet
Prabhava (Special actions): diuretic, demulcent, nutritive

Nutritional Information:

- Quinoa has more calcium than milk and is very high in lysine, iron, phosphorus, B- complex vitamins and vitamin E
- Highest protein content of any grain. The World Health Organization declared quinoa to be a least equal to milk in its protein quantity
- Excellent for tonifying the kidneys and adrenals
- Excellent for the heart and circulatory system
- Is a complete protein and has an amino acid profile similar to milk

Rice

Dosha: tridoshic, increases *kaph*a if taken in excess
Rasa (Taste): sweet, astringent
Virya (Energy): cooling, neutral

Vipaka (Post-digestive effect): sweet
Prabhava (Special actions): tonic, demulcent, nutritive, laxative

Nutritional Information:

- High vitamin B- complex content
- Excellent for promoting healthy digestion
- Good for the mind and nervous system
- Alleviates cough, thirst, fever, edema and arthritis
- Harmonizes the spleen, pancreas, and stomach
- Assists in eliminating toxins from the body
- White basmati rice is the easiest type of rice to digest
- Brown rice has the most B- complex vitamins of all the grains, but it is more difficult to digest and assimilate (it is best for those with very high *agni*)

Rye

Dosha: decreases *pitta* and *kapha*, increases *vata*
Rasa (Taste): astringent
Virya (Energy): heating
Vipaka (Post-digestive effect): pungent
Prabhava (Special actions): diuretic

Nutritional Information:

- Rye has a good amount of protein, eleven B vitamins, iron and other minerals
- An excellent grain for *kapha* types as it has the most lysine of any grain and aids in weight loss
- Builds muscle tissue and promotes energy and endurance
- Good for liver function

Wheat

Dosha: decreases *pitta* and *vata*, increases *kapha*

Rasa (Taste): sweet, astringent
Virya (Energy): cooling
Vipaka (Post-digestive effect): sweet
Prabhava (Special actions): nutritive, aphrodisiac

Nutritional Information:

- Excellent for nourishing all the *dhatus* (seven tissue layers: lymph, blood, muscle, fat, bone, marrow and nerve, reproductive)
- Alleviates cough, thirst, fever, edema and arthritis
- Its *sattvic* nature makes is perfect for meditation and yoga
- Reduces physical and mental stress
- Tonifies the liver, spleen, pancreas and stomach
- The best grain for *vata-* type constitutions
- While wheat is one of the most nourishing grains, many people have sensitivities or allergies to wheat and gluten. In *kapha* types it can create *ama*. Wheat should be avoided if there are toxins in the system or inflammatory conditions like arthritis, rheumatism, gout, etc. White, processed, refined wheat flour is *tamasic* (dull) and clogs the body with toxins. It is best to eat only unprocessed, whole grain wheat.
- Kamut is a relative of wheat and often can replace wheat for those who have wheat sensitivities or allergies. However, it still has a good amount of gluten so for those with celiac and gluten intolerances, kamut should also be avoided.

Legumes

Legumes tend to be sweet and astringent in nature. In general, they decrease *pitta* and *kapha*. As they often cause gas they tend to aggravate *vata*, except for mung and soybeans. Most legumes are *rajasic* (energetic) and stimulate the body, the mind and the senses. They are great for breaking up stagnant energy. Other than mung beans and soybeans, legumes are not traditionally part of a yogic diet. As mung beans are *sattvic* in nature they are often taken as mung dahl soup or as part of kichari. Together, legumes and grains are a great combination and make a complete protein containing all essential amino acids. As beans are made of earth and air, they are hard to digest. It is best to cook them very well, using spices and a light oil (such as ghee).

Aduki Beans

Dosha: decrease *pitta* and *kapha*, increase *vata* if taken in excess
Rasa (Taste): sweet, astringent
Virya (Energy): cooling/neutral
Vipaka (Post-digestive effect): pungent
Prabhava (Special actions): diuretic, alterative, heart tonic

Nutritional Information:

- Excellent for the heart, blood and circulatory system
- Good for convalescence and children's development
- Detoxify the body and remove excess heat (both internal and external)
- Cleanse the blood and reduce swelling
- Good for excess *pitta- kapha-* type disorders such as leukorrhea, jaundice, ascites, diarrhea, edema, boils, obesity, etc
- Strong diuretic properties make them good for the kidneys
- Aduki beans are easier to digest then most other beans

Black Gram (Masha)

Dosha: decreases *pitta*, increases *vata* greatly and *kapha* mildly
Rasa (Taste): sweet, astringent
Virya (Energy): cooling
Vipaka (Post-digestive effect): sweet

Prabhava (Special actions): nutritive, demulcent, aphrodisiac, nervine, lactagogue

Nutritional Information:

- Excellent for alleviating diarrhea, dysentery, indigestion and other digestive disorders
- Good for general debility and weakness
- Beneficial against liver disorders, hemorrhoids, arthritis, cystitis, gout and rheumatism
- Tonic for the reproductive system, as it increases semen and the flow of breast milk

Chickpeas/Garbanzos

Dosha: decrease *pitta* and *kapha*, increase *vata*
Rasa (Taste): sweet
Virya (Energy): cooling
Vipaka (Post-digestive effect): pungent
Prabhava (Special actions): diuretic, nutritive, aphrodisiac, astringent

Nutritional Information:

- Contain calcium, potassium, iron, and vitamins A and C
- Promote strength and increase energy
- Good for the reproductive system and counter general debility
- Tonic for the brain
- Support the spleen, pancreas, stomach and heart

Kidney, Navy and Pinto Beans

Dosha: decrease *pitta* and *kapha*, increase *vata*
Rasa (Taste): astringent; navy beans sweet
Virya (Energy): heating; pinto beans cooling
Vipaka (Post-digestive effect): pungent
Prabhava (Special actions): nutritive, aphrodisiac, cardiac tonic

Nutritional Information:

- Rich in nutrients, protein and fiber
- Excellent for healing all types of bleeding disorders
- Alleviate thirst, fever and all types of excess *pitta* disorders
- Kidney beans reduce swelling and edema

Lentils

Dosha: decrease *pitta* and *kapha,* increase *vata* if taken in excess or under cooked
Rasa (Taste): sweet, astringent
Virya (Energy): cooling, except red lentils, which are heating and can aggravate *pitta*
Vipaka (Post-digestive effect): sweet, except red lentils, which are pungent
Prabhava (Special actions): nutritive, mildly diuretic

Nutritional Information:

- High in calcium, magnesium, phosphorus, sulphur, protein and vitamin A
- Excellent for strengthening vitality
- Great for the kidneys and adrenals
- As they do not contain sulphur, they do not produce as much gas as other beans
- Help to reduce cholesterol and control blood sugar levels
- Reduce high blood pressure
- Prevent hemorrhoids by regulating the bowels

Mung Beans

Dosha: tridoshic
Rasa (Taste): sweet, astringent
Virya (Energy): cooling

Vipaka (Post-digestive effect): sweet
Prabhava (Special actions): refrigerant, antipyretic, alterative, hemostatic

Nutritional Information:

- Easiest of all legumes to digest
- Excellent for convalescence
- Good for the liver, kidney and gall bladder
- Treat febrile diseases, fevers, immune weaknesses, digestive disorders and cancer
- Great for detoxification
- A paste can be made and applied externally to burns, rashes, sores, mastitis, inflamed joints, swollen breasts, etc

Peanuts

Dosha: increase all *doshas*; okay for *vata* and *kapha* occasionally
Rasa (Taste): sweet, astringent
Virya (Energy): heating
Vipaka (Post-digestive effect): sweet
Prabhava (Special actions): tonic, laxative

Nutritional Information:

- Contain a high content of vitamin B- complex
- Excellent source of protein
- Tonic for the kidney
- Good for lactation
- Help to alleviate constipation

Caution: Peanuts are near the top of the list of common food allergens. People with liver weakness, candida albicans, cancer, immune weakness, digestive disorders, inflammation, arthritis, rheumatism and gout should avoid peanuts. They are one of the most chemically laden crops. They are often grown alongside cotton, which is sprayed with extremely toxic chemicals. The USDA allows a small amount of aflatoxin, a carcinogenic mold, to be present in peanuts and peanut products. This toxin causes free radicals, damages nerve tissue, decreases immunity and threatens the overall health of the body.

Soybeans

Dosha: decrease all *doshas*, increase *pitta* if taken in excess
Rasa (Taste): sweet, astringent
Virya (Energy): cooling
Vipaka (Post-digestive effect): pungent
Prabhava (Special actions): diuretic, demulcent

Nutritional Information:

- Excellent source of protein, calcium and magnesium
- Contain beta- carotene and vitamins B1, B2, and B3
- Soybeans are easier to digest than tofu
- Balance female hormonal levels
- Restore pancreatic function
- Help to alleviate effects of menopause
- Have anti- cancer properties
- Slow osteoporosis
- Strengthen kidneys and adrenals
- Are a good source of iron so help in cases of anemia and other blood deficiencies
- Improve circulation and help with detoxification

Tempeh

Dosha: decreases all *doshas*
Rasa (Taste): sweet, astringent
Virya (Energy): cooling
Vipaka (Post-digestive effect): pungent

Prabhava (Special actions): diuretic, demulcent

Nutritional Information:

- Excellent source of easily digested protein
- One of the best sources of B12
- Increases the natural energy of the body
- Good source of omega 3 fatty acids
- Good for general health and immunity
- Due to its fermentation, it is much easier to digest than other soy products

Nuts and Seeds

Most nuts and seeds decrease *vata* and increase *pitta* and *kapha*. Almost all nuts and seeds are sweet in taste and are warming. They are a major tonic food. They are nutritive, strengthening, and rejuvenating. Of all plant products, nuts and seeds are the best source of protein and fats. They strengthen nerve tissue, reproductive tissue and fat tissue. They build healthy blood and muscles. They are perfect in a yogic diet because they are a *sattvic* food that builds *ojas*.

Almonds

Dosha: decrease *vata*, increase *pitta* and *kapha*
Rasa (Taste): sweet, bitter
Virya (Energy): heating
Vipaka (Post-digestive effect): sweet
Prabhava (Special actions): nutritive, demulcent, nervine, aphrodisiac, laxative, rejuvenative

Nutritional Information:

- Good source of protein (are 18% protein), as well as calcium, magnesium, iron, phosphorus, potassium and vitamin B- complex
- They contain high amounts of alpha tocopherol vitamin E

- Great for the nervous system and the mind; ease stress
- Strengthen the kidneys, adrenals and reproductive system
- Counter general weakness
- Great for convalescence and childhood development
- Excellent lung and heart tonic
- Contain anti- cancer protease inhibitors and the phytonutrient phytosterol
- They are the only nut that is alkalizing

Brazil Nuts

Dosha: decrease *vata*, mildly increase *pitta* and greatly increase *kapha*
Rasa (Taste): sweet, astringent
Virya (Energy): heating
Vipaka (Post-digestive effect): sweet
Prabhava (Special actions): nutritive, tonic

Nutritional Information:

- One of the only nuts containing a substantial amount of vitamin C
- Great source of calcium and healthy fats
- Have anti- cancer and anti- tumour properties

Cashews

Dosha: decrease *vata*, increase *pitta* and greatly increase *kapha*
Rasa (Taste): sweet
Virya (Energy): heating
Vipaka (Post-digestive effect): sweet
Prabhava (Special actions): nutritive, tonic, expectorant

Nutritional Information:

- Excellent protein source: they are 20% protein
- High in vitamin A, potassium and magnesium
- Nutritive tonic for the deep tissue

Coconuts

Dosha: decrease *vata* and *pitta* and increase *kapha*
Rasa (Taste): sweet
Virya (Energy): cooling
Vipaka (Post-digestive effect): sweet
Prabhava (Special actions): refrigerant, diuretic, demulcent, emollient

Nutritional Information:

- Have general nutritive qualities
- Help build fat and muscle tissue
- Counteract weakness due to malnutrition
- Are tonic for the heart, but not if there is high cholesterol
- The water from coconuts alleviates thirst and constipation

Flax Seeds

Dosha: decrease *vata* and *kapha*, mildly increase *pitta*
Rasa (Taste): sweet, astringent
Virya (Energy): neutral
Vipaka (Post-digestive effect): sweet
Prabhava (Special actions): anti- inflammatory, anti- viral, antifungal, antibacterial

Nutritional Information:

- Have large amounts of essential fatty acids
- Good for alleviating bronchial congestion and constipation
- Tonic for the stomach and colon
- Strengthen the immune system due to their high content of linoleic acids
- Help prevent cancer and clear obstructions to the heart arteries
- Alleviate rheumatoid arthritis and other inflammatory conditions

Hazelnuts

Dosha: decrease *vata*, increase *pitta* and *kapha*
Rasa (Taste): sweet, astringent
Virya (Energy): heating
Vipaka (Post-digestive effect): sweet
Prabhava (Special actions): nutritive, tonic

Nutritional Information:

- Have restorative properties and combat chronic fatigue
- Good against hypoglycaemia and candida
- Crushed, they are good against chronic cough
- Are the second highest source of calcium of any nut (almonds are first)

Hemp Seeds

Dosha: tridoshic, slightly increase *pitta* in excess
Rasa (Taste): sweet, astringent
Virya (Energy): heating
Vipaka (Post-digestive effect): sweet
Prabhava (Special actions): nutritive, tonic

Nutritional Information:

- High content of all amino acids
- Excellent source of protein
- Contain large amounts of dietary fiber
- Alleviate constipation and help remove *ama* from the colon
- Strengthen the nerve tissue and help build healthy blood
- Improve the health of the skin, bones, teeth, nails and hair
- Help with inflammatory conditions like arthritis
- Hemp seed oil has numerous healing properties because it contains large amounts of omegas 3, 6 and 9

Lotus Seeds

Dosha: decrease *pitta* and *vata* and increase *kapha*
Rasa (Taste): sweet, astringent
Virya (Energy): heating
Vipaka (Post-digestive effect): sweet
Prabhava (Special actions): nutritive, tonic, calmative, aphrodisiac, rejuvenative

Nutritional Information:

- Lotus seeds are up to 20% protein
- Excellent for strengthening *ojas*
- Great tonic for the reproductive system
- Good for infertility or sexual debility
- Strengthen the kidneys, adrenals, and overall vitality and wellbeing
- Nourish the heart and nervous system

Pecans

Dosha: decrease *vata*, increase *pitta* and *kapha*
Rasa (Taste): sweet, astringent
Virya (Energy): heating
Vipaka (Post-digestive effect): sweet
Prabhava (Special actions): nutritive, aphrodisiac, laxative, nervine

Nutritional Information:

- A good source of potassium and vitamin A
- Excellent for the blood, bone marrow and nerve tissue
- Tonic for the reproductive system
- Act as a laxative, especially for children and the elderly
- Rejuvenate energy and vitality

Pine Nuts

Dosha: decrease *vata*, increase *pitta* and *kapha*
Rasa (Taste): sweet, astringent
Virya (Energy): heating
Vipaka (Post-digestive effect): sweet
Prabhava (Special actions): nutritive, tonic, rejuvenative, demulcent

Nutritional Information:

- Tonic for the nerves and the reproductive system
- Reduce stress and anxiety
- Good treatment for debility, wasting and overall debility
- Excellent for convalescence
- Have a healing effect on the lungs
- Treat dizziness and *vata* type disorders such as arthritis and rheumatism

Pistachios

Dosha: decrease *vata*, increase *pitta* and *kapha*
Rasa (Taste): sweet, astringent
Virya (Energy): heating
Vipaka (Post-digestive effect): sweet
Prabhava (Special actions): tonic, sedative, nervine

Nutritional Information:

- Filled with iron, potassium, phosphorus and magnesium
- Contain a good amount of protein, calcium and vitamin A
- Excellent against anemia, neurasthenia and general debility
- Tonic for the muscles tissue
- Help restore vital energy to the whole body
- Reduce hypertension
- Purify the liver, kidneys and blood

• Alleviate constipation

Pumpkin Seeds

Dosha: tridoshic; in excess, decrease *pitta* and *kapha* and increase *vata*
Rasa (Taste): sweet, bitter
Virya (Energy): heating
Vipaka (Post-digestive effect): sweet
Prabhava (Special actions): anti- parasitical, vermifuge

Nutritional Information:

• Contain a large amount of protein Contain some calcium and B vitamins
• Good source of omega 3 fatty acids, iron, zinc, phosphorus and vitamin A
• Excellent for removing parasites and worms (tapeworm, pinworm, roundworm)
• Good for treating painful gout
• Have a healing effect on the liver, gall bladder, colon, spleen, pancreas and stomach

Sesame Seeds

Dosha: decrease *vata*, increase *pitta* and *kapha*
Rasa (Taste): sweet, astringent, bitter
Virya (Energy): heating
Vipaka (Post-digestive effect): pungent
Prabhava (Special actions): nutritive, tonic, rejuvenative

Nutritional Information:

• High in vitamin E, iron, phosphorus, niacin, thiamine and the amino acids methionine and tryptophan
• Excellent source of calcium, however they should be soaked to make the calcium available to the body

- Sesame seeds are over 35% protein, which is more than any other nut
- Nourish all of the *dhatus*
- Excellent for every internal organ. Great for convalescence
- Help with the growth of skin, bones, hair, teeth, nails, etc
- Counteract general debility and malnutrition
- Build *ojas* and strengthen the immune system
- Sesame seed milk alleviates intestinal disorders such as colitis, gastritis, indigestion, constipation and heartburn
- Great for all types of *vata* disorders
- Sesame oil is extremely beneficial to all the *doshas* and is a vital part of ayurvedic treatment

Sunflower Seeds

Dosha: tridoshic
Rasa (Taste): sweet, astringent
Virya (Energy): cooling/neutral
Vipaka (Post-digestive effect): sweet
Prabhava (Special actions): nutritive, tonic

Nutritional Information:

- Excellent for treating febrile or infectious diseases
- Tonic for the reproductive system and lungs. Overall energy tonic
- Cleanse the lymphatic system of toxins
- Alleviate constipation
- Great source of protein (more than beef)
- Contain large amounts of calcium, phosphorus, iron and vitamins A, B- complex, D and E
- A rejuvenative for the spleen, and pancreas

Walnuts

Dosha: decrease *vata*, increase *pitta* and *kapha*
Rasa (Taste): sweet
Virya (Energy): heating
Vipaka (Post-digestive effect): sweet
Prabhava (Special actions): nutritive, aphrodisiac, laxative, nervine, anti- parasitic (unripe green hulls)

Nutritional Information:

- High content of omega 3 fatty acids, potassium, magnesium and vitamin A
- Excellent for the blood, bone marrow, and nerve tissue
- Tonic for both the male and female reproductive systems, especially for impotency and involuntary nocturnal emissions
- Have laxative properties, especially for the elderly
- Treat parasites and worms
- Alleviate swelling, inflammation and pain
- Lower cholesterol levels

Dairy

Dairy can be one of the most nourishing foods that we can eat. However, it can also be one of the most toxic. In the current modern age, fertilizers, pesticides, chemicals and hormones are used at all stages of commercial dairy production. In addition, the pasteurization and homogenization of dairy has a toxic effect on human health. Consuming this kind of dairy is not advisable. We must take extra special care to make sure the diary we eat is from animals that have not been treated with hormones and antibiotics, have been fed organic grass, and have lived freely on a range. Dairy products are most beneficial when consumed raw (unpasteurized and unhomogenized). As a general rule, dairy should come from animals treated with love and understanding, not cruelty and ignorance. This will ensure that the dairy we consume is of a pure, *sattvic* nature.

In general, dairy is sweet and cooling. It decreases *vata* and *pitta*, and increases *kapha*. Dairy from well- treated animals is the most *sattvic* of all foods. It nurtures all the *dhatus,* and is excellent for promoting calmness and clarity of mind. This is why it is such a vital part of the traditional yogic diet.

Dairy counteracts emaciation, debility, wasting diseases and sexual weakness. It is great for convalescence. It is the best food for building *ojas.*

Dairy is contraindicated if there are toxins in the body, especially in the colon or lungs. Also, due to poor dairy production standards, more and more people are developing sensitivities or intolerances to dairy products. It is advisable to consult an ayurvedic practitioner to ensure that consuming dairy is beneficial to one's constitution.

It is very important to understand that dairy products should not be consumed with certain foods. Dairy combined with the wrong food can lead to poor digestion, weak assimilation and toxicity in the body. Dairy does not combine well with meat, fish, yeast, fruit, nuts, green leafy vegetables or nightshades (tomatoes, potatoes, bell peppers, eggplants). Dairy products should be used in moderation, and the appropriate dairy type (buffalo, cow, goat, sheep, etc.) and form (milk, buttermilk, cheese, yogurt, etc.) should be chosen for one's individual constitution.

Butter

Dosha: decreases *pitta* and *vata,* increases *kapha*
Rasa (Taste): sweet
Virya (Energy): cooling
Vipaka (Post-digestive effect): pungent
Prabhava (Special actions): nutritive, aphrodisiac

Nutritional Information:

• Excellent for nourishing, strengthening and rejuvenating the body

- Good for convalescence and overall debility
- Improves digestion
- Improves skin complexion
- Counteracts sexual debility
- Helps to heal hemorrhoids, paralysis and bronchitis
- Good for all types of *vata* and *pitta* disorders
- Best used by developing youth and the elderly

Buttermilk

Dosha: decreases *vata*, increases *pitta* and *kapha*
Rasa (Taste): sweet, sour
Virya (Energy): cooling
Vipaka (Post-digestive effect): sweet
Prabhava (Special actions): diuretic, digestive stimulant, astringent

Nutritional Information:

- Excellent for indigestion and malabsorption due to low *agni*
- Good for emaciation, convalescence, and general debility
- Reduces edema, hemorrhoids, anorexia, anemia and blood weakness
- Tonic for the spleen

Cheese/Paneer

Dosha: Hard cheese decreases all *doshas*, but it is a little hard for *vata* to digest, and will increase *pitta* if used in excess. Soft cheese decreases *vata* and *pitta* and increases *kapha*. Goat cheese is okay in moderation for all doshas.
Rasa (Taste): sweet, sour
Virya (Energy): heating
Vipaka (Post-digestive effect): sour
Prabhava (Special actions): nutritive, astringent

Nutritional Information:

- Excellent for treating diarrhea and bleeding disorders
- Builds all bodily tissues
- Strengthens *ojas* and the reproductive system

Cream

Dosha: decreases *vata* and *pitta*, increases *kapha*
Rasa (Taste): sweet
Virya (Energy): cooling
Vipaka (Post-digestive effect): sweet
Prabhava (Special actions): rejuvenative, nutritive, aphrodisiac, calming, laxative

Nutritional Information:

- Excellent for weakness and convalescence
- Builds all the *dhatus,* but especially the reproductive tissue
- Strengthens the lungs and stomach
- Counteracts dry cough, bleeding, fever, thirst and all types of *vata- pitta-* related disorders

Ghee (Clarified Butter)

Dosha: decreases *vata* and *pitta*, increases *kapha* in excess
Rasa (Taste): sweet
Virya (Energy): cooling
Vipaka (Post-digestive effect): sweet
Prabhava (Special actions): tonic, emollient, antacid, rejuvenative, nutritive, aphrodisiac

Nutritional Information:

- Excellent for weakness and convalescence
- Builds all the *dhatus,* but especially the reproductive tissue
- Improves mental clarity and intelligence

- Added to our meal, it helps us assimilate the food we eat
- Builds *ojas*
- Improves the skin, liver, quality of the voice, kidneys, brain and nerves. It also improves eyesight and motor functions
- Harmonizes all the *agnis* (digestive fires) of the body
- Promotes longevity and vitality
- Excellent against immune disorders, fevers and most *vata- pitta-* related disorders
- Used as a transport system for taking medicinal herbs because it delivers the nutrients and energy of the herbs to all *dhatus*
- Ghee is by far the best oil to consume

Ice Cream

Dosha: decreases *pitta*, increases *vata* and *kapha;* increases *ama* in all bodies
Rasa (Taste): sweet
Virya (Energy): cooling
Vipaka (Post-digestive effect): sweet
Prabhava (Special actions): None!

Nutritional Information:

- Cold dairy products with sugar are not healthy. They create stagnation and *ama* (toxins) in the body and mind. They should be avoided!
- Ice cream also weakens the digestive fire. It is specifically contraindicated for TB, all *kapha-* related disorders, *ama*, fever, constipation, alcoholism, sugar addictions, and disorders of the spleen, pancreas and digestive system
- Daily of consumption of ice cream can lead to hypoglycemia, diabetes, toxic lymph and blood, cysts and tumours
- Frozen yogurt has similar qualities as ice cream but with less sugar
- There are now ice cream alternatives made with rice, cashew and

coconut milks. These are a somewhat healthier choice. However, food combining principles and Ayurvedic guidelines still apply. Moderation is advisable

Kefir

Dosha: decreases *vata*, increases *pitta* and *kapha*
Rasa (Taste): sour
Virya (Energy): heating
Vipaka (Post-digestive effect): sour
Prabhava (Special actions): digestive stimulant

Nutritional Information:

- Increases digestive fire and absorption
- Good for low appetite and anorexia
- Best if taken plain (or with spices), without sugar or fruit

Milk

Dosha: decreases *vata* and *pitta*, increases *kapha*
Rasa (Taste): sweet
Virya (Energy): cooling
Vipaka (Post-digestive effect): sweet
Prabhava (Special actions): *sattvic*, rejuvenative, nutritive, aphrodisiac, calming, laxative

Nutritional Information:

- Excellent for weakness and convalescence
- Builds all the *dhatus,* but especially the reproductive tissue
- Promotes longevity and rejuvenation
- Counteracts exhaustion and dizziness
- Nourishes the skin, may be used externally as well
- Tonic for the stomach and lungs

- Good for treating dry cough, throat, fever and thirst Reduces bleeding
- Great for almost all *pitta-* related disorders
- Great for the elderly and debilitation
- Builds *ojas* and is wonderful for the mind, memory, brain and nerves
- The following concoction benefits *kapha:* Boil raw milk for a couple minutes. Add spices such as ginger, cinnamon, and cardamom Consume while hot
- Milk boiled with nervine herbs (*brahmi, jatamansi*, etc) promotes sleep and counteracts insomnia and nervous tension

Yogurt

Dosha: sweet yogurt decreases *vata* and *pitta*, increases *kapha*; sour yogurt decreases *vata*, increases *pitta* and *kapha* as well as *ama;* sweet and sour yogurt has mixed effects
Rasa (Taste): sweet, sour
Virya (Energy): cooling
Vipaka (Post-digestive effect): sweet
Prabhava (Special actions): digestive stimulant, nutritive, astringent

Nutritional Information:

- Excellent for weakness and convalescence
- Nourishes all the *dhatus,* especially the reproductive tissue
- Aids in the digestion of other foods
- Rejuvenates healthy flora and bacteria in the intestines
- Helps dissolve malignant tumors and cancer
- Good against low immunity, flu, colds, diarrhea, anorexia, anemia, cholesterol and digestive system infections
- Whey cleanses the *nadis,* and increases appetite and mental clarity
- Lassi (yogurt mixed with water and spices) promotes digestion

for all three doshas. *Vata* and *pitta* people should mix equal parts yogurt and water. *Kapha* individuals should mix one part yogurt and three parts water. For all consitutions, ginger, cinnamon, cardamom, black pepper and saffron can be added.

Oils

Oils are generally either sweet or bland, and they can be either warming or cooling. All oils reduce *vata* and most oils increase *pitta* and *kapha*. Oils can be used both internally and externally. They are an integral of Ayurvedic therapies. For example, oils are a vital part of the Ayurvedic cleansing program known as *panchakarma*. They are frequently used in massage to soften the skin and muscles. They also promote the detoxification and decongestion of the tissues. When they are absorbed through the skin, they nurture the deep tissues and large intestines. They are wonderful for counteracting most *vata* disorders. Oils should be avoided when there is *ama* in the system, especially if the blood is toxic. Oil massage is also contraindicated in the case of cancer, so as not to circulate the toxins.

Almond Oil

Dosha: decreases *vata*, increases *pitta* and *kapha*
Rasa (Taste): sweet, sometimes bitter
Virya (Energy): heating
Vipaka (Post-digestive effect): sweet
Prabhava (Special actions): expectorant, nutritive, demulcent, nervine, aphrodisiac, laxative, rejuvenative

Nutritional Information:
- Contains high amounts of alpha tocopherol vitamin E
- Soothes skin and muscles
- Internally, it is a good laxative
- Provides relief for muscle tension, aches and pain

- Reduces stretch marks and wrinkles
- Alleviates coughs and wasting disorders of the lungs and kidneys

Avocado Oil

Dosha: decreases *vata* and *pitta*, increases *kapha*
Rasa (Taste): sweet
Virya (Energy): cooling
Vipaka (Post-digestive effect): sweet
Prabhava (Special actions): nutritive, demulcent, tonic

Nutritional Information:

- Avocado oil has all of the same properties as the fruit. It is even more nutritive
- High in vitamin E. It is also high in monounsaturated fat and calories
- Excellent source of protein, chlorophyll, carbohydrates, calcium, phosphorus, copper, cobalt and vitamins A, B- complex and C
- Trace source of inositol
- Contains fourteen minerals that regulate body functions and stimulate growth
- Great for salads Don't cook with the oil
- Strengthens muscles and the liver
- Excellent for nourishing the skin and joints
- Easily absorbed through the skin
- One of the most important foods in combating cancer
- The fatty substances have a beneficial effect on the body, while animal fats have a harmful effect
- Combats the negative effects of a meat- based diet
- Helps with digestive issues, general debility, rheumatism, skin infections and kidney problems. Normalizes liver and pancreas functions

• Aids in red blood cell regeneration and prevent anemia

Castor Oil

Dosha: decreases *vata* and *pitta,* increases *kapha* in excess
Rasa (Taste): sweet, bitter
Virya (Energy): heating
Vipaka (Post-digestive effect): sweet
Prabhava (Special actions): purgative, antispasmodic, analgesic

Nutritional Information:

• Cleanses the channels of *ama*

• Excellent against constipation, epilepsy, arthritis, and nerve and muscle pain

• External compresses of the oil heal wounds, sprains, bruises, sores and various other injuries

• External packs can detoxify tumours and swellings, and ease pain and menstrual cramps

• Best oil for *vata* to ingest for cleansing and purgation. It is said that when castor oil enters the body all *vata* disturbances leave

• Internally, it alleviates enlarged prostate glands, fevers, hernias and pain/swelling in the waist, genitals, abdomen and back

Coconut Oil

Dosha: decreases *vata* and *pitta,* increases *kapha*
Rasa (Taste): sweet
Virya (Energy): cooling
Vipaka (Post-digestive effect): sweet
Prabhava (Special actions): emollient, refrigerant, tonic

Nutritional Information:

• Excellent for reducing excess *pitta* because it is easily assimilated

• Nourishes and softens the skin

- Alleviates inflammatory conditions of the skin such as psoriasis, eczema, sunburn, chapped lips and dryness
- Reduces dry coughs, fevers, burning in the lungs and other excessive heat disorders
- Increases the reproductive tissue

Corn Oil

Dosha: increases *vata* and *pitta*, decreases *kapha*
Rasa (Taste): sweet, astringent
Virya (Energy): heating
Vipaka (Post-digestive effect): pungent
Prabhava (Special actions): demulcent, diuretic

Nutritional Information:

- Alleviates difficult urination
- Very nourishing for the skin; great for massage
- Unless organic and non- GMO, the use of corn or its products is not advisable

Flaxseed Oil

Dosha: decreases *vata* and *kapha*, increases *pitta*; inceases *kapha* in excess
Rasa (Taste): sweet
Virya (Energy): heating
Vipaka (Post-digestive effect): pungent
Prabhava (Special actions): expectorant, lubricant, laxative

Nutritional Information:

- Excellent source of omega 3 essential fatty acids
- Removes excess mucus from the body
- Regulates female hormones
- Helps clean the colon. Great for sore throats and coughs

Mustard Oil

Dosha: decreases *vata* and *kapha*, increases *pitta*
Rasa (Taste): pungent
Virya (Energy): heating
Vipaka (Post-digestive effect): pungent
Prabhava (Special actions): stimulant, demulcent

Nutritional Information:

- Excellent for most *vata* and *kapha-* related disorders
- Great for both internal and external use
- Helps alleviate coughs, colds, congestion, heaviness of the joints and limbs, arthritis, rheumatism, abdominal pain and sprains
- Loosens mucus in the lungs
- Reduces inflammation

Olive Oil

Dosha: decreases *vata* and *pitta*, increases *kapha* in excess
Rasa (Taste): sweet
Virya (Energy): cooling
Vipaka (Post-digestive effect): sweet
Prabhava (Special actions): mildly laxative

Nutritional Information:

- High vitamin E content
- Wonderful for the liver and gallbladder, as it softens and eliminates stones
- Reduces cholesterol and is great on salads and vegetables
- Great for massage due to its light nature
- Regulates blood pressure and diabetes
- Great to cook with as it is one of the most stable oils

Safflower Oil

Dosha: decreases *vata,* mildly increases *pitta* and *kapha*
Rasa (Taste): sweet, astringent
Virya (Energy): heating
Vipaka (Post-digestive effect): pungent
Prabhava (Special actions): laxative, emmenagogue

Nutritional Information:

- Has immune boosting properties
- As massage oil, it is okay for *kapha* due to its light nature
- Increases circulation and is good for the blood and nervous system when used in massage
- It is not traditionally used that frequently in ayurvedic cooking or healing therapies
- Oleic- rich safflower oil is up to 80% monounsaturated fats, which gives it a high heat resistance and thus makes it good for cooking

Sesame Oil

Dosha: decreases *vata,* increases *pitta* and *kapha* (slightly)
Rasa (Taste): sweet, bitter
Virya (Energy): heating
Vipaka (Post-digestive effect): sweet
Prabhava (Special actions): rejuvenative, tonic, sedative, laxative, nutritive

Nutritional Information:

- Sesame oil is considered the best oil, especially for *vata*
- In Ayurveda, it is commonly used in massage due to its ability to deeply penetrate the skin
- Nourishes and detoxifies all the *dhatus*
- Avoid if there are excess *pitta* conditions, especially on the skin
- Nourishes and reduces *vata*

- Used to eliminate parasites
- It is said that if high quality, properly processed sesame oil is used (internally or externally), it can assist in healing almost any disease
- Helps the lungs, kidneys, brain, nervous system and muscles Improves eyesight, voice quality, hair, teeth, bones, nails and skin complexion Good for children and the elderly
- Treats stress, debility, convalescence, spasms, strains, constipation and coughs
- Excellent staple in a yogic diet
- Strengthens the immune system and builds *ojas*
- A good antioxidant

Sunflower Oil

Dosha: relatively *tridoshic*, will increase *kapha* in excess
Rasa (Taste): sweet, astringent
Virya (Energy): cooling
Vīpaka (Post-digestive effect): sweet
Prabhava (Special actions): nutritive

Nutritional Information:
- Contains a high amount of omega 3 essential fatty acids. High vitamin E content
- Should not be used for cooking
- Great for the skin
- Alleviates sunburns, rashes and excess heat conditions
- When applied externally, is good for lungs and coughs

Sweeteners

Sweeteners generally decrease *vata* and *pitta,* and increase *kapha.* In excess, all sweeteners will increase and derange the *doshas.* Most sweeteners act as a tonic, demulcent, diuretic, laxative, preservative, refrigerant and calmative. They are good for general debility and rejuvenation. Many Ayurvedic healing formulas use a sweetener in their base. For example, *chaywanyaprash,* an Ayurvedic rejuvenative formula, uses honey with ghee as its base. High quality organic sugar will support the bodily tissues, while processed, artificial and devitalized sugar is poisonous to the body.

Fruit Sugar

Dosha: decreases *vata* and *pitta*, increases *kapha*
Rasa (Taste): sweet
Virya (Energy): cold
Vipaka (Post-digestive effect): sweet
Prabhava (Special actions): laxative

Nutritional Information:
- Builds bodily tissue
- Of all the fruit sugars, date and grape sugar are the best
- If fruit sugars are not organic, they may have come from third world countries that allow the use of harsh chemicals like DDT (known to cause cancer).

Honey

Dosha: decreases *vata* and *kapha*, increases *pitta* in excess
Rasa (Taste): sweet
Virya (Energy): heating
Vipaka (Post-digestive effect): sweet
Prabhava (Special actions): laxative, nutritive, emollient, expectorant, tonic, rejuvenative. Externally: antibacterial, antibiotic, astringent, demulcent

Nutritional Information:
- Raw, uncooked honey is the most medicinal of all sweeteners

- Contains similar properties as the flower from which it came
- Builds *ojas* and strengthens the *dhatus* and immunity
- Used as a vehicle for delivering herbs to the deep tissue of the body
- Excellent for the mind and nerves
- Expels phlegm, fat, mucus, and other toxins from the body
- Dissolves hard masses such as tumors, cysts, polyps and fibroids
- Destroys poison in the body
- Heals skin conditions
- Heating honey destroys the medicinal properties and makes it toxic. It is acceptable to add to hot tea that has cooled for a minimum of five minutes

Jaggery

Dosha: decreases *vata*, increases *pitta* and *kapha*
Rasa (Taste): sweet
Virya (Energy): heating
Vipaka (Post-digestive effect): sweet
Prabhava (Special actions): tonic, rejuvenative

Nutritional Information:

- Properties are similar to sucanat or turbinado in properties
- Contains minerals and is a good sweetener to use in case of debility or weakness
- Contains vitamins, minerals and other micronutrients
- Helps with anemia and burning urination
- Organic, unprocessed, high quality jaggery contains chromium, which makes it very beneficial to those with diabetes
- Good for the relief of muscle spasms and pain

Maple Syrup

Dosha: decreases *pitta*, increases *vata* if used in excess and increases *kapha*
Rasa (Taste): sweet
Virya (Energy): cooling
Vipaka (Post-digestive effect): sweet
Prabhava (Special actions): nutritive, demulcent

Nutritional Information:

- High quality organic maple syrup is one of the best sweeteners
- Beneficial for coughs, fever and burning conditions
- Helps alleviate many high *vata* and *pitta* disorders
- *Caution:* Like white sugar, maple syrup can cause insulin and adrenaline reactions. Additionally, it should be avoided if there is candida, parasites, tumours, cysts, polyps, fibroids, cancer or immune weakness

Molasses

Dosha: decreases *vata*, increases *pitta* and *kapha*
Rasa (Taste): sweet
Virya (Energy): heating
Vipaka (Post-digestive effect): sweet
Prabhava (Special actions): nutritive, tonic

Nutritional Information:

- Molasses, especially the blackstrap variety, contains a large amount of iron, calcium and potassium
- It is good for building blood. Strengthens the heart, lungs, stomach, spleen and pancreas. Strengthens muscles
- Alleviates general weakness and debility
- Treats coughs

• Good sweetener to use during pregnancy and lactation. Good for treating many gynecological issues

Raw Cane Sugar (Turbinado/Sucanat)

Dosha: decreases *vata* and *pitta*, increases *kapha*
Rasa (Taste): sweet
Virya (Energy): cold
Vipaka (Post-digestive effect): sweet
Prabhava (Special actions): laxative

Nutritional Information:

• Builds bodily tissue
• Is a natural aphrodisiac
• Calms the nerves

White/ Processed Sugar

Dosha: greatly disturbs all the *doshas*
Rasa (Taste): sweet
Virya (Energy): cooling
Vipaka (Post-digestive effect): sweet

Nutritional Information:

• White sugar is toxic to the body It is treated by the body as a poison
• Leaches minerals, vitamins and nutrients from the body
• Disturbs the entire digestive system
• Weakens the immune system and feeds bacteria, viruses and infections
• Deranges the metabolism of fat and water
• Destroys the liver and pancreas
• Creates more disturbances than any other common food we consume

Miscellaneous

Carob

Dosha: balances all *doshas*
Rasa (Taste): sweet, astringent
Virya (Energy): heating
Vipaka (Post-digestive effect): sweet
Prabhava (Special actions): nutritive, demulcent

Nutritional Information:

- Contains calcium and other minerals
- Good for treating general weakness
- An excellent substitute for chocolate

Chocolate

Dosha: increases all *doshas*
Rasa (Taste): sweet, sour, bitter
Virya (Energy): heating
Vipaka (Post-digestive effect): sweet
Prabhava (Special actions): stimulant, aphrodisiac, calmative

Nutritional Information:

- Contains some minerals, especially dark organic chocolate
- Chocolate beans have more health benefits than processed chocolate
- Good mood enhancer Counteracts depression and hypotension, but can be addictive
- Combined with white sugar, it becomes extremely toxic
- Numerous reports show that raw cacao beans contain numerous minerals and anti-oxidants and are beneficial when used in moderation

Salt

Dosha: decreases *vata*, increases *pitta* and *kapha*
Rasa (Taste): salty
Virya (Energy): heating
Vipaka (Post-digestive effect): sweet
Prabhava (Special actions): laxative

Nutritional Information:

- Makes food soft and easy to digest
- Good for gargling Soothes the mucus membranes
- Relaxes muscular tension through its softening ability
- Removes toxins from the body
- Best if used in moderation In excess, it will aggravate all the *dhatus*, weaken digestion, disturb the blood, cause water retention and bring on other *kapha* related disorders

Vinegars

Dosha: decreases *vata*, increases *pitta* and *kapha*
Rasa (Taste): sour
Virya (Energy): heating
Vipaka (Post-digestive effect): sour
Prabhava (Special actions): digestive and circulatory stimulant

Nutritional Information:

- Promote the production of hydrochloric acid, which is necessary for digestion
- Help menstruation by reducing cramping
- Assist in post- digestive processes

PART TWO

Recipes

Please note that most of these recipes are made traditionally using ghee. If you are vegan, you may substitute the ghee with another oil or with Earth Balance (a vegan, vegetable-based buttery spread). Please feel free to experiment with the recipes and come up with your own creations!

Ghee (clarified butter)

In Ayurveda, ghee is highly regarded as being one of the most *sattvic* foods. It is beneficial for all three *doshas*, and is the healthiest of all oils. It can be used in any recipe, in place of any oil.

Melt one pound of organic unsalted butter in a saucepan on medium heat. The better the quality of butter the better the ghee will be. As the butter melts, it will begin to boil, and white froth will float to the top while sediments will settle to the bottom. Do not stir the butter. Be sure the butter boils consistently by maintaining a consistent temperature. Allow the butter to boil until the bubbling noise quiets down, the sediment at the bottom of the pan starts to turn a golden brown (check the color of the sediment by slowly tilting the pot), and the liquid under the froth begins to turn an amber color (it usually takes about 18- 20 minutes). Let the cooked ghee cool for 15- 20 minutes, then line a fine mesh strainer with cheesecloth and strain the ghee into a sterilized glass jar. Discard the sediment. The ghee will turn hard when cooled. It is not necessary to refrigerate. If it is good quality ghee and made correctly, it should keep for over a year. Be careful not to get water in the container when using the ghee, or it may spoil. Many Ayurvedic formulas mix medicinal herbs with ghee, as it has the ability to deliver the healing qualities of the herbs deep into the body.

Salads

Oh love, where are you going?
Who are you looking for?
Your Beloved is right here.
She lives in your own neighborhood.
Her face is real.
She hides behind screens calling for you.
While you search and lose yourself
In the wilderness and in the desert.
Cease looking for flowers.
There blooms a garden in your own home.
While you go looking for trinkets,
The treasure house awaits you
In your own being.
There is no need for suffering.
God is here.

— *Rumi*

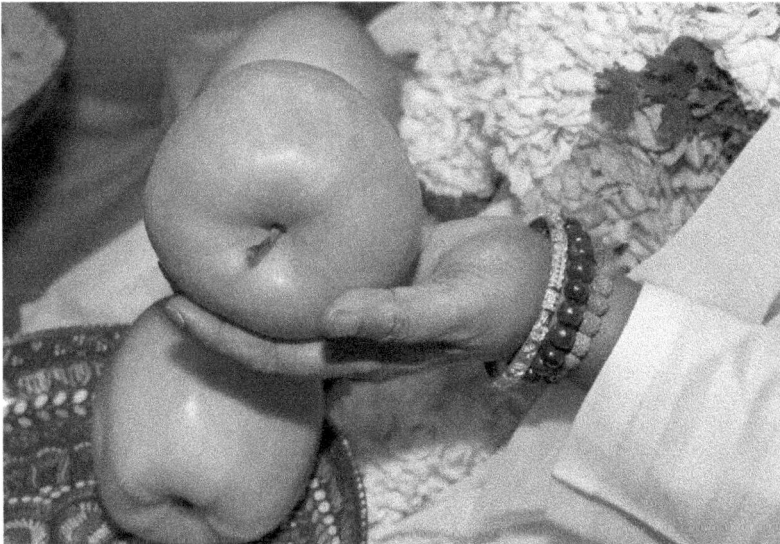

Ambika's Agar Salad

Tridoshic
Serves: 2-3
Ingredients:
2 cups agar
¼ cup parsnips, grated
1 Tbs toasted sesame seeds or gamasio
½ tsp organic cane sugar (sucanat, turbinado, rapidura, etc.)
½ - 1 tsp black pepper fresh ground
2 Tbs fresh cilantro, chopped
1 Tbs fresh basil, chopped
1 tsp fresh dill, chopped
1 tsp fresh squeezed lemon or sweet lime juice
2 tsp balsamic vinegar or apple cider vinegar
2 Tbs water
1 Tbs extra virgin olive oil or ghee
1 heaping tsp nutritional flakes

Note: This salad also tastes great with Annie's Goddess Dressing (available in most health food stores across the United States and England). If you use the Annie's Goddess dressing, leave out the lemon juice, vinegar, water and oil.

Instructions:
Rinse the seaweed and soak in water for 20 minutes. Rinse the seaweed again. Mix all the ingredients in a large bowl. Stir for several minutes. Cover and let sit for 5 minutes.

Satchitananda Seaweed Salad

Tridoshic
Serves: 3-4
Ingredients:
¼ cup dulse
½ cup agar
¼ cup arame
¼ cup hiziki
½ cup carrots, grated
½ cup beets, grated
½ tsp organic cane sugar (sucanat, turbinado, rapidura, etc)
½ - 1 tsp black pepper fresh ground
2 Tbs fresh cilantro, chopped
1 Tbs fresh basil, chopped
1 tsp fresh mint, chopped
1 tsp fresh dill, chopped
½ tsp fresh tarragon or ¼ tsp dry
2 tsp fresh squeezed lemon juice
2 tsp balsamic vinegar or apple cider vinegar
2 Tbs water
1 Tbs extra virgin olive oil or ghee

Note: This salad tastes great with Annie's Goddess Dressing (available in most health food stores across the United States and England). If you use the Annie's Goddess Dressing, leave out the lemon juice, vinegar, water and oil.

Instructions:
Wash the seaweed and soak in fresh water for 20 minutes. Rinse the seaweed again. Mix all the ingredients in a large bowl. Stir for several minutes. Cover and let sit for 5 minutes.

Shivaji's Sundried Tomato and Seaweed Salad

Tridoshic
Serves: 3-4
Ingredients:
¼ cup hiziki
1 cup agar
¼ cup arame
½ cup sundried tomatoes, chopped into small pieces
¼ cup celery, chopped
½ tsp organic cane sugar (sucanat, turbinado, rapidura, etc)
½ - 1 tsp black pepper fresh ground
2 Tbs fresh cilantro, chopped
1 Tbs fresh basil, chopped
1 tsp fresh dill, chopped
1 tsp freshly squeezed lemon juice
1 tsp balsamic vinegar or apple cider vinegar
2 Tbs water
1 Tbs extra virgin olive oil or ghee

Note: This salad tastes great with Annie's Goddess Dressing (available in most health food stores across the United States and England). If you use this, leave out the lemon juice, vinegar, water and oil.

Instructions:
Wash the seaweed and soak in fresh water for 20 minutes. Rinse the seaweed again. Mix all the ingredients in a large bowl. Stir for several minutes. Cover and let sit for 5 minutes.

Sita's Seaweed and Seeds Salad

Tridoshic
Serves: 3-4
Ingredients:
2 cups agar
½ cup arame
3 Tbs hemp seeds
2 Tbs pumpkin seeds
1 Tbs sunflower seeds
½ tsp organic cane sugar (sucanat, turbinado, rapidura, etc)
½ - 1 tsp black pepper fresh ground
2 Tbs fresh cilantro, chopped
1 Tbs fresh basil, chopped
1 tsp fresh mint, chopped
1 Tbs fresh dill, chopped
½ tsp fresh tarragon or ¼ tsp dry
2 tsp fresh squeezed lemon juice
2 tsp balsamic vinegar or apple cider vinegar
2 Tbs water
1 Tbs extra virgin olive oil or ghee

Note: This salad tastes great with Annie's Goddess Dressing or Raspberry Vinnegrette (available in most health food stores across the United States and England). If you use these, leave out the lemon juice, vinegar, water and oil.

Instructions:
Wash the seaweed and soak in fresh water for 20 minutes. Rinse the seaweed again. Mix all the ingredients in a large bowl. Stir for several minutes. Cover and let sit for 5 minutes.

Cinmayi's Carrot and Pea Salad

Tridoshic, slightly + vata
Serves: 4-5
Ingredients:
2 cups grated carrots
2 cups green peas (if using frozen, defrost first or boil for a couple of minutes)
¼ cup celery, chopped
½ tsp organic cane sugar (sucanat, turbinado, rapidura, etc.)
½ - 1 tsp sea salt or to taste
½ - 1 tsp black pepper fresh ground
1 Tbs fresh cilantro, chopped
1 Tbs fresh basil, chopped
1 tsp fresh mint, chopped
½ tsp fennel seeds
1 tsp fresh dill, chopped
½ tsp fresh tarragon or ¼ tsp dry
2 tsp fresh squeezed lemon juice
2 tsp balsamic vinegar or apple cider vinegar
2 Tbs water
1 Tbs extra virgin olive oil or ghee

Instructions:
Mix all the ingredients in a large bowl. Stir for several minutes. Let sit for 5 minutes.

Brahmananda Carrot Beet Raita

-vata, +pitta, =kapha
Serves: 4
Ingredients:
1 cup plain yogurt (if you are vegan you can use soy yogurt)
1 cup beets grated

1 large carrot grated
1/8 tsp cloves
1/8 tsp cinnamon
a pinch of hing (asafoetida) powder
¼ tsp sea salt
¼ tsp black pepper powder
1/8 tsp organic cane sugar

Instructions:
In a medium to large bowl, mix the yogurt and spices. Add the beets and carrots and stir well. Cover and let sit for 5 minutes. Refrigerate. Serve cold.

Chandra's Carrot Cucumber Salad

-vata, pitta, +kapha
Serves: 2-3
Ingredients:
2 cups grated carrots
½ cup cucumber,chopped
½ tsp organic cane sugar (sucanat, turbinado, rapidura, etc.)
½ - 1 tsp sea salt or to taste
½ - 1 tsp black pepper fresh ground
1 Tbs fresh cilantro, chopped
1 Tbs fresh basil, chopped
1 tsp fresh mint, chopped
1 tsp fresh dill, chopped
½ tsp fresh tarragon or ¼ tsp dry
2 tsp fresh squeezed lemon juice
2 tsp balsamic vinegar
1 tsp nutritional flakes
1 tsp de- shelled hemp seeds
2 Tbs water
1 Tbs hemp seed oil, extra virgin olive oil or ghee

Instructions:
Mix all the ingredients in a large bowl. Stir for several minutes. Cover and let sit for 5 minutes.

Edible Enlightenment Veggie Salad

Tridoshic, slightly +vata
Serves: 4-5
Ingredients:
½ cup alfalfa sprouts
½ cup clover sprouts
½ cup bean sprouts
½ cup radish sprouts
¼ cup beets, grated
¼ cup carrots, grated
¼ cup, chopped tomato
¼ cup parsnips, grated
¼ cup red cabbage, chopped
¼ cup celery, chopped
¼ cup green onions, chopped
¼ cup green peas
1 inch ginger, grated
¼ cup almonds, chopped or put through a food processor
1 Tbs de- shelled hemp seeds
1 tsp organic cane sugar (sucanat, turbinado, rapidura, etc.)
½ - 1 tsp sea salt or to taste or 1tsp Braggs Liquid Amino Acids
½ - 1 tsp black pepper fresh ground
1½ Tbs nutritional flakes
1 Tbs fresh cilantro, chopped
1 Tbs fresh basil, chopped
1 tsp fresh mint, chopped
1 Tbs fresh dill, chopped
½ tsp fresh tarragon or if fresh is not available, use ¼ tsp dry
2 Tbs fresh squeezed lemon juice

1 Tbs organic extra virgin olive oil
1 Tbs organic apple cider vinegar or red wine vinegar

Instructions:
Mix all the ingredients in a large bowl. Stir for several minutes. Cover and let sit for 5 minutes.

Gayatri's Great Garden Salad

Tridoshic, slightly +vata
Serves: 4
Ingredients:
½ cup grated beets
½ cup grated carrots
¼ cup grated daikon
¼ cup grated parnsips
¼ cup celery, chopped
¼ cup red clover sprouts
¼ cup alfalfa sprouts
¼ cup daikon radish sprouts
1 Tbs sunflower seeds
1 Tbs hemp seeds
¼ cup cilantro, chopped
1 Tbs fresh dill, chopped
1 Tbs fresh basil, chopped
1 tsp fresh lemon juice
1 tsp apple cider vinegar, balsamic vinegrette or red wine vinegar
1 tsp hemp seed or olive oil
½ tsp organic cane sugar or agave
¼ tsp sea salt
¼ tsp coarse ground black pepper
¼ tsp cayenne pepper

Instructions:
Mix all ingredients in a bowl, cover and let sit 5 minutes.

Gauri's Greens

-pitta and kapha, +vata
Serves: 4-5
Ingredients:
1 cup spinach, chopped
½ cup kale, chopped
¼ cup mustard greens, chopped
½ cup green chard, chopped
¼ cup collard greens, chopped
¼ cup bokchoy, chopped
¼ cup dandelion greens, chopped
½ cup alfalfa sprouts
¼ cup celery, chopped
¼ cup green onions, chopped
¼ cup green peas
1 tsp pumpkin seeds
1 tsp crushed or chopped almonds
1 tsp organic cane sugar (sucanat, turbinado, rapidura, etc)
½ - 1 tsp sea salt or to taste or 1 tsp Braggs Liquid Amino Acids
½ - 1 tsp black pepper fresh ground
1½ Tbs nutritional flakes
1 Tbs fresh cilantro, chopped
1 Tbs fresh basil, chopped
1 tsp fresh mint, chopped
1 Tbs fresh dill, chopped
½ tsp fresh tarragon or if fresh is not available use ¼ tsp dry
2 Tbs fresh squeezed lemon juice
1 Tbs extra virgin olive oil
1 Tbs organic apple cider vinegar or red wine vinegar

Instructions:
Mix all the ingredients in a large bowl. Stir for several minutes. Add a little water if necessary to make slightly wet. Cover and let sit for 5 minutes.

Turiya Thai Salad

Tridoshic, slightly +vata
Serves: 2-3
Ingredients:
1½ Tbs organic raw cane sugar (turbinado, sucanat, etc.)
1- 2 Tbs lime or lemon juice
2 cups raw green papaya, shredded
6 green beans, chopped
1 clove garlic minced
1½ Tbs soy sauce or tamari sauce or Braggs Liquid Amino Acids
3 hot chili peppers, chopped
5 small cherry tomatoes
2 Tbs peanuts (traditional) or cashews or almonds

Instructions:
First the papaya is peeled and shredded using a food processor or regular cheese grater with medium to large sized holes. Cut the whole papaya in half and remove the seeds before peeling. Smash the garlic, tomatoes and beans all together. Chop the chili peppers and add the green papaya, nuts, soy sauce (or similar), lime/lemon juice and sugar. Firmly mix it all up together with clean hands. This is the best way to mix the juices and flavors. Alternatively, you can use a large wooden spoon, or other utensil such as a spatula, to mash it all together so it is mixed well.

Tattvamayi's Traditional Green Papaya Salad

Tridoshic, slightly +vata
Serves: 3
Ingredients:
1½ Tbs organic raw cane sugar (turbinado,sucanat, etc)
1- 2 Tbs sweet lime or lemon juice
2 cups raw green papaya, shredded
1 cup green cabbage, chopped into small pieces
6 green beans, chopped
1 clove garlic minced
1½ Tbs soy sauce or tamari sauce or Braggs Liquid Amino Acids
3- 4 chili peppers, chopped
2 large tomatoes cut into small pieces
2 Tbs peanuts (traditional) or cashews or almonds

Instructions:
Cut the whole papaya in half and remove the seeds before peeling. Now peel the papaya and shred it using a food processor or regular cheese grater with medium to large holes. Add all the ingredients in a large mixing bowl. Firmly mix it all up together with clean hands. This is the best way to mix the juices and flavors. Alternatively, you can use a large wooden spoon, or other utensil, such as a spatula, to mash it all together so it is mixed well.

Gurupriya's Green Goddess Papaya Salad

Tridoshic, slightly +vata
Serves: 3-4
Ingredients:
1½ Tbs organic raw cane sugar (turbinado, sucanat , etc)
2 Tbs sweet lime or lemon juice
2 cups raw green papaya, shredded
½ cup mung bean sprouts long style

1 medium size tomato, chopped into small pieces
1 large clove of garlic minced
1½ Tbs soy sauce or tamari sauce or Braggs Liquid Amino Acids
2 chili peppers, chopped
2 Tbs peanuts (traditional) or cashews or almonds, chopped in a
food processor or coffee grinder so they are a chunky powder
3 Tbs cilantro, chopped
2 Tbs basil, chopped
2- 3 Tbs green onions, chopped
1- 2 Tbs tamarind paste

Instructions:
First the papaya is peeled and shredded using a food processor or
regular cheese grater with medium to large sized holes. Cut the
whole papaya in half and remove the seeds before peeling. Add all
the ingredients into a large mixing bowl. Firmly mix it all up together
with clean hands. This is the best way to mix the juices and flavors.
Alternatively, you can use a large wooden spoon, or other utensil,
such as a spatula, to mash it all together so it is mixed well.

Para Shakti's Spicy Green Papaya Salad

Tridoshic, slightly +vata
Serves: 3-4
Ingredients:
1½ Tbs organic raw cane sugar (turbinado, sucanat, etc)
2 Tbs sweet lime or lemon juice
2 cups raw green papaya, shredded
½ cup mung bean sprouts, long style
1 medium size tomato, chopped into small pieces
1 large clove of garlic minced
2 inches fresh ginger grated
1 tsp black pepper finely ground
1½ Tbs soy sauce or tamari sauce or Braggs Liquid Amino Acids

4-5 hot chili peppers, chopped
2 Tbs peanuts (traditional) or cashews or almonds, chopped in a food processor or coffee grinder so they are a chunky powder
¼ cup cilantro, chopped
3 Tbs basil, chopped
¼ cup green onions, chopped
1- 2 Tbs tamarind paste

Instructions:
First the papaya is peeled and shredded using a food processor or regular cheese grater with medium to large size holes. Cut the whole papaya in half and remove the seeds before peeling. Add all of the ingredients to a large mixing bowl. Firmly mix it all up together with clean hands. This is the best way to mix the juices and flavors. Alternatively, you can use a large wooden spoon, or other utensil such as a spatula, to mash it all together so it is mixed well.

Vidya Root Vegetable Green Papaya Salad

Tridoshic, slightly +vata
Serves: 3-4
Ingredients:
2 Tbs organic raw cane sugar (turbinado, sucanat, etc)
3 Tbs lime or lemon juice
2 cups raw green papaya, shredded
½ cup mung bean sprouts long style
¼ cup beets, grated
¼ cup carrots, grated
¼ cup daikon, grated
¼ cup parsnips, grated
1 medium size tomato, chopped into small pieces
2 large cloves of garlic, minced
2 inches fresh ginger grated
1 tsp black pepper finely ground

2 Tbs soy sauce or tamari sauce or Braggs Liquid Amino Acids
2- 3 chili peppers, chopped
3 Tbs peanuts (traditional) or cashews or almonds, chopped in a
food processor or coffee grinder so they are a chunky powder
¼ cup cilantro, chopped
3 Tbs basil, chopped
¼ cup green onions, chopped
2 Tbs tamarind paste

Instructions:
Cut the whole papaya in half and remove the seeds before peeling.
Now peel the papaya is peeled and shredded using a food processor
or regular cheese grater with medium to large sized holes. Add all of
the ingredients to a large mixing bowl. Firmly mix it all up together
with clean hands. This is the best way to mix the juices and flavors.
Alternatively, you can use a large wooden spoon, or other utensil
such as a spatula, to mix it well.

Savitri's Green Papaya Sprout Salad

-pitta and kapha, +vata
Serves: 3-4
Ingredients:
2 Tbs organic raw cane sugar (turbinado, sucanat, etc)
2- 3 Tbs sweet lime or lemon juice
2 cups raw green papaya, shredded
½ cup mung bean sprouts, long style
¼ cup daikon sprouts
¼ cup clover sprouts
¼ cup brocolli sprouts
¼ cup sunflower sprouts
¼ cup alfalfa sprouts
1 medium size tomato, chopped into small pieces
1 large clove of garlic minced

1 inch fresh ginger grated
1 tsp black pepper finely ground
2 Tbs soy sauce or tamari sauce or Braggs Liquid Amino Acids
2 chili peppers, chopped
2 Tbs peanuts (traditional) or cashews or almonds, chopped in a food processor or coffee grinder so they are a chunky powder
¼ cup cilantro, chopped
2 Tbs basil, chopped
¼ cup green onions, chopped
1- 2 Tbs tamarind paste

Instructions:
Cut the whole papaya in half and remove the seeds before peeling. Now the papaya is peeled and shredded using a food processor or regular cheese grater with medium to large sized holes. Add all of the ingredients to a large mixing bowl. Firmly mix it all together with clean hands. This is the best way to mix the juices and flavors. Alternatively, you can use a large wooden spoon, or other utensil such as a spatula, to mash it all together so it is mixed well.

Note: If all the different sprouts are not available, simply add more of your favorite sprouts that are available.

Hrdaya Herbed Beet Salad

Tridoshic
Serves: 2-3
Ingredients:
2 cups beets, grated
½ cup tomato, chopped
½ tsp organic cane sugar (sucanat, turbinado, rapidura, etc)
½ - 1 tsp sea salt or to taste
½ - 1 tsp black pepper fresh ground
1- 2 Tbs fresh cilantro, chopped

1 Tbs fresh basil, chopped
1 tsp fresh mint, chopped
1 tsp fresh dill, chopped
½ tsp fresh tarragon or ¼ tsp dry
2 tsp fresh squeezed lemon juice
1 Tbs extra virgin olive oil or ghee

Instructions:
Mix all the ingredients in a large bowl. Stir for several minutes.
Cover and let sit for 5 minutes.

Self-Realized Rainbow Salad

Tridoshic, slightly +vata
Serves: 4-5
Ingredients:
1 cup beets, grated
2 cups spinach, chopped
1 cup carrots, grated
10 black olives sliced
4- 5 whole artichoke hearts sliced in halves or quarters
3 small bell peppers thinly sliced length- wise: 1 green, 1 yellow, 1 red
3 Tbs sundried tomato, chopped
1 stalk of celery, chopped
½ tsp organic cane sugar (sucanat, turbinado, rapidura, etc)
½ - 1 tsp sea salt or to taste
½ - 1 tsp black pepper fresh ground
¼ tsp cumin powder
1 tsp de- shelled hemp seed
1 tsp pumpkin seed
1 Tbs balsamic vinegar
1 Tbs fresh squeezed lemon juice
1 tsp nutritional flakes
1 Tbs hemp seed oil or extra virgin olive oil

Instructions:
Mix all the ingredients in a large bowl. Stir for several minutes. Cover and let sit for 5 minutes.

Raghupati's Root Veggie Salad

Tridoshic, slightly +vata
Serves: 3-4
Ingredients:
1 cup beets, grated
1 cup carrots, grate
¼ cup daikon radish, grated
½ cup parsnips, grated
¼ cup celery, chopped
½ tsp organic cane sugar (sucanat, turbinado, rapidura, etc)
½ - 1 tsp sea salt or to taste or 1 tsp Braggs Liquid Amino Acids
½ - 1 tsp black pepper fresh ground
1- 2 Tbs fresh cilantro, chopped
1 Tbs fresh basil, chopped
1 tsp fresh mint, chopped
1 tsp fresh dill, chopped
½ tsp fresh tarragon or ¼ tsp dry
2 tsp fresh squeezed lemon juice
1 Tbs extra virgin olive oil or ghee
1 tsp balsamic vinegar
1 Tbs water

Instructions:
Mix all the ingredients in a large bowl. Stir for several minutes. Cover and let sit for 5 minutes.

Shankara's Simple Beet Root Salad

Tridoshic
Serves: 2-3
Ingredients:
2 cups beets, grated
½ tsp organic cane sugar (sucanat, turbinado, rapidura, etc)
½ - 1 tsp sea salt or to taste
½ - 1 tsp black pepper fresh ground
¼ tsp cumin powder
¼ tsp coriander powder
1 tsp cilantro, chopped
1 tsp fresh squeezed lemon juice
1 tsp extra virgin olive oil

Instructions:
Mix all the ingredients in a large bowl. Stir for several minutes.
Cover and let sit for 5 minutes.

Shambo's Super Sunflower Salad

Tridoshic, slightly +vata
Serves: 3
Ingredients:
2 cups fresh sunflower sprouts
½ cup long mung bean sprouts
2 Tbs sunflower seeds
¼ cup grated carrots
2 Tbs cilantro, chopped
1 Tbs parsley, chopped
1 tsp dill (fresh or dry)
1 Tbs balsamic, red wine or apple cider vinegar
1 tsp organic cane sugar
1 tsp hemp seed oil, olive or sesame oil (or 1/3rd tsp of each)

1 Tbs fresh squeezed lemon juice

Instructions:

Mix everything together in a bowl. Cover and let sit for 10 minutes.

Sarada's Special Spicy Salad

-pitta and kapha, +vata
Serves: 3-4
Ingredients:
1 large red cabbage, finely, chopped
1 12 - inch daikon radish, grated
1 medium carrot, grated
2 small or 1 large hot chili pepper, chopped
1 Tbs shredded coconut
1 Tbs fresh squeezed lemon
1- 2 Tbs fresh cilantro
1 tsp dill (fresh or dry)
1 Tbs balsamic or apple cider vinegar
1 tsp organic cane sugar
¼ tsp cumin
3 Tbs water
1 Tbs hemp seed oil or olive oil

Instructions:

Mix all the ingredients in a large bowl. Stir for several minutes. Add a little water if necessary to make moist. Cover and let sit for 5 minutes.

Santosha Spinach Cranberry Salad

-pitta and kapha, slightly +vata
Serves: 3-4
Ingredients:
3 cups spinach, chopped

¼ cup dried cranberries
1 Tbs de- shelled hemp seeds
1 tsp sunflower seeds
¼ cup celery, chopped
1 Tbs walnuts
1 Tbs organic almonds (crushed or, chopped, by hand or in a food processor)
1 tsp organic cane sugar (sucanat, turbinado, rapidura, etc)
½ - 1 tsp sea salt or to taste or 1 tsp Braggs Liquid Amino Acids
½ - 1 tsp black pepper freshly ground
¼ tsp cumin powder
1 tsp fresh cilantro, chopped
1 tsp fresh basil, chopped
1 tsp fresh dill, chopped
½ tsp fresh tarragon or if fresh is not available use ¼ tsp dry
1 Tbs freshly squeezed lemon juice
1 Tbs hemp seed oil or extra virgin olive oil
1 Tbs organic apple cider vinegar

Instructions:
Mix all the ingredients in a large bowl. Stir for several minutes. Add a little water if necessary to make slightly wet. Cover and let sit for 5 minutes.

Siddhesvari's Succulent Sprout Salad

-pitta and kapha, +vata
Serves: 2-3
Ingredients:
½ cup red clover sprouts
½ cup alfalfa sprouts
½ cup daikon radish sprouts
½ cup sunflower sprouts
1 cup whole mung bean sprouts
¼ cup cilantro, chopped

1 Tbs fresh dill, chopped
1 Tbs fresh basil, chopped
1 tsp fresh lemon juice
1 tsp apple cider vinegar, balsamic vinegrette or red wine vinegar
1 tsp hemp seed or olive oil
½ tsp organic cane sugar or agave
¼ tsp sea salt
¼ tsp coarse ground black pepper
¼ tsp cayenne pepper

Instructions:
Mix all ingredients in a bowl. Cover and let sit 5 minutes.

Satguru's Supreme Spinach Salad

-pitta and kapha, +vata
Serves: 4
Ingredients:
3 cups spinach, chopped
½ cup kale, chopped
¼ cup carrots, grated
¼ cup celery, chopped
1 tsp organic cane sugar (sucanat, turbinado, rapidura, etc)
½ - 1 tsp sea salt or to taste or 1 tsp Braggs Liquid Amino Acids
½ - 1 tsp black pepper fresh ground
¼ tsp cumin powder
1 Tbs fresh cilantro, chopped
1 tsp fresh basil, chopped
1 tsp fresh dill, chopped
½ tsp fresh tarragon, or if fresh is not available, use ¼ tsp dry
1 Tbs freshly squeezed lemon juice
1 tsp sunflower seeds
1 tsp hemp seed oil or extra virgin olive oil
1 Tbs organic apple cider vinegar

Instructions:
Mix all the ingredients in a large bowl. Stir for several minutes. Add a little water if necessary to make moist. Cover and let sit for five minutes.

Valsala's Vegetable Medley Salad

Tridoshic, slightly +vata
Serves: 4-5
Ingredients:
1 cup collard greens, chopped into small pieces
½ cup beets grated
½ cup carrots grated
½ cup, chopped tomato
½ cup parsnips grated
¼ cup red cabbage, chopped
¼ cup celery, chopped
¼ cup green onions, chopped
¼ cup green peas
1 tsp organic cane sugar (sucanat, turbinado, rapidura, etc)
½ - 1 tsp sea salt or to taste or 1 tsp Braggs Liquid Amino Acids
½ - 1 tsp black pepper fresh ground
2 Tbs fresh cilantro, chopped
1 Tbs fresh basil, chopped
1 tsp fresh mint, chopped
1Tbs fresh dill, chopped
½ tsp fresh tarragon or if fresh is not available use ¼ tsp dry
1- 2 Tbs freshly squeezed lemon juice
2 Tbs water
1 tsp nutritional flakes
1 tsp de- shelled hemp seed
1 Tbs hemp seed oil or extra virgin olive oil
1 Tbs organic apple cider vinegar

Instructions:
Mix all the ingredients in a large bowl. Stir for several minutes. Cover and let sit for five minutes.

Hrim Kali's Hawaiian Heaven

Tridoshic, slightly +kapha
Serves: 2
Ingredients:
½ cup pineapple cut into small squares
½ cup papaya cut into small squares
1 cup mango, ripe but not too ripe so it cuts properly
1 Tbs shredded coconut
1 tsp freshly squeezed lemon juice
Pinch of cayenne pepper

Instructions:
Add all the ingredients in a bowl and mix with a spoon. Enjoy!

Perfectly Purna Papaya Salad

-vata and pitta, +kapha
Serves: 2
Ingredients:
2 cups ripe papaya cut into squares
½ cup dates, chopped
1 Tbs freshly squeezed lemon juice

Instructions:
Put cut papaya in a large bowl. Add the dates and lemon juice. Stir and serve.

Berry Bhakti Salad

Tridoshic
Serves: 2
Ingredients:
1 cup blueberries
½ cup blackberries
½ cup raspberries
1 cup strawberries cut into quarters

Instructions:
Mix in a bowl and enjoy!

Prashanta's Paradise

Serves: 2
Tridoshic, slightly +kapha
Ingredients:
¼ cup mango
¼ cup papaya
¼ cup pineapple
¼ cup blueberries
¼ cup red grapes
½ of a peach
1 Tbs dry shredded coconut
1 Tbs freshly squeezed lemon juice

Instructions:
Chop the mango, papaya, pineapple and peach into small squares.
Place all fruit in a large mixing bowl. Add the coconut and lemon.
Mix. Enjoy!

Kerala Fruit Delight

-vata and pitta, +kapha
Serves: 2-3
Ingredients:
2 cups bananas
½ cup dates
½ cup mango
½ cup papaya
¼ cup shredded coconut
1 Tbs freshly squeezed lemon juice

Instructions:
Cut the banana into thin slices. Chop the dates into small pieces. Cut the papaya and mango into small squares. Add the coconut and lemon juice and mix.

Optional: Add a pinch of cayenne pepper to your personal serving.

Soups

*What is the use of sitting inside a room with all the doors and
windows closed and complain that it is dark,
while the sun is shining brightly outside?
If we just open the doors of our hearts, we can receive
the grace that God is constantly showering upon us.*

— Amma

A Taste of Heaven

Tridoshic
Serves: 3-4
Ingredients:
1 cup carrots, chopped into small, thin rounds
1 cup asparagus, chopped
1 cup beets, chopped
1 tsp ginger grated
½ tsp sea salt or to taste
¼ tsp black pepper
½ tsp cumin powder
½ tsp coriander powder
¼ tsp cayenne pepper
1 Tbs garlic minced
2 Tbs ghee
1 tsp cilantro, chopped
3 cups water

Instructions:
Heat the ghee on medium heat in a pot and sauté the spices and
vegetables (except the cilantro) for about 4- 5 minutes. Add water
and bring to a boil. Reduce heat to low and simmer covered for about

25 minutes, stirring occasionally, until vegetables are soft. Remove from heat, mix in the cilantro and cover. Let sit for five minutes.

Chinnamasta's Carrot Celery Celebration

Tridoshic
Serves: 3-4
Ingredients:
2 cups carrots, chopped into small, thin rounds
½ cup onions, chopped
1 cup celery, chopped
2 tsp ginger grated

½ tsp sea salt or to taste
1/8 tsp black pepper
¼ tsp cumin powder
¼ tsp coriander powder
1 clove
1 vegetable bouillon cube
1 Tbs garlic, chopped
1 small bay leaf
1 Tbs ghee
1 tsp parsley, chopped
1 tsp cilantro, chopped
3 cups water

Instructions:
Heat the ghee in a pot and sauté the bay leaf, cumin, coriander, garlic, ginger, onions, celery and carrots for about 3- 4 minutes. Add water and vegetable bouillon, and bring to a boil. Reduce heat to low and simmer covered for about 20 minutes, until vegetables are soft. Add salt and pepper and remove from heat. Mix in the cilantro and parsley, cover, and let sit for five minutes.

Gita's Cilantro Ginger Soup

Tridoshic, slightly +pitta
Serves: 2-3
Ingredients:
1 cup cilantro, chopped
4 oz. ginger grated
½ tsp cumin seeds
1 tsp turmeric powder
2 Tbs ghee or Earth Balance Vegan Spread
¼- ½ tsp sea salt or to taste
¼ tsp coriander powder
½ tsp black pepper fresh ground

10 oz. almond or hemp milk
2½ cups water

Instructions:
Grate the ginger and mash it into a paste in a bowl. Heat the ghee and sauté the cumin seeds and ginger together. Add the turmeric, black pepper, salt and water. When the water boils, add the milk. Bring to a boil and reduce to low heat. Cook for about 3- 4 minutes. Stir frequently to prevent boiling over. Remove from heat and add cilantro. Cover and let sit for five minutes. Add salt to taste.

Ganapati's Ginger Soup

-vata and kapha, +pitta
Serves: 2-3
Ingredients:
6 oz. ginger grated
½ tsp cumin seeds
1 tsp turmeric powder
2 Tbs ghee or Earth Balance Vegan Spread
¼- ½ tsp sea salt or to taste
¼ tsp coriander powder
¼ - ½ tsp black pepper fresh ground
10 oz. almond or hemp milk
2 cups water
1 Tbs cilantro, chopped

Instructions:
Grate the ginger and mash it into a paste in a bowl. Heat the ghee and sauté the cumin seeds and ginger together. Add the turmeric, black pepper, salt and water. When the water boils add the milk. Bring it to a boil and reduce to low heat. Cook for about 3- 4 minutes. Stir frequently to prevent boiling over. Remove from heat and add cilantro. Cover and let sit for five minutes. Add salt to taste.

Mata Rani Root Soup

Tridoshic
Serves: 4-5
Ingredients:
4- 5 cups water
1 cup beets, chopped
1 cup carrots, chopped into thin rounds
½ cup burdock root, chopped into thin rounds
½ cup parsnips, chopped into small pieces
3 tsp black pepper
2 tsp cayenne pepper
2 inch ginger freshly grated
2 tsp cumin powder
½ tsp turmeric
1 tsp, chopped garlic
1 tsp coriander powder
¼ tsp fenugreek powder
1/8 tsp hing (asafoetida)
½ tsp sea salt
2 Tbs ghee
2 tsp cilantro, chopped

Instructions:
Sauté in ghee all of the ingredients, except the cilantro, in a large stainless steel pot for about 3- 4 minutes. Add the water and bring to a rolling boil. Reduce heat to low and simmer for about 45 minutes. Remove from heat and add the cilantro. Cover and let sit for five minutes.

Kapha Balancing Soup

Tridoshic
Serves: 4-5
Ingredients:
4- 5 cups water
½ cup carrots grated
½ cup onions, chopped
1 cup dark leafy greens (kale, collards, mustard, chard, etc), chopped
3 tsp black pepper
2 tsp cayenne pepper
2 inch ginger freshly grated
2 tsp cumin powder
½ tsp turmeric
1 Tbs basil, chopped
½ tsp sea salt
2 tsp cilantro, chopped

Instructions:
Put all of the ingredients in a large stainless steel pot and boil. Reduce heat to low and simmer for about 45- 50 minutes. Remove from heat and add the cilantro. Cover and let sit for five minutes.

Kapha Balancing Soup II

Tridoshic
Serves: 4-5
Ingredients:
4- 5 cups water
½ cup kale grated
¼ cup green onions, chopped
1 cup broccoli cut into small florets
½ cup cauliflower cut into small florets
3 tsp black pepper

2 tsp cayenne pepper
2 inch ginger freshly grated
2 tsp cumin powder
½ tsp turmeric
1 Tbs basil, chopped
½ tsp sea salt or Braggs Liquid Amino Acid
2 tsp cilantro, chopped

Instructions:
Put all of the ingredients in a large stainless steel pot and bring to a rolling boil. Reduce heat to low and simmer for about 45- 50 minutes. Remove from heat and add the cilantro. Cover and let sit for five minutes.

Pitta Balancing Soup

Tridoshic
Serves: 4-5
Ingredients:
½ cup basmati rice
6- 7 cups water
1 cup kale, chopped
½ cup celery, chopped
½ cup carrots grated
½ cup fennel bulb, chopped
1 tsp fennel seed powder
¼ tsp cumin powder
¼ tsp coriander powder
1 Tbs cilantro, chopped
¼ - ½ tsp sea salt or to taste

Instructions:
Wash the rice. Boil water in a large heavy- bottomed pot. Add the rice, the vegetables (except the kale), fennel, cumin and coriander. Reduce heat to medium- low, cover the pot and let simmer for 20-

30 minutes. Now reduce the heat to low and add the kale and cover. Cook another 20 minutes. Remove from heat and add the cilantro and salt. Let sit for five minutes.

Pitta Balancing Soup II

Tridoshic
Serves: 4-5
Ingredients:
½ cup basmati rice
6- 7 cups water
½ cup kale, chopped
½ cup chard, chopped
½ cup beets, chopped
½ cup carrots grated
½ cup fennel bulb, chopped
1 tsp fennel seed powder
¼ tsp cumin powder
¼ tsp coriander powder
1 Tbs cilantro, chopped
¼ - ½ tsp sea salt or to taste

Instructions:
Wash the rice. Boil water in a large heavy- bottomed pot. Add the rice, vegetables (except the kale and chard), fennel, cumin and coriander. Reduce heat to medium- low, cover the pot and let simmer for 20- 30 minutes. Now reduce the heat to low and add the kale and chard and cover. Cook another 20 minutes. Remove from heat and add the cilantro and salt. Let sit for five minutes.

Vata Balancing Soup

Tridoshic
Serves: 4-5
Ingredients:
¼ cup basmati rice
6- 8 cups water
1 cup, chopped kale
½ cup carrots grated
½ cup beets, chopped into small pieces
3- 4 Tbs daikon grated
1/8 tsp black pepper
1/8 tsp ground cumin
1/8 tsp ground coriander
1/8 tsp turmeric
1 Tbs cilantro, chopped
½ tsp fresh ginger root minced
¼ tsp sea salt or to taste

Instructions:
Wash and drain the rice. Boil the water in a large, heavy- bottomed stainless steel pot. Add all the ingredients except the cilantro and kale. Reduce heat to medium- low, cover the pot and let simmer for 20- 30 minutes. Then reduce to low heat, add the kale and cook another 30 minutes. Remove from heat. Mix in the cilantro and cover and let sit five minutes. Add more salt to taste.

Vata Balancing Sweet Potato Soup

Tridoshic
Serves: 4-5
Ingredients:
¼ cup basmati rice
6- 8 cups water

1 cup kale, chopped
1 cup sweet potato cut into small thin pieces
½ cup carrots, chopped into small thin round pieces
3- 4 Tbs daikon grated
1/8 tsp black pepper
1/8 tsp ground cumin
1/8 tsp ground coriander
1/8 tsp turmeric
1 tsp cilantro, chopped
½ tsp fresh ginger root minced
¼ tsp sea salt or to taste

Instructions:
Wash and drain the rice. Boil the water in a large, heavy- bottomed stainless steel pot. Add all the ingredients, except the cilantro and kale. Reduce heat to medium- low, cover the pot and let simmer for 20- 30 minutes. Then reduce to low heat, add the kale and cook another 30 minutes. Remove from heat. Mix in the cilantro, cover and let sit for five minutes. Add more salt to taste.

Shanti Seaweed Soup

Tridoshic, slightly + kapha
Serves: 3-4
Ingredients:
¼ cup dulse
½ cup agar
¼ cup arame
¼ cup hiziki
½ cup grated carrots
½ cup beets, grated
4- 5 cups water
1 tsp black pepper fresh ground
2 Tbs fresh cilantro, chopped

1 Tbs fresh basil, chopped
1 tsp cumin powder
1 tsp fresh dill, chopped
½ tsp fresh tarragon or ¼ tsp dry
1 Tbs extra virgin olive oil or ghee
¼ tsp sea salt or to taste

Instructions:
Bring water to a boil. Add seaweed, beets and carrots. Cook for 5-7 minutes. Add all other ingredients and cook for a few minutes. Remove from heat, cover and let sit for five minutes.

Svatantra Spicy Greens Soup

Tridoshic, slightly +pitta
Serves: 4-5
Ingredients:
1 cup each of kale, collards and chard, chopped
4- 5 cups water
2 tsp organic corn flour dissolved in 2 Tbs water
1 tsp cayenne pepper or 1 red hot chili pepper, chopped
2- 3 Tbs ghee
1 Tbs cilantro freshly, chopped
½ tsp black pepper freshly ground
½ tsp sea salt or to taste
1 tsp nutritional flakes (optional)

Instructions:
Heat the ghee on medium heat in a large saucepan, add the, chopped greens and chili (if using fresh) and sauté on low heat for about 5- 6 minutes. Now, add the water and spices, including chili if using dry. Bring to boil on medium heat. Next, add the corn flour and simmer on low heat for about 4- 5 minutes. Remove from heat and add the cilantro. Cover and let sit for five minutes. If using nutritional flakes, add now.

Suddha's Spicy Greens Soup

-vata and kapha, +pitta
Serves: 4
Ingredients:
1 cup each of kale, spinach, chopped
½ cup each of bokchoy and mustard greens, chopped
4- 5 cups water
2 tsp organic corn flour dissolved in 2 Tbs water
1 Tbs strong cayenne pepper or 3 red hot chili pepper, chopped
2- 3 Tbs ghee
3 Tbs cilantro freshly, chopped
½ tsp black pepper freshly ground
1 tsp garlic finely, chopped or minced
1 Tbs ginger finely, chopped or minced
½ tsp sea salt or to taste
1 tsp nutritional flakes (optional)

Instructions:
Heat the ghee in a saucepan or large pot and add the, chopped greens, garlic, ginger and chili (if using fresh) and sauté on low heat for about 5- 6 minutes. Now, add the water and spices. Bring to boil on medium heat. Next, add the corn flour and simmer on low heat for about 4- 5 minutes. Remove from heat and add the cilantro. Cover and let sit for five minutes. If using nutritional flakes, add now.

Selfless Service Soup

-vata and kapha, +pitta
Serves: 3-4
Ingredients:
2 large onions, chopped
4 cups water
2 tsp organic corn flour dissolved in 2 Tbs water

1 tsp cayenne pepper or 1 red hot chili pepper, chopped
2 Tbs ghee
1 Tbs cilantro freshly, chopped
½ tsp black pepper freshly ground
½ tsp sea salt or to taste

Instructions:

Heat the ghee in a saucepan and add the, chopped onions and chili (if using fresh). Sauté on low heat for about 8 minutes or until they are well browned. Now, add the water and spices. Bring to boil on medium heat. Next, add the corn flour and simmer on low heat for about 3- 4 minutes. Remove from heat and add the cilantro. Cover and let sit for five minutes. Add salt to taste.

SadaShiva's Spicy Seaweed Soup

Tridoshic
Serves: 4
Ingredients:
½ cup agar
¼ cup arame
¼ cup hiziki
¼ cup grated daikon
2 inches fresh ginger grated
2- 3 red hot chili peppers, chopped
½ cup yellow or red onions, chopped
4 cups water
1 tsp black pepper fresh ground
2 Tbs fresh cilantro, chopped
1 Tbs fresh basil, chopped
1 tsp cumin powder
¼ tsp coriander powder
1 tsp fresh dill, chopped
½ tsp fresh tarragon or ¼ tsp dry

1 Tbs extra virgin olive oil or ghee
Sea salt to taste

Instructions:
Bring water to a boil. Add seaweed, beets and carrots and cook for 5- 7 minutes. Mix all the ingredients in and cook for a few minutes. Remove from heat, cover and let sit for five minutes.

Kanyakumari's South Indian Subji Soup
(Tomato, Bell Pepper, Eggplant and Potato)

Tridoshic
Serves: 4-5
Ingredients:
1 cup eggplant cut into small pieces (¼ inch)
1 cup bell pepper, chopped
1 cup potato, chopped into small squares/pieces
2 cups tomato, chopped
1 tsp ginger grated
½ tsp sea salt or to taste
¼ tsp black pepper
½ tsp cumin powder
½ tsp coriander powder
¼ tsp cayenne pepper
1 tbsp garlic minced
2 Tbs ghee
1 tsp cilantro, chopped
3 cups water

Instructions:
Heat the ghee on medium heat in a pot and sauté the spices and vegetables (except the cilantro) for about 4- 5 minutes. Add water and bring to a boil. Reduce heat to low, cover and simmer for about 35- 40 minutes, or until vegetables are soft. Stir occasionally. Remove from heat and mix in the cilantro. Cover and let sit for five minutes.

Vegetables

Love cannot contain two. It can contain only one. Love is purnam; it is fullness. In Love's constant and devoted remembrance, 'you' and 'I' dissolve and disappear. Love alone remains. The entire universe is contained in that pure, undivided love. Love is endless; nothing can be excluded from it. Love is all- pervasive.

– Amma

Lalitamba's Lemon Pepper Broccoli

Tridoshic

Serves: 2-3

Ingredients:

2 large broccoli crowns cut into florets
1 cup of water
3 - 4 Tbs lemon juice
½ tsp fresh ground black pepper
½ tsp sea salt or to taste or 1 Tbs Braggs Liquid Amino Acids
2 Tbs ghee (Vegans can use extra virgin olive oil.)
1 tsp grated lemon peel
1 Tbs cilantro finely, chopped

Instructions:

Boil or steam broccoli for about 5- 6 minutes. Turn heat down to low and cook another 4 - 5 minutes (until broccoli is just soft). In a saucepan heat the ghee. Add the broccoli, salt, pepper and lemon,and sauté for about 2 - 3 minutes. Remove from heat, mix in the cilantro, cover and let sit for five minutes. Serve with basmati rice, jasmine rice or rice noodles.

Ananda Aloo Gobi Mutter

Tridoshic

Serves: 4

Ingredients:

1 cup water
2 cups cauliflower, chopped
2 cups potatoes, chopped
1 medium size tomato, chopped
1 cup green peas
3 Tbs ghee
1 tsp cumin seeds

½ tsp fennel seeds
¼ tsp fenugreek seeds
½ tsp turmeric
½ tsp cayenne pepper
½ tsp coriander powder
¼ tsp black pepper powder
½ tsp sea salt or to taste
1 tsp organic cane sugar (turbinado, sucanat, etc)
3 Tbs cilantro finely, chopped

Instructions:
Heat ghee on medium heat in a wok or pot. Add the cumin, fennel and fenugreek seeds and stirfry for a couple of minutes. Next, add the cauliflower. On low to medium heat, lightly stirfry for 3- 4 minutes. Add the peas and stirfry for a few more minutes, stirring occasionally. Now add the potatoes, turmeric, cayenne and coriander. Mix well. Add water, cover with a tight fitting-lid, and cook on low flame for 10- 12 minutes. Now add the tomatoes, salt and sugar and mix together. Add a little water if necessary. Cover and cook for 8- 10 minutes or until potatoes are soft. When finished, remove from heat and let it sit covered for five minutes. Mix in cilantro and let sit another minute or two. Serve with rice.

Amritanandini's Asparagus

Tridoshic
Serves: 2
Ingredients:
2 cups asparagus stems, chopped
½ cup water
1 tsp lemon juice
1 tsp cumin powder
¼ tsp turmeric powder
¼ tsp paprika

¼ tsp black pepper
1/8 tsp coriander
1/8 tsp sea salt or 1 tsp Braggs Liquid Amino Acids
½ cup blanched, sliced almonds
2 Tbs ghee

Instructions:
Heat the ghee on medium heat in a saucepan. Add the spices and sauté for a minute or two. Add the asparagus and sauté for 3- 4 minutes. Add the water and cover. Cook until asparagus is tender (about 10 minutes). Stir frequently and add more water if necessary to prevent sticking. When the asparagus is finished, add the lemon juice and almonds, cover and remove from heat. Let sit for five minutes. Add more salt or Braggs to taste. Serve with rice, dahl, kichari.

Omkara Okra Masala

Tridoshic
Serves: 2-3
Ingredients:
2 Tbs ghee
3- 4 green chilies, chopped
1 Tbs ginger, chopped into small pieces
4 large onions, chopped into small pieces
½ tsp turmeric powder
1½ lbs. okra washed, dried and cut into small strips lengthwise or into 5- 6 rings per okra
¼ tsp black pepper
¼ tsp sea salt or to taste

Instructions:
Heat the ghee on medium heat in a saucepan and stir fry the green chilies and ginger slightly until the ginger turns a light brown. Add the onions and stirfry on medium heat for 2- 3 minutes or until onions are just about to brown. Stir in the turmeric. Add the okra

and cook briefly on high heat until it is well covered with ghee and spices and. Now, add in the salt and cook on low for 10- 12 minutes or until okra is soft and well cooked. Sauté for a few more minutes, until the okra is well fried. Add a little more ghee if necessary to avoid sticking. Cover and let sit for five minutes. Serve with rice.

Bhagarati's Broccoli and Peas

Tridoshic
Serves: 2-3
Ingredients:
1 onion, chopped into small pieces
2 cups broccoli, chopped into florets
1 cup green peas
2 Tbs ghee
a pinch of hing (asafoetida)
½ tsp turmeric powder
½ tsp cayenne pepper
½ tsp cumin powder
¼ tsp coriander powder
¼ tsp black pepper powder
1/8 tsp ginger powder
¼- ½ tsp sea salt or to taste

Instructions:
Steam or boil broccoli and peas until slightly soft. Heat ghee in a saucepan and sauté the onions until they are just about to start browning. Now, add the spices and sauté for a minute or two. Add the broccoli and peas and sauté for 3- 5 minutes. Add a little more ghee if necessary to avoid sticking. Cover and let sit for a few minutes. Serve with rice.

Bhadra Tarini's Benevolent Brocolli

Tridoshic
Serves: 3
Ingredients:
3 cups broccoli florets
3 or 4 hot green peppers, chopped
1- inch fresh ginger grated
1 tsp of cumin seeds
¼ tsp turmeric powder
¼ tsp coriander
¼ tsp black pepper freshly ground
2 Tbs of ghee
2 cups water
¼ tsp sea salt or to taste

Instructions:
Steam or boil the broccoli for 6- 7 minutes, remove from heat and cover. Mix the grated ginger and chili together with ¼ tsp water. Heat the ghee in a saucepan or wok and add the cumin seeds, ginger, chili and black pepper. Stirfry for 1- 2 minutes. Now add the broccoli and the rest of the spices and sritfry for about five minutes. Add a little water if needed. Remove from heat, cover and let sit for a few minutes. Serve with basmati or jasmine rice or rice noodles.

Compassion in Action Carrot Spinach Curry

Tridoshic
Serves: 3-4
Ingredients:
4 Tbs ghee
3 lbs. spinach, chopped
2 cups carrots, chopped
1 large onion, chopped

1 Tbs ginger freshly grated
1/8 tsp hing (asafoetida)
½ tsp turmeric
½ tsp cayenne pepper
1½ tsp sea salt or to taste
1 tsp cumin powder
½ tsp coriander powder
½ tsp black pepper

Instructions:
Heat the ghee on medium heat in a large pan. Add the carrots, onions and spinach. Stirfry the veggies for a couple of minutes. Add the turmeric, cayenne pepper and salt. Stirfry until the spinach is slightly soft. Add 2½ cups of water and the other spices. Cook on a medium to medium- high heat for about 15- 20 minutes (stirring frequently) or until just a little liquid is left and the carrots are soft. Cover and let sit five minutes. Serve with basmati or jasmine rice.

Cidananda's Cashew Broccoli (Baked or Stirfried)

Tridoshic
Serves: 2
Ingredients:
1 large head of broccoli (approximately 2½ cups, cut)
3 Tbs green onion, chopped
2 Tbs ghee
2 tsp organic cane sugar (turbinado, sucanat, rapidura)
1 tsp apple cider or red wine vinegar
½ tsp black mustard seeds
¼ tsp sea salt
¼ tsp cumin seeds
1 cup dry roasted cashews, finely, chopped (This can be done in a food processor.)
1½ cups water

Instructions:
Option 1:
Pre- heat oven to 350°F (175°C). Cook broccoli in water until slightly soft. Sauté onions in ghee for about a minute and add the other spices. Drain first, then put the broccoli in an oiled (with ghee or olive oil) baking dish and cover with onions. Sprinkle with the roasted cashews and bake for 15- 20 minutes. Serve with rice or rice noodles.

Option 2:
Cook broccoli in water until slightly soft. Sauté onions in ghee for about a minute and add the other spices. Drain the broccoli and add to spices. Add the cashews and a little more ghee if too dry. Stirfry about five minutes. Cover and let sit five minutes. Serve with rice or rice noodles.

Cit Shakti's Chili Okra

Tridoshic
Serves: 2-3
Ingredients:
3 cups okra
3 Tbs ghee
2- 3 large chili peppers, chopped into small pieces, or 1 tsp strong cayenne pepper
¼ - ½ tsp sea salt or to taste
¼ tsp black pepper freshly ground

Instructions:
Wash and dry the okra. Cut into small round pieces. Heat ghee on medium heat in a wok or saucepan and stirfry the chili peppers for a few minutes. Add the okra, sea salt and black pepper, stirring frequently until the okra is cooked, approximately 10- 12 minutes. Cover and let sit five minutes. Serve with rice.

Bhairavi's Coconut Eggplant Extravaganza

Tridoshic, slightly +kapha
Serves: 2-3
Ingredients:
3 cups eggplant
1 large garlic clove crushed or finely, chopped
3 whole large garlic cloves
1 tsp grated ginger
3 Tbs tamarind paste (available in Indian grocery stores or the international food section of most natural food stores)
1/8 tsp turmeric
½ tsp sea salt
½ tsp black pepper
¼ tsp cumin powder
¼ tsp cayenne pepper
3- 4 Tbs ghee
3½ oz. coconut milk
1 Tbs cilantro, chopped
2 medium size green chilies, chopped

Instructions:
Slice the eggplant into rounds about ½ inch thick. Place the slices on top of each other, and slice again into ½ inch strips. Place the eggplant pieces in a bowl. Add the crushed garlic, ginger, tamarind paste, turmeric, salt and chili powder. Mix together. Let sit 15- 20 minutes. Meanwhile, peel the three whole garlic cloves and crush. Heat the ghee on medium heat, add garlic and stir until garlic is light golden brown. Add the eggplant mixture and stirfry until cooked, about 12- 15 minutes. Remove from heat and add the coconut milk and green chilies. Heat again and stirfry until it starts to simmer, then remove from heat. Add the cilantro, cover and let sit about five minutes. Serve with basmati or jasmine rice.

Kapila's Coconut Vegetable Curry

Tridoshic, slightly +kapha
Serves: 4-5
Ingredients:
1 cup broccoli florets
1 cup cauliflower florets
1 cup carrots, chopped into small pieces
1 cup green peas
1 large garlic clove, crushed
3 large garlic cloves
1 Tbs grated ginger
3 Tbs tamarind paste (available in Indian grocery stores or the international food section of most natural food stores)
1/8 tsp turmeric
½ tsp sea salt
½ tsp black pepper
½ tsp cumin powder
½ tsp coriander powder
¼ tsp cayenne pepper
3- 4 Tbs ghee
4 oz. (½ cup) coconut milk
2 Tbs cilantro, chopped into small pieces
2 medium sized green chilies, chopped

Instructions:
Boil or steam the vegetables for about 7- 8 minutes. Keep the water. Peel the three whole garlic cloves and crush a little but keep whole as much as possible. Heat the ghee in a pan over medium flame. Add the garlic and stir until light golden brown. Add the vegetables and spices and stirfry until they are almost cooked, about 10 minutes. Add a little of the vegetable water if necessary. Add the coconut milk and green chilies. Stirfry until it starts to simmer and then remove

from heat. Add the cilantro, cover and let sit for about five minutes. Serve with basmati or jasmine rice.

Chudamani's Curry

Tridoshic
Serves: 3-4
Ingredients:
2 cups green peas
2 cups carrots, chopped into very small pieces
2 Tbs ghee
1 cup onions, chopped
1 large garlic clove, chopped fine
1 inch ginger grated
1 tsp cumin seed
½ tsp sea salt
1 tsp black pepper
1 tsp turmeric
1 tsp coriander powder
1/8 tsp cumin powder
¼ cup tomato mashed into pulp/purée
1/8 tsp cayenne pepper
3 Tbs cilantro, chopped fine

Instructions:
Heat the ghee in large pan. Add onions and sauté until clear or slightly brown. Purée garlic and ginger in blender with small amount of water and add to onions. Add the other spices, not the cilantro. Cook for 8- 10 minutes, stirring frequently. Now, add the tomato purée, carrots and green peas. Cook about 15- 20 minutes. When finished, add the cilantro and cover. Let it sit five minutes. Serve with rice.

Durga's Eggplant and Sweet Potato Curry

Tridoshic, slightly + kapha
Serves: 4
Ingredients:
4 medium eggplants sliced
4 medium sweet potatoes sliced
4 medium tomatoes sliced
1 tsp cayenne pepper
1 tsp turmeric
½ tsp ginger powder
¼ tsp fenugreek powder
1 tsp cumin powder
1 tsp coriander powder
4 Tbs ghee
4 cups water
1 heaping tsp organic cane sugar
½- 1 tsp sea salt or to taste or 1 Tbs Braggs Liquid Amino Acids
2 Tbs cilantro, chopped

Instructions:
Heat the ghee in a saucepan. Add the tomatoes, spices and sugar. Saute on medium heat for a few minutes until the tomatoes are soft. Add the sweet potatoes and eggplants and stirfry about five minutes. Now, add the water and cook covered on medium heat for 4- 5 minutes or until the vegetables are fully cooked. Remove from heat and add the cilantro. Cover and let sit about five minutes. Serve with rice.

Gauri Shankara's Garlic Okra

Tridoshic
Serves: 2-3
Ingredients:
3 cups okra washed and dried
3 Tbs ghee
2- 3 large garlic bulbs (about 2- 3 Tbs), finely, chopped or thinly sliced
½tsp sea salt
¼ tsp black pepper powder
1 cup water for steaming okra

Instructions:
Cut okra into small round pieces. Steam the okra for five minutes on high. Heat ghee in a wok or saucepan on medium heat and stirfry garlic until slightly brown. Add the okra, sea salt and pepper stirring frequently until the okra is cooked (soft), approximately 8- 10 minutes. Cover and let sit five minutes. Serve with rice.

Ganga Ghee Root Vegetables

Tridoshic
Serves: 4-5
Ingredients:
3 large parsnips, peeled and chopped
3 large white potatoes, peeled and chopped
3 large carrots, peeled and chopped
3 medium sweet potatoes, peeled and chopped
4 Tbs ghee
1/8 tsp hing (asafoetida)
2 tsp black mustard seeds
1 tsp coriander powder
1 tsp cumin seeds

2 bay leaves
¼ tsp sea salt
½ tsp black pepper freshly ground

Instructions:
Preheat oven to 375°F (200°C). In a saucepan bring some lightly salted water to a boil. Add vegetables, boil for 3- 4 minutes, then drain. Heat the ghee in a saucepan on medium heat. Add veggies and hing and sauté until they are slightly brown at the edges. Add the mustard seeds, cumin seeds and bay leaves. Cook for another minute or so and then add salt and pepper. Put everything (asafoetida) (asafoetida) in a glass oven dish and bake for 35 minutes, stirring occasionally. Serve with rice.

Optional: Add 1 Tbs of fresh, chopped cilantro the last minute it is in the oven.

Gopi's Golden Veggie Jubilee

Tridoshic
Serves: 2-3
Ingredients:
2 large yellow zucchini, cut into long slices or thin circles
1 large white or yellow onion, chopped
1 large yellow or orange bell pepper
2 medium red or yellow tomatoes, chopped
1 large garlic clove
¼ tsp turmeric powder
¼ tsp dry red chili flakes
1 small fresh cayenne pepper, chopped
¼ tsp sea salt
¼ tsp black pepper powder
¼ tsp cumin powder
¼ tsp coriander powder

3 Tbs ghee

Instructions:
First heat the ghee in a frying pan, pot or wok. Add onions and sauté until they are clear. Add turmeric, garlic and dried chilies. Sauté for a minute and add the other vegetables and spices. Cook for 8- 10 minutes until veggies are soft (or until desired consistency). When done, cover and let sit for five minutes. Serve with rice or rice noodles.

Pranada's Perfect Pea Paradise

Tridoshic
Serves: 2-3
Ingredients:
2 cups green peas
1 tomato, chopped into small pieces
½ cup (4 oz) coconut milk
2 inches ginger grated
5 cloves of garlic
¼ tsp turmeric
3 cardamom pods
1 tsp cayenne pepper or 3 large chili peppers, chopped
½ tsp cumin powder
¼ tsp coriander powder
2 Tbs ghee
½ tsp sea salt or to taste

Instructions:
Heat ghee in pan and add tomato, ginger and garlic, stirfry for 1- 2 minutes. Then add coconut milk, spices and peas. Cook for about 12- 15 minutes until peas are soft. Stir frequently. When finished, remove from heat, mix in the cilantro, cover and let sit another five minutes. Serve with basmati rice, jasmine rice or other grain dish.

Giridhara's Spicy Green Peas

Tridoshic
Serves: 2-3
Ingredients:
3 cups green peas
3 hot green chilis, chopped
1 small red onion, chopped
1- inch fresh ginger grated
1 tsp of cumin seeds
¼ tsp black mustard seeds
¼ tsp turmeric powder
¼ tsp fenugreek powder
¼ tsp coriander
¼ tsp black pepper freshly ground
3 Tbs of ghee
2 cups water
¼ tsp sea salt or to taste

Instructions:
Steam or boil the peas for 6- 7 minutes, remove from heat and cover. Mix the grated ginger and chilis together with ¼ tsp water. Heat the ghee in a saucepan or wok and add the onions, cumin, mustard seeds, ginger, chili and black pepper. Stirfry 1- 2 minutes. Add the peas and the rest of the spices and stirfry about five minutes. Add a little water if needed. Remove from heat, cover and let it sit for a few minutes. Serve with basmati rice, jasmine rice or other grain dish or rice noodles.

Hamsa's Herbed Beets

Tridoshic
Serves: 2-3
Ingredients:
2 cups beets cut into small pieces
1 cup yellow or red onions, chopped into small pieces
2 tsp garlic minced
1 Tbs fresh basil, chopped
1 tsp dry dill
1 tsp oregano
Pinch of saffron
½ tsp black pepper freshly ground
2 Tbs cilantro, chopped
2 Tbs ghee
¼ - ½ tsp sea salt or to taste

Instructions:
Boil or steam the beets for five minutes. Heat the ghee, add the spices and onions for 1- 2 minutes. Add the beets and all the spices, and sauté for about five minutes. Remove from heat and add the salt and cilantro. Cover and let sit for five minutes. Add salt to taste. Serve with rice or another grain such as millet or quinoa.

Jagadamba's Green Glory

Tridoshic
Serves: 4
Ingredients:
2 cups collard greens, chopped
2 cups kale, chopped
2 cups mustard greens or chard, chopped
1 cup of water
1 medium white or yellow onion, chopped into small pieces

½ tsp fresh ground black pepper
½ tsp sea salt or to taste or 1Tbs Braggs Liquid Amino Acids
2 Tbs ghee (Vegans can use olive oil or Earth Balance Vegan Spread.)
1 tsp fresh tarragon, chopped
1 Tbs fresh dill, chopped
1 Tbs fresh basil, chopped
1 Tbs cilantro finely, chopped
¼- ½ tsp cayenne pepper (optional)

Instructions:
Steam the greens for 5- 6 minutes. Turn heat down to low and cook another 3- 4 minutes until they are just soft. In a saucepan heat the ghee and stirfry the onion for a few minutes until brown. Add the greens, salt, pepper and the fresh herbs (except the cilantro) and sauté for about 2- 3 minutes. If you are using cayenne pepper, add it at this time. Remove from heat, mix in the cilantro, cover and let sit for five minutes. Serve with basmati rice, jasmine rice or other grain dish or rice noodles.

Kali's Kale Sauté

Tridoshic
Serves: 1-2
Ingredients:
2 cups kale, chopped into small pieces
¼ tsp sea salt or to taste
¼ tsp black pepper powder or to taste (Freshly ground is best.)
1/8 tsp turmeric powder
1/8 tsp cumin powder
1 Tbs ghee

Instructions:
Steam the kale for 10- 12 minutes. Meanwhile, heat the ghee in a saucepan with turmeric, cumin and black pepper, and sauté for about 1 minute. Add the cooked kale and salt, and sauté for 2- 3

minutes. Save the steamed kale water and if needed add a couple tablespoons to the sauté. Cover and let sit for a few minutes. Serve with rice or rice noodles.

Karuna Coconut Vegetable Delight

Tridoshic, slightly +kapha
Serves: 3-4
Ingredients:
3 cups (total) of chopped vegetables: mixture of carrots, eggplant, potatoes, zucchini, squash, onions, peas
2 cups coconut milk
2 Tbs ghee
½ tsp cardamom powder
¼ tsp black pepper
1- 2 whole cinnamon sticks about 2 inches long
2- 3 bay leaves broken into 2- 3 small pieces each
2 inches ginger, , chopped Into small pieces or thinly sliced
½ tsp sea salt or to taste

Instructions:
First boil the vegetables until almost cooked, and save the stock. Heat ghee in a saucepan, add all spices except the ginger, and stirfry for 1- 2 minutes. Then add the ginger and stirfry for a few more minutes. Now, add the vegetables and sauté for 2- 3 minutes. Add 1½ cups of the vegetable stock and one cup of coconut milk. Cook on high for 8- 10 minutes, then lower the heat and simmer until the vegetables are cooked. Remove from heat, add one cup of coconut milk. Cover and let sit five minutes. Serve with rice or rice noodles.

Lambodara's Lemon Broccoli

Tridoshic
Serves: 3-4
Ingredients:
4 cups broccoli cut into small florets
1 Tbs olive oil
2½ tsps lemon peel grated
1/8 tsp crushed red pepper or cayenne pepper

Alternative version:
1/8 tsp crushed black peppercorns
1/8 tsp salt
1/8 tsp ginger powder

Instructions:
Steam broccoli until a little tender (or as you like), cover and let sit a couple of minutes. drain water. Heat olive oil on medium heat in a skillet and add lemon peel and crushed red pepper. Stir until peel begins to brown, or approximately 30 seconds. Add broccoli and salt and stirfry for about 1 minute. Serve with rice, rice noodles or other grain dish.

Maha Ratih Mystic Vegetables

Tridoshic, slightly +kapha
Serves: 4-5
Ingredients:
2 cups cauliflower, cut into small florets
1 cup carrots, cut into small pieces
1 lb of potatoes, cut into small- size pieces
½ lb paneer, cut into medium- size pieces
1 cup green peas
3 oz cashews, cut into small pieces

5 tomatoes: 1 tomato is to be cut into small pieces and the others, blended
3 big onions: 1 onion will be sliced and the others, blended
2 green chilies, finely chopped
¼ tsp turmeric powder
2 tsp coriander powder
2 tsp cumin powder
1/8 tsp cayenne pepper powder
1/8 tsp cardamom powder
1- inch ginger, grated
1 large clove of garlic, chopped finel½ cup ghee
3 Tbs cilantro finely, chopped

Instructions:
Rapidly boil the vegetables for about five minutes then reduce to low heat for five minutes. Strain the water. Heat half of the ghee in a pot and add the sliced onion, half of each dry spice, half of the ginger, half of the garlic and half of the chilies. Stirfry for a few minutes. Next, add the steamed vegetables and paneer, and stirfry for five minutes or until all the veggies are cooked. Remove from heat and add cilantro. Serve with any grain dish.

To make the masala:
Blend together 2 onions and 4 tomatoes in a blender with a little water so that it makes a purée. Water quantity will vary depending on the quality and size of the tomatoes. Heat the ghee and add the rest of the ginger and garlic. When the ginger and garlic are slightly brown, add tomato- onion purée and stirfry a few minutes. Then add the, chopped cashew nuts and stirfry for 3- 4 minutes. Add the rest of the green chilies and the rest of the dry spices. Stirfry for five minutes on low flame. Add ¼ cup water and boil for a couple minutes.

Nine Gems Korma

Tridoshic
Serves: 4-6
Ingredients:
½ cup white potatoes, chopped
½ cup carrots, chopped
½ cup green peas, chopped
½ cup green beans, chopped
½ cup cauliflower florets, chopped
½ cup bell pepper, chopped
½ cup red cabbage, chopped
½ cup yellow zucchini, chopped
½ cup broccoli florets, chopped
½ cup tomato purée
2 medium white or yellow onions
3 tsp ginger, grated
1 Tbs garlic, mashed or finely, chopped
¼ tsp sea salt or to taste
1 tsp turmeric
2 tsp cayenne
1 tsp coriander
2 tsp cumin
6 Tbs ghee
1 cup milk and water (If vegan, unsweetened almond milk goes best.)
10- 15 cashews
15 raisins
2 Tbs cilantro, chopped

Instructions:
With the exception of the red cabbage, steam or boil the vegetables for 7- 8 minutes. Add the red cabbage in for the last 3 minutes. Cover and let sit. In a different pan, heat the ghee and sauté the onions, ginger and garlic until they turn a light golden brown. Add

the cashews, raisins, cilantro and spices and cook 2- 3 more minutes on medium heat. Now add the tomato purée. Stir frequently, cooking for 3- 4 minutes. Add the milk and water, and bring to a boil. Reduce the heat and add all the vegetables to the sauce and cook for 5- 7 minutes. Remove from heat and stir in the cilantro. Cover and let sit for five minutes. Serve with rice or grain dish.

Nataraja's North Indian Spinach

Tridoshic
Serves: 2-3
Ingredients:
4- 5 Tbs ghee
3 lb spinach, chopped
1 Tbs ginger, freshly grated
1/8 tsp hing (asafoetida)
½ tsp turmeric
½ tsp cayenne pepper
1 ¼ tsp sea salt
½ tsp cumin powder
½ tsp coriander powder
¼ tsp black pepper

Instructions:
Heat the ghee in a large pan on medium. Add the hing (asafoetida) (asafoetida) and then the spinach. Stirfry the spinach for 1 minute. Then add the turmeric, cayenne pepper and salt. Stirfry until the spinach becomes slightly soft. Add 1½ cups of water and the other spices. Cook on a medium heat for about 15 minutes, or until just a little liquid is left. Stir every few minutes. Turn the heat to low and mash up the spinach with spoon until it becomes slightly creamy. Cook for a couple more minutes. Cover and let sit for five minutes. Serve with rice or grain dish.

Supriya's Sauteed Okra

Tridoshic
Serves: 1-2
Ingredients:
1 cup okra, chopped
1 Tbs ghee
½ tsp turmeric
½ tsp cumin powder
½ tsp coriander powder
1/8 tsp sea salt or to taste
1/8 tsp hing (asafoetida) (asafoetida)
½ tsp black pepper powder
¼ tsp ginger powder or ½ inch fresh ginger grated
1- 2 Tbs cilantro, chopped

Instructions:
Wash okra thoroughly. Heat the ghee in a saucepan and add the okra. Sauté the okra, stirring frequently, until it is slightly brown at the edges and a little crispy (about 7 minutes). Add the salt and spices. Sauté for about 5 more minutes. Add more ghee if necessary. When done, mix in cilantro, cover and let sit for five minutes. Serve with rice or quinoa dish.

Roots of Creation

Tridoshic
Serves: 2-3
Ingredients:
1 medium white daikon radish, cut into thin pieces
1 large beet, chopped into thin pieces
2 large carrots, chopped into thin pieces
12 inches of burdock (gobo) root, cut into thin pieces
1 bunch green onions (scallions), chopped

10 almonds, soaked, peeled and slivered
3 Tbs ghee
2 oz water
¼ tsp sea salt
¼ tsp black pepper

Instructions:
Wash and slice all the vegetables into thin pieces. Heat the ghee in a large frying pan or wok. Add almonds and onions and sauté for a couple of minutes. Mix in the vegetables, salt and pepper and stirfry for 3- 4 minutes. Add 2 oz of water, cover and cook for about 6- 7 minutes, stirring frequently. Taste and add more salt and pepper if needed. When veggies are soft, cover and let sit for five minutes. Serve with rice, rice noodles or grain dish.

Additional option: Fresh cilantro and basil also goes well with this dish. Add 1 Tbs each of fresh cilantro and basil.

Shyama's Seaweed Beets

Tridoshic, slightly +kapha
Serves: 2-3
Ingredients:
2 cups beets, cut into small pieces
1 Tbs hijiki
1 Tbs arame
1 Tbs agar
1 Tbs wakame
1 Tbs dulse
2 tsp garlic, minced
1 Tbs fresh basil, chopped
1 tsp dry dill
1 tsp oregano
½ tsp black pepper, freshly ground

2 Tbs cilantro, chopped
3 Tbs ghee
¼ - ½ tsp sea salt or to taste

Instructions:
Soak the seaweeds in 1 cup of water for five minutes, then rinse. Steam the seaweed for five minutes. Heat the ghee and sauté the beets for a few minutes. Then add spices and seaweed and sauté for few more minutes. Remove from heat, add the salt and cilantro and cover. Let sit for five minutes. Add salt to taste. Serve with rice, millet or quinoa.

Ocean of Ojas

Tridoshic, slightly +kapha
Serves: 4
Ingredients:
1 cup beets, cut into small pieces
1 cup carrots, cut into thin rounds
1 cup green peas
1 cup broccoli florets
1 Tbs hijiki
1 Tbs arame
2 Tbs agar
1 Tbs wakame
1 Tbs dulse
2 tsp garlic, minced
1 Tbs fresh basil, chopped
1 tsp dry dill
1 tsp oregano
½ tsp black pepper, freshly ground
2 Tbs cilantro, chopped
4 Tbs ghee

½- 1 tsp sea salt or to taste or 1 Tbs Braggs Liquid Amino Acids

Instructions:
Soak the seaweeds in 1 cup of water for five minutes, then rinse. Steam the vegetables for 8- 10 minutes. Heat the ghee and sauté the vegetables for a few minutes. Add a little water if necessary to prevent sticking. Then add spices and seaweed and sauté for few more minutes. Remove from heat and add the salt and cilantro and cover. Let sit for five minutes. Add salt to taste. Serve with rice, millet or quinoa.

Sneha Sesame Broccoli

Tridoshic
Serves: 3-4
Ingredients:
4 cups broccoli florets
1 tsp ginger, grated
½ tsp sea salt or 1 Tbs Braggs Liquid Amino Acids
1 Tbs organic toasted sesame oil
1 Tbs lemon juice
1- 2 Tbs toasted sesame seeds
1 tsp black pepper powder

Instructions:
Mix the ginger, Braggs Liquid Amino Acid (or salt), sesame oil, lemon and let it sit. Steam broccoli until slightly soft, then add the sauce. Add the sesame seeds, and black pepper and mix. Cover and let sit for five minutes. Serve with rice, rice noodles or grain dish.

Sri Mayi's Spicy Beets

Tridoshic, slightly +pitta
Serves: 3-4
Ingredients:
3 cups beets, cut into small pieces
2 medium sized tomatoes, chopped
1 cup yellow or red onions, chopped into small pieces
2 tsp garlic, minced
1 Tbs hot cayenne pepper
1 tsp coriander powder
1 tsp cumin powder
½ tsp black pepper, freshly ground
3 Tbs cilantro, chopped
3 Tbs ghee
¼ tsp sea salt (or salt to taste)

Instructions:
Boil or steam the beets for five minutes. Blend the tomatoes with a little water into a creamy paste. Add all the spices and sauté the beets for about 5 more minutes. Add the tomatoes and cook another few minutes until the sauce starts to simmer. Remove from heat, add the salt and cilantro, and cover. Let this sit for five minutes. Add salt to taste. Serve with rice, millet or quinoa.

Saraswati's Spicy Cauliflower

Tridoshic, slightly +pitta
Serves: 3
Ingredients:
3 cups cauliflower, cutsinto medium-size florets
1 cup yellow or red onions, chopped into small pieces
2 Tbs garlic, minced
1 Tbs cayenne pepper (strong)

1 tsp turmeric powder
1 Tbs coriander powder
1 Tbs cumin powder
½ tsp black pepper, freshly ground
2 medium sized tomatoes, chopped
¼ cup cilantro, chopped
3 Tbs ghee
¼ tsp sea salt or to taste

Instructions:

Boil or steam the cauliflower for about 5- 6 minutes. Blend the tomatoes with a little water into a creamy paste. Heat the ghee and sauté the spices for a minute or two and add the cauliflower. Add all the spices and sauté until the cauliflower is slightly brown or golden. Add the tomato and cook another few minutes until the sauce starts to simmer. Remove from heat and add the salt and cilantro and cover. Let this sit for five minutes. Add salt to taste. Serve with rice, millet or quinoa.

Cetana Rupa Cauliflower of Creation

Tridoshic
Serves: 2-3
Ingredients:
3 large garlic cloves, finely chopped
2- inches fresh ginger root, thinly sliced or finely chopped
1 large head of cauliflower cut into small florets
1 Tbs olive oil or ghee
½ tsp cumin seed
½ tsp mustard seed
2- 3 hot green or red chilies, chopped into small pieces
¼- ½ tsp sea salt
½ tsp black pepper powder
¼ tsp coriander powder

¼ tsp turmeric powder
1/8 tsp hing (asafoetida)
Optional: an additional pinch of cayenne pepper for those who like
it really hot!

Instructions:
Heat olive oil or ghee in a pan and add the cumin and mustard seeds.
Cook until they pop, then and add the garlic, ginger, cauliflower
and chilies. Sauté for 5- 7 minutes until the cauliflower is lightly
browned, adding a little water if it starts to stick. Sprinkle in the
salt, pepper and herbs. Add 4 Tbs water and stir, then cover and
cook for 2 or 3 minutes more (until cauliflower is slightly soft). If
you prefer the cauliflower softer, add a little more water and cook
until it is done to your preference. Serve with rice, millet or quinoa.

Kali Kapalini's Spicy Kale and Broccoli

Tridoshic, slightly +pitta
Serves: 3-4
Ingredients:
2 cups broccoli, cut into florets
2 cups kale, chopped
1 cup of water
1 small red onion, chopped into small pieces
3 or 4 hot chili peppers (or 1 heaping tsp cayenne pepper)
½ tsp fresh ground black pepper
½ tsp sea salt or to taste or 1 Tbs Braggs Liquid Amino Acids
2 Tbs ghee (Vegans can use olive oil or Earth Balance Vegan Spread.)
1 tsp lemon peel, grated
1 Tbs cilantro, finely chopped

Instructions:
Boil or steam broccoli and kale for about 5- 6 minutes. Turn heat
down to low and cook another 3- 4 minutes until broccoli and kale
are just soft. In a saucepan heat the ghee and stirfry the onion and

chili for a few minutes until they start to brown. Mix this with the broccoli, kale, salt and pepper and sauté for about 2- 3 minutes. If you are using cayenne pepper, add it at this time. Remove from heat and mix in the cilantro, cover and let sit for five minutes. Serve with rice, rice noodles or grain dish.

Radharani's Roots

Tridoshic
Serves: 3
Ingredients:
1 cup burdock root, chopped into thin rounds
½ cup beets, chopped
½ cup carrots, chopped
½ cup parsnips, chopped
¼ cup green onions, chopped
¼ cup green peas
1 tsp dill
1 tsp basil
1 Tbs cilantro
½ tsp oregano
½ tsp tarragon
½ tsp sea salt or 1 Tbs Braggs Liquid Amino Acids
½ tsp fine ground black pepper

Instructions:
Chop the vegetables into small pieces. In a large stainless steel pot, boil 2 cups of water. Steam the vegetables for 7 minutes and remove from heat. In a large bowl mix the vegetables, herbs, salt and pepper and mix together thoroughly. Cover for a few minutes and let sit. Serve with rice or grain dish.

Sarvaga's Steamed Green Garden

Tridoshic, slightly +vata
Serves: 2-3
Ingredients:
1 cup kale
½ cup collard greens
½ cup bokchoy
¼ cup arugula
¼ cup dandelion greens
¼ cup mustard greens
¼ cup chard
1 tsp dill
1 tsp basil
1 Tbs cilantro
½ tsp sea salt or 2 tsp Braggs Liquid Amino Acids
½ tsp fine ground black pepper

Instructions:
Chop all the greens. In a large stainless steel pot, boil 2 cups of water. Steam the greens for five minutes and remove from heat. In a large bowl add the greens, herbs, salt and pepper and mix thoroughly. Cover for a few minutes and let sit. Serve with any grain dish.

Bhavatarini's Green Bean Curry

Tridoshic
Serves: 3-4
Ingredients:
1 lb fresh string beans
½ lb fresh zucchini, chopped into thin rounds
1 large white or yellow onion, chopped into small pieces
3- 4 Tbs ghee
1 tsp cumin powder

1 tsp coriander powder
½ tsp turmeric powder
¼ tsp cayenne
½ tsp garlic, minced/finely, chopped
¼ tsp black mustard seeds
¼ tsp fresh ground black pepper
¼ tsp sea salt or to taste

Instructions:
Wash the string beans and cut into 1 to 2- inch pieces. Heat the ghee in a deep frying pan or wok on medium heat and sauté the onions and mustard seeds for a couple of minutes (until the seeds pop or the onions are slightly browned). Then add the spices and sauté for another minute. Now add the string beans, mix and cover for 3- 4 minutes. Then add the zucchini, cover and cook for 8- 10 minutes. Add a little water if necessary. Once the beans and zucchini are soft, remove from heat and cover. Let it sit for about 5 mintues. Serve with rice, rice noodles, quinoa or millet.

Shiva's Subji

Tridoshic, slightly +kapha
Serves: 4
Ingredients:
2 cups bell peppers, chopped
2 cups potatoes, chopped
2 tomatoes medium- size, chopped
2 cups eggplant, cut into small quarter- inch squares
1 cup green peas
3 Tbs ghee
1 tsp cumin seeds
½ tsp fennel seeds
¼ tsp fenugreek seeds
½ tsp turmeric

½ tsp cayenne pepper
½ tsp coriander powder
¼ tsp black pepper powder
¼- ½ tsp sea salt or to taste
1 tsp organic cane sugar (turbinado, sucanat)
3 Tbs cilantro ,finely chopped

Instructions:

Heat the ghee in a large saucepan or pot. Add the cumin, fennel and fenugreek seeds and stirfry for a couple of minutes. Next, add the eggplant and bell peppers. On a low to medium heat, lightly stirfry for 4- 5 minutes. Now, add the peas and stirfry for a few more minutes stirring occasionally. Now add the potatoes, turmeric powder, cayenne powder, coriander powder and mix well. Add 1 cup of water and cover it with a tight- fitting lid. Cook on medium-low for 10- 12 minutes. Now add the tomatoes, salt and sugar, and mix together. Add a little water if necessary. Cover it and cook for 10- 12 minutes (or until potatoes are soft). When finished, remove from heat and let it sit covered for another five minutes. Then mix in the cilantro and let it sit another minute or two. Serve with rice or grain dish.

Shakti's Subji

Tridoshic
Serves: 4
Ingredients:
2 cups broccoli, cut into florets
2 cups sweet potatoes, chopped into small pieces
2 tomatoes, medium- size, chopped
2 cups cauliflower, cut into florets
1 cup green peas
4 Tbs ghee
1 tsp cumin seeds

½ tsp fennel seeds
¼ tsp fenugreek seeds
½ tsp turmeric
½ tsp cayenne pepper
½ tsp coriander powder
¼ tsp black pepper powder
sea salt to taste
1 tsp organic cane sugar (turbinado, sucanat)
3 Tbs cilantro, finely chopped

Instructions:
Heat the ghee in a large saucepan or pot. Add the cumin, fennel and fenugreek seeds and stirfry for a couple of minutes. Next, add the broccoli and cauliflower. On a low to medium heat lightly stirfry them in the ghee for 3- 4 minutes. Now, add the peas and stirfry for a few more minutes, stirring occasionally. Now add the potatoes, turmeric powder, cayenne powder, coriander powder and mix well. Add 2 cups of water and cover it with a tight fitting lid. Cook on medium- low for 10- 12 minutes. Now add the tomatoes, salt and sugar, and mix together. Add a little more water if necessary. Cover it and cook for 8- 10 minutes or until potatoes are soft. Remove from heat and let it sit covered for another five minutes, then mix in the cilantro and let it sit another minute or two. Serve with rice or grain dish.

Thai Tofu Tapas Curry

-vata, slightly +pitta and kapha
Serves: 3-4
Ingredients:
12 oz package of extra firm tofu (organic, non- GMO) cut in ½-inch cubes
1½ cups (12 oz) coconut milk
1 large broccoli, cut into florets

1 cup chopped carrots
1 large bunch of green onions, chopped
1 large red onion, chopped into small pieces
2-3 red or green hot chili peppers, chopped
3 cloves of garlic, chopped
2 Tbs fresh lemongrass, chopped (Available in most asian/Indian grocery stores. If you can't find fresh, dry is okay.)
1 can baby corn (organic, non- GMO)
2 Tbs Thai green curry paste
3 Tbs ghee or olive oil
½ tsp sea salt or to taste

Instructions:

In a medium- sized frying pan or wok, heat the ghee or olive oil. Add tofu and stirfry until it is golden brown on all sides. Remove tofu. Stirfry the red onions and garlic until slightly brown. Add more oil if necessary. Now, add all the other vegetables and lemongrass and stirfry for about five minutes. Then add the tofu, green curry paste and coconut milk. Cook until the coconut milk simmers. Reduce to low heat and cook another 3- 5 minutes. Remove from heat and let sit for five minutes. Salt to taste. Best served with basmati rice, jasmine rice, millet or quinoa.

Triloka Thai Vegetable Curry

Tridoshic, slightly +kapha
Serves: 3-4
Ingredients:
2 cups (16 oz) coconut milk
1 medium broccoli, cut into florets (about 1½ cups)
1 cup green peas
1 cup carrots, chopped into small pieces
1 large bunch of green onions, chopped
1 large bunch of cilantro, chopped

3 cloves of garlic, chopped
2 Tbs fresh lemongrass, chopped (available in most Asian/Indian grocery stores. If you can't find fresh dry is ok)
2 Tbs Thai green curry paste
4 Tbs ghee or olive oil
Sea salt to taste (approximately ½ tsp)

Instructions:
In a medium- sized frying pan or wok, heat the ghee or olive oil. Add all the vegetables and lemongrass and sauté about 8 minutes, stirring frequently. Add a little more oil if necessary. Then add the green curry paste and coconut milk and cook until the coconut milk simmers. Reduce to low heat and cook another 3- 5 minutes. Remove from heat, add the cilantro and let sit for five minutes. Salt to taste.

Note: If you prefer curry thicker or thinner just add (thinner) or reduce (thicker) coconut milk as desired. Best served with basmati rice, jasmine rice, rice noodles or another grain dish.

Varada's Veggie Medley

Tridoshic
Serves: 3-4
Ingredients:
3 large bell peppers (to create variety use 1 orange, 1 red and 1 green)
2 cups green peas
3 large carrots
2 medium sweet potatoes
4-5 Tbs ghee
1/8 tsp hing (asafoetida)
2 tsp black mustard seeds
1 tsp coriander powder
½ tsp dry basil
1 tsp cumin seeds

2 bay leaves
¼ tsp sea salt
¼ tsp organic cane sugar (sucanat, turbinado, etc)
½ tsp black pepper, freshly ground

Instructions:
Preheat oven to 375°F (200°C). Bring 2 cups of lightly salted water to a boil in a saucepan. Cut the vegetables into chunks and boil them for 3- 4 minutes, then drain. Heat the ghee in a saucepan on medium heat. Add vegetables and hing, and sauté until they are slightly brown at the edges. Add the remaining spices and cook for 1- 2 minutes. Now add salt and pepper. Put everything in a baking dish and bake for five minutes, mixing the vegetables occasionally. Optional: Add 1 Tbs of fresh, chopped cilantro the last minute it is in the oven.

Kichari

The opportunity to love and serve others
should be considered a rare gift,
a blessing from God.

— *Amma*

Immortal Bliss Kichari (Traditional)

Tridoshic
Serves: 4
Ingredients:
2 cups whole mung beans
1 cup basmati rice
6 cups water
2 Tbs ghee
¾ tsp sea salt
½ tsp ground black pepper
½ tsp ground ginger
1 Tbs ground cumin
1 Tbs ground coriander
1 Tbs turmeric

Instructions:

Soak mung beans and basmati rice for a couple of hours then rinse until water runs clear. Bring 6 cups of water to a boil. Add the beans and rice, bring to a boil, then reduce the temperature to low and cook for 5 minutes. Keep covered. Stir every 3 minutes and add more water if necessary. After about half an hour, heat on low the ghee and spices, in a saucepan for about five minutes. Add to the kichari. Cook another 5- 10 minutes. Remove from heat, cover and let sit for 10 minutes before serving. You may add a tablespoon of plain yogurt and additional fresh cilantro to your personal serving. If you prefer it spicy, you may add a half teaspoon cayenne pepper or a couple of, finely chopped chili peppers.

Kamala's Kaivalya Kichari

Tridoshic, slightly +vata
Serves: 4-5
Ingredients:
2 cups split yellow mung dhal
2 cups basmati rice
1- inch ginger, fresh grated
¼ cup fresh cilantro, finely chopped
2 Tbs ghee
½ tsp turmeric
½ tsp coriander powder
1½ tsp cumin seeds
½ tsp black mustard seeds
½ tsp sea salt
1/8 tsp hing (asafoetida)
1 cup tomatoes, finely chopped
8- 10 cups water

Instructions:
Soak mung beans and rice for a couple of hours then rinse until water runs clear. Bring seven cups of water to a boil. While waiting for the water to boil, heat a stainless steel pot or saucepan on medium heat and add ghee, mustard seeds, turmeric, hing (asafoetida) (asafoetida), cumin and coriander. Stir all together for a couple of minutes. Add basmati rice, mung dhal, tomatoes and stir. Next add the mixture to the water, along with the salt, and bring to a boil. Cook for 10 minutes on medium heat then turn to low, cover, and simmer until both dhal and rice are soft, stirring frequently. Remove from heat. Add the cilantro leaves. Let it sit for 10 minutes before serving.

Kalavati's Kichari

Tridoshic
Serves: 3-4
Ingredients:
1 cup basmati rice
1 cup mung dhal
1 onion, chopped
1 cup brocolli, chopped
1 carrot, grated
1 small beet grated
1 tsp turmeric
½ tsp chili powder
1/8 tsp hing (asafoetida) powder
½ tsp cumin powder
½ tsp sea salt
¼ tsp black pepper
2 tsp ghee
¼ cup, chopped cilantro

Instructions:
Soak mung beans and basmati rice for a couple of hours then rinse until water runs clear. Boil 8 cups of water. While waiting for water to boil, sauté on medium heat the ghee, cumin and black pepper. After a couple of minutes, add the onions and stirfry 2- 3 minutes. Then add the rest of the vegetables (except tomato) and stir. Now add turmeric, chili, hing (asafoetida) and salt, and stir on high heat for 1 minute. Add tomato, rice and beans, and stir again for a few minutes. Add everything to boiling water. Cover and cook for 20- 25 minutes, stirring frequently. Remove from heat, add cilantro, cover and let sit for 10 minutes before serving.

Gunavati's Kichari Gobi

Tridoshic
Serves: 4-5
Ingredients:
1½ cup split yellow mung dhal
1½ cup basmati rice
1 cup cauliflower
1 inch ginger, freshly grated
¼ cup fresh cilantro, chopped
2 Tbs ghee
½ tsp turmeric
½ tsp coriander powder
1½ tsp cumin seeds
½ tsp black mustard seeds
½ tsp sea salt
1/8 tsp hing (asafoetida)
1 cup tomatoes, finely chopped
8 cups water

Instructions:
Soak mung beans and basmati rice for a couple of hours then rinse until water runs clear. Bring seven cups of water to a boil. While waiting for the water to boil, heat a saucepan on medium heat and add ghee, mustard seeds, turmeric, hing (asafoetida), cumin and coriander. Stir for a couple of minutes. Add basmati rice, mung dhal, tomatoes and stir. Next add the mixture to the water, along with the sale, and bring to a boil. Cook for 10 minutes on medium heat then turn to low, cover, and simmer until both dhal and rice are soft, stirring frequently. After 15- 20 minutes, once the dhal has softened, add the cauliflower. When caulifolower softens, remove from heat. Add the cilantro leaves. Let it sit for 10 minutes before serving.

Vairagya Vegetable Kichari

Tridoshic

Serves: 4

Ingredients:

½ cup mung beans or red or green lentils
1 cup basmati rice
2 Tbs ghee
2½ tsp sea salt
½ tsp black pepper
2 tsp coriander powder
1 tsp cumin seeds
½ tsp turmeric powder
½ tsp black pepper
½ tsp fennel seeds
½ tsp black mustard seeds
2 Tbs ginger, freshly grated root
4 cups of, chopped vegetables of your choice: beets, carrots, celery, zucchini, spinach, bell peppers, cauliflower, broccoli or green peas

Instructions:

Soak the beans and rice for several hours then thoroughly rinse. In a large stainless steel pot, bring six cups of water to a boil. Once boiling, add beans, rice and ginger. Cover pot and boil on medium heat for 20 minutes. Meanwhile, in a saucepan, sauté on medium heat: ghee, cumin, fennel and mustard seeds. Sauté until mustard seeds crackle and the others begin to brown. Add black pepper, coriander and turmeric. Fry momentarily. Add this to the beans and rice. Add the salt and vegetables. Bring to a moderate boil. Add water if necessary. Cover and simmer for 20 minutes, briefly stirring every 2- 3 minutes. Remove from heat but keep covered. Let sit for 10 minutes before serving.

Chittachora's Carrot Kichari

Tridoshic
Serves: 3-4
Ingredients:
1 cup basmati rice
1 cup mung dhal
2 carrots diced
1 tsp turmeric powder
1 tsp cumin seeds
½ tsp coriander powder
1 inch of fresh ginger, finely chopped or grated
1 very small pinch (1/8 tsp) of hing
¼ tsp black pepper powder
2 Tbs ghee

Instructions:
Soak mung beans and basmati rice for a couple of hours then rinse until water runs clear. Bring seven cups of water to a boil. While waiting for the water to boil, heat the ghee on medium heat. Add the cumin and ginger. Fry for a minute and then add the rice and mung dhal. Stir for a few seconds, then add to the boiling water. Now add the remaining spices. Stir every two or three minutes. After about 10 minutes, add the carrots. Cook until all water is absorbed (about 25 minutes). Let it sit for 10 minutes before serving.

Karuna Sagar Kichari

Tridoshic, slightly +kapha
Serves: 3-4
Ingredients:
1 cup mung beans or red/green lentils
1 cup basmati rice
2 Tbs ghee
1 tsp sea salt
½ tsp black pepper
2 tsp coriander powder
1 tsp cumin seeds
½ tsp turmeric powder
½ tsp black pepper
½ tsp fennel seeds
½ tsp black mustard seeds
2 Tbs freshly grated ginger root
1/8 cup each dried agar, arame, dulse and wakame

Instructions:
Soak the beans and rice for several hours then rinse thoroughly. Bring 6 cups of water to a boil. Add the beans and ginger. Cover and boil on medium heat for 20 minutes. Soak seaweeds in 1- 2 cups hot water for 20 minutes and rinse. In a saucepan, heat on medium heat ghee, cumin, fennel and mustard seeds. Sauté until mustard seeds crackle and the others begin to brown. Add the black pepper, coriander and turmeric, and fry momentarily. Add this to the mung beans. Bring to a moderate boil. Stir in rice. Simmer for 20- 25 minutes with lid on. After 10 minutes add the seaweeds. If necessary, add more water. Stir briefly every 2- 3 minutes. Remove from heat, keep covered, and let sit for 10 minutes before serving.

Panduranga's Palak Kichari

Tridoshic
Serves: 3-4
Ingredients:
1 cup basmati rice
1 cup mung dhal
2 cups spinach, chopped
1 tsp turmeric powder
1 tsp cumin seeds
½ tsp coriander powder
¼ cup cilantro, chopped
1 inch of fresh ginger, finely chopped or grated
1 very small pinch of asafoetida (1/8 tsp)
¼ tsp black pepper powder
2 Tbs ghee

Instructions:
Soak mung beans and basmati rice for a couple of hours then rinse until water runs clear. Bring 8 cups of water to a boil. While waiting for the water to boil, heat the ghee in a saucepan on medium heat. Add the cumin and ginger and stirfry for 1 minute. Add the rice and mung dhal, stir for a minute, then add to boiling water. Add the other spices. Stir every 2-3 minutes. After about 10 minutes add the spinach. Cook until all water is absorbed (about 25 minutes). Remove from heat, add the cilantro, cover and let sit 10 minutes before serving.

Ram Prasad's Root Vegetable Kichari

Tridoshic
Serves: 4-6
Ingredients:
2 cup whole mung beans
1 cups basmati rice
8 cups water
1 cup beets, chopped
1 cup carrots, chopped
1 cup parsnips, chopped
2 Tbs ghee
¾ tsp sea salt
½ tsp ground black pepper
½ tsp ground ginger
1 Tbs ground cumin
1 Tbs ground coriander
1 Tbs turmeric

Instructions:

Soak mung beans and basmati rice for a couple of hours then rinse until water runs clear. Bring 8 cups of water to a boil. Add the beans and rice, bring to a boil, then reduce the temperature to low and cook for 45 minutes. Keep covered. Stir every 3 minutes and add more water if necessary. After about a half an hour, stirfry on low heat the ghee, vegetables and spices for about five minutes. Add to the kichari. Cook another 5- 10 minutes. Remove from heat and let sit for 10 minutes before serving. You may add a tablespoon of plain yogurt and fresh cilantro to your personal serving. If you prefer it spicy, you may add a half teaspoon cayenne pepper or a couple of, finely chopped chili peppers.

Trimurtih Vegetable Kichari

Tridoshic
Serves: 5-6
Ingredients:
2 cups split yellow mung dhal
½ cup each of basmati rice, millet and barley (can use quinoa instead of barley)
¼ cup carrots, grated or chopped
¼ cup zucchini, chopped
¼ cup green peas
¼ cup beets, chopped
1 inch ginger, freshly grated
¼ cup fresh cilantro, finely chopped
2 Tbs ghee
½ tsp turmeric
½ tsp coriander powder
1½ tsp cumin seeds
½ tsp black mustard seeds
½ tsp sea salt
1/8 tsp hing (asafoetida)
1 cup, finely chopped tomatoes
8 cups water

Instructions:
Soak beans and grains together for a couple of hours then rinse until water runs clear. Bring seven cups of water to a boil. While waiting for the water to boil, heat the ghee on medium heat and add the vegetables (except tomatoes), mustard seeds, turmeric, hing (asafoetida), cumin and coriander. Stirfry for 2 minutes. Next, add grains, mung dhal and tomatoes, and stirfry a few more minutes. Add the mixture to the boiling water, along with the salt, and bring to a boil again. Cover and cook for 15- 20 minutes on medium heat, stirring frequently. Reduce heat to low, cover and simmer until both dhal

and grains are soft, stirring frequently. Remove from heat, add the cilantro leaves, cover and let sit 10 minutes before serving.

Tridoshic Garden Herb Kichari

Tridoshic
Serves: 4
Ingredients:
1½ cups whole green mung beans
2 cups basmati rice
8 cups water
1 cup cilantro, chopped
1 cup fresh basil, chopped
½ cup fresh dill, chopped
2 Tbs ghee
1 tsp sea salt
½ tsp ground black pepper
½ tsp ground ginger
1 tsp ground cumin
½ tsp ground coriander
½ tsp turmeric

Instructions:
Soak mung beans and basmati rice for a couple of hours then rinse until water runs clear. Bring 8 cups of water to a boil. Add the beans and rice, bring to a boil, then reduce the temperature to low and cook for 45 minutes. Keep covered. Stir every 3 minutes and add more water if necessary. After about a half an hour, heat the ghee and dry spices, in a saucepan for about five minutes. Add to the kichari. Cook another 5- 10 minutes. Remove from heat, add the fresh herbs and let sit for 10 minutes before serving. You may add a tablespoon of plain yogurt and additional fresh cilantro to your personal serving. If you prefer it spicy you may add a half teaspoon cayenne pepper or a couple of , finely chopped chili peppers.

Pavitra Garden Kichari

Tridoshic
Serves: 4
Ingredients:
2 cups whole mung beans
1 cup basmati rice
8 cups water
1 cup spinach, chopped
1 cup green peas
1 cup broccoli
2 Tbs ghee
¾ tsp sea salt
½ tsp ground black pepper
½ tsp ground ginger
1 Tbs ground cumin
1 Tbs ground coriander
1 Tbs turmeric

Instructions:
Soak mung beans and basmati rice for a couple of hours then rinse until water runs clear. Bring 8 cups of water to a boil. Add the beans and rice, bring to a boil, then reduce the temperature to low and cook for five minutes. Keep covered. Stir every 3 minutes and add more water if necessary. After about a half an hour, heat the ghee, vegetables and spices, in a saucepan for five minutes. Add to the kichari. Cook another 5- 10 minutes. Remove from heat, cover and let sit for 10 minutes before serving. You may add a tablespoon of plain yogurt and additional fresh cilantro to your personal serving. If you prefer it spicy you may add a half teaspoon cayenne pepper or a couple of chili peppers, chopped.

Amartya's Western Style Kichari

Tridoshic
Serves: 4-6
Ingredients:
2 cups split green mung dhal
2 cups basmati rice
1 inch ginger, freshly grated
¼ cup fresh cilantro, finely chopped
2 Tbs ghee
½ tsp dried dill or 1 tsp fresh, chopped
½ tsp dried basil powder or 3 or 4 fresh basil leaves, chopped fine
1 tsp cumin seeds
½ tsp dried tarragon
½ tsp sea salt
¼ tsp dried oregano
¼ cup tomatoes, finely chopped
8 cups water

Instructions:
Soak beans and grains together for a couple of hours then rinse until water runs clear. Bring seven cups of water to a boil. While waiting for the water to boil, heat the ghee on medium heat and add the spices. Stirfry for 2 minutes. Add the rice, dhal and tomatoes, and stirfry 3-5 minutes. Add to the boiling water, along with the salt, and bring to a boil again. Cover and cook for 15- 20 minutes on medium heat, stirring frequently. Reduce heat to low, cover and simmer until both dhal and grains are soft, stirring frequently. Remove from heat, add the cilantro leaves, cover and let sit for 10 minutes before serving.

Vivek's Vegetable Barley Kichari

Tridoshic

Serves: 4-6

Ingredients:

2 cups mung beans or red/green lentils
1 cup barley
2 Tbs ghee
2 tsp sea salt
½ tsp black pepper
2 tsp coriander powder
1 tsp cumin seeds
½ tsp turmeric powder
½ tsp black pepper
½ tsp fennel seeds
½ tsp black mustard seeds
2 Tbs freshly grated ginger
3 cups chopped vegetables of your choice: beets, carrots, celery, zucchini, spinach, bell peppers, cauliflower, broccoli or green peas

Instructions:

Soak the beans for several hours then rinse until water runs clear. Bring to a boil 8 cups of water and add beans and ginger. Cover and boil on medium heat for 20 minutes. On medium- low heat, sauté ghee, cumin, fennel and mustard seeds. Sauté until mustard seeds crackle and the others begin to brown. Add black pepper, coriander and turmeric powder. Stirfry momentarily. Add this to the mung beans. Add the vegetables and salt. Bring to a moderate boil. Stir in barley. Add water if necessary. Cover and simmer for 15- 20 minutes. Stir briefly every 2- 3 minutes. Remove from heat, keep covered and let sit for 10 minutes before serving.

Tripura Sundari's Three Grain Kichari

Tridoshic

Serves: 5-6

Ingredients:

2 cups split yellow mung dhal

½ cup each of basmati rice, millet and barley

1 inch ginger, freshly grated

¼ cup freshly cilantro, finely chopped

2 Tbs ghee

½ tsp turmeric

½ tsp coriander powder

1½ tsp cumin seeds

½ tsp black mustard seeds

½ tsp sea salt

1/8 tsp hing (asafoetida)

1 cup tomatoes, finely chopped

8 cups water

Instructions:

Soak mung beans and basmati rice for a couple of hours then rinse until water runs clear. Bring 7 cups of water to a boil. While waiting for the water to boil, heat the ghee on medium heat and add mustard seeds, turmeric, hing (asafoetida), cumin and coriander. Stir all together for 2 minutes. Add rice, dhal and tomatos and stir. Add the mixture and salt to the water, and bring to a boil. Cover and cook for 15- 20 minutes on medium heat, stirring frequently. Reduce heat to low and continue cooking until both dhal and grains are soft, also stirring frequently. Remove from heat, add the cilantro leaves, cover and let sit for 10 minutes before serving.

Kalika's Kichari Quinoa

Tridoshic
Serves: 4-5
Ingredients:
2 cups mung dhal
1½ cups quinoa
2 tsps (heaping) ghee
¼ tsp black mustard seeds
¼ tsp cumin seeds
¼ tsp cayenne pepper
¼ tsp sea salt
½ tsp ground cumin
½ ground coriander
½ turmeric
1 pinch (1/8 tsp) hing (asafoetida)
1- inch ginger, freshly grated root
7 cups water
¼- ½ cup fresh cilantro, chopped

Instructions:
Soak the mung beans for one to two hours. Wash the mung beans and quinoa together until water runs clear. Bring 7 cups of water to a boil. While waiting for water to boil, heat ghee and mustard seeds in a large saucepan on medium heat until seeds begin to pop. Add remaining spices and cook 1- 2 minutes. Then add a little water to the spices to prevent burning. Add the mung beans, quinoa and salt. Add everything to the boiling water and cook for 10 minutes. Cover, reduce to medium- low heat and cook until both the mung beans and quinoa are soft (about 30 minutes), adding water as necessary. Remove from heat, add the cilantro leaves, cover and let sit 10 minutes before serving.

Milarepa's Millet Kichari

Tridoshic
Serves: 4-5
Ingredients:
2 cups split yellow mung dhal
1 cup red or yellow millet
1 inch ginger, freshly grated
½ cup fresh cilantro, finely chopped
2 Tbs ghee
½ tsp turmeric
½ tsp coriander powder
1½ tsp cumin seeds
½ tsp black mustard seeds
½ tsp sea salt
1/8 tsp hing (asafoetida)
1 cup tomatoes, finely chopped
8 cups water

Instructions:

Soak mung beans and millet for a couple of hours and then rinse until water runs clear. Bring 7 cups of water to a boil. While waiting for the water to boil, heat a large saucepan on medium heat and add ghee, mustard seeds, turmeric, hing (asafoetida), cumin and coriander. Stir for 2- 3 minutes. Add millet, mung dhal and tomatoes. Stir. Add the mixture and salt to the boiling water. Bring to a boil again and then cook for 5 minutes on medium heat, stirring frequently. Reduce to low heat, cover, and cook until dhal and millet are soft, stirring ever 2- 3 minutes. Remove from heat, add the cilantro leaves, cover and let sit for 10 minutes before serving.

Bhadrakali's Barley Kichari

-pitta and kapha, +vata
Serves: 3-4
Ingredients:
2 cups split yellow mung dahl
1 cup barley
1- inch fresh ginger, grated
¼ cup fresh cilantro, finely chopped
2 Tbs ghee
½ tsp turmeric
½ tsp coriander powder
1½ tsp cumin seeds
½ tsp black mustard seeds
½ tsp sea salt
1/8 – 1/16 tsp hing (asafoetida)
1 cup tomatoes, finely chopped
8 cups water

Instructions:
Soak mung beans and barley for an hour, then rinse until water runs clear. Bring seven cups of water to a boil. While waiting for water to boil, heat a stainless steel pot or saucepan on medium heat and add ghee, mustard seeds, turmeric, hing, cumin and coriander. Stir for a couple of minutes. Add barley, mung dahl, tomatoes and stir. Add the mixture to the boiling water, add the salt and bring to a boil again. Cook for fiveminutes on medium heat, stirring frequently. Turn to low, cover, and simmer until both dal and rice are soft. Stir frequently! Remove from heat. Add the cilantro leaves. Let it sit for 10 minutes before serving.

Grains

Love and beauty are within you. Try to express them through your actions and you will definitely touch the very source of bliss. Do not be satisfied with your ordinary state of worldly consciousness. There is a supreme state of blissfulness, an all- knowing and all- powerful state that can be attained by every one of you. Direct your mind and activities toward this end and strive to achieve the ultimate goal.

– Amma

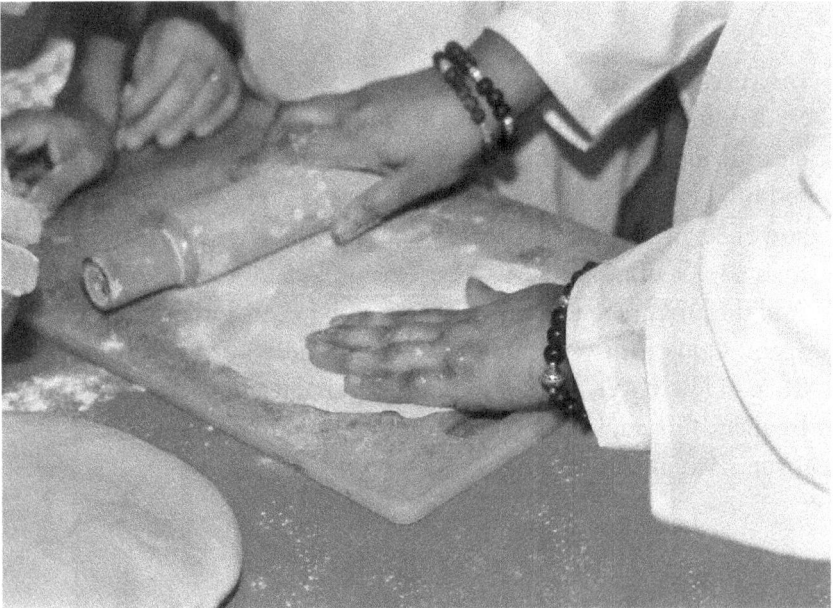

Kerala Ghee Dosa

Tridoshic
Serves: 6 dosas
Ingredients:
(Urad dhal and rice flour are usually available at Indian grocery stores.
Pre- made dosa mixtures are also available.)
1 cup urad dhal flour
1 cup rice flour
½ tsp sea salt
1/8 tsp hing (asafoetida)
2- 2½ cups water
Ghee

Instructions:
Combine the flours, salt and hing (asafoetida) in a large mixing bowl. Add the water slowly, mixing while pouring it. It should be like a thin pancake mixture. Cover the batter with a cloth and let it sit overnight at room temperature. Do not refrigerate it.
In a non- stick frying pan, warm the pan and add about ½ tsp ghee. Add about 1/3 of a cup of the batter and spread it around with the back of a large spoon until it is thin. Cook just like a pancake. It will turn a golden brown on the bottom. Flip just like a pancake. If the pan is dry add a little more ghee. Cook until it is done. Repeat until you have made all the dosas. Serve with coconut chutney, sambar or vegetable masala.

Chapathi

Tridoshic
Serves: 10-12 chapathis
Ingredients:
4 cups organic whole wheat flour
2 cups water
1 tsp sea salt
Ghee, safflower or olive oil

Instructions:
In a large mixing bowl, combine the flour and salt. Add the water a little at a time, mixing with hands each time. Add the water until the dough is thick and non- sticky. Cover the bowl with a clean cloth and let sit for about 30 minutes. Now, make little balls (about the size of a golf ball or small egg), with the dough. Roll the balls in flour and flatten them with your hands or a rolling pin. The chappathi should be thin. Add a little oil to one side and then sprinkle a little flour on top. Repeat on other side. Heat a non- stick pan and place the chappathi in the pan. Add a little oil to the top and cook until the chappathi bubbles slightly and the bottom edges brown (about 3 minutes). Flip, add a few drops of oil to the top and cook for a couple of minutes until the chappthi is done. Serve with any curry, kichari, dhal, rice or soup.

Ghee Rice

Tridoshic, +kapha
Ingredients:
2 cups basmati rice
4 cups water
1 tsp fresh ground black pepper
½ tsp sea salt
2 Tbs ghee

Instructions:
Rinse the rice. Boil the water, add the rice and simmer for 20 minutes. In the last five minutes, add in the ghee, salt and pepper. Stir in well. Cook until rice is soft. Remove from heat and serve. Great with any vegetable dish or dhal.

Caraka's Cumin Rice

Tridoshic
Serves: 2-3
Ingredients:
2 cups basmati rice
4 cups water
2- 3 whole cloves
½ tsp fresh ground black pepper
2 whole bay leaves
3 tsp cumin seeds
½ tsp sea salt
2 Tbs ghee

Instructions:
Rinse the rice. Boil the water. Meanwhile, heat the ghee in a saucepan and add all of the spices except the salt. Sauté 1- 2 minutes then remove from heat. When water is boiling, add the rice and spices. Turn heat down to low, cover and let the rice cook for 20 minutes. Stir occasionally to prevent sticking. Remove from heat and serve. Goes great with any vegetable dish or dhal.

Lola's Lovely Lemon Dill Rice

Tridoshic
Serves: 2-3
Ingredients:
2 cups basmati rice
2 Tbs fresh dill
1 Tbs ghee
4 cups water
¼- ½ tsp sea salt
¼ tsp black pepper, freshly ground.
1 Tbs cilantro freshly, chopped
2 Tbs freshly squeezed lemon or lime juice

Instructions:
Rinse the rice. Boil the water, add the rice and simmer for 20 minutes. Add the ghee, dill, salt and pepper, and cook a few more minutes until rice is soft. Remove from heat. Mix in the lemon/lime juice and cilantro. Cover and let sit for five minutes before serving.

Sambhavi's Cilantro Ghee Rice

Tridoshic
Serves: 2-3
Ingredients:
2 cups basmati rice
4 cups water
1 tsp fresh ground black pepper
½ tsp sea salt
1 cup fresh cilantro, chopped
3 Tbs ghee

Instructions:
Rinse the rice. Boil 4 cups of water, add the rice and simmer for about 20 minutes or until soft. In the last five minutes, add the

ghee, salt and pepper. Stir in well. When done, remove from heat, mix in the cilantro, cover and let sit for five minutes. Great with any vegetable dish or dhal.

Narada's Bhakti Basil Rice

Tridoshic
Serves: 2-4
Ingredients:
2 cups basmati rice
8 tomatoes, chopped
½ cup basil, chopped
1 onion, chopped into small pieces
3- 4 Tbs olive oil
1 large bulb garlic, minced
¼ tsp sea salt or to taste
¼ tsp black pepper, freshly ground or to taste
¼ tsp cloves powder
¼ tsp oregano
1 Tbs cilantro, chopped
¼ tsp cayenne pepper (optional)
6 cups water

Instructions:
Rinse the rice. Boil 6 cups of water and simmer the rice for about 20 minutes. Then remove from heat, cover and let sit. Heat the olive oil and sauté the tomatoes, garlic, onions and spices, except the cilantro and basil, for about ten minutes. Then add the basil. Add everything to the rice and cook another 8- 10 minutes or until the rice is soft. When the rice is finished, remove from heat, add the cilantro, cover and let sit for 5 minutes.

Gopika's Garden Herb Basmati Rice

Tridoshic
Serves: 2-3
Ingredients:
2 cups basmati rice
4 cups water
½ cup fresh basil, chopped
½ tsp black pepper powder
1 Tbs fresh dill, chopped
1 tsp dried oregano
¼ cup cilantro, chopped
¼ tsp thyme
½ tsp sea salt
2 Tbs ghee

Instructions:
Rinse the rice. Boil the water and simmer the rice for 25 minutes. Meanwhile, heat the ghee in a saucepan on medium heat and add the spices, except the salt. Sauté 1- 2 minutes then remove from heat. After cooking the rice for 15 minutes, add the spices and salt. Reduce heat to low, cover and let the rice cook another 10 minutes or so until rice is soft. Stir occasionally to prevent sticking. Remove from heat and serve. Serve with any vegetable dish or dhal.

Rudra's Coconut Rice

Tridoshic, slightly +kapha
Serves: 2-3
Ingredients:
2 cups basmati rice
4 cups water
1 cup shredded coconut
1 tsp fresh ground black pepper

½ tsp sea salt
¼ tsp cumin powder
2 Tbs ghee

Instructions:
Rinse the rice. Boil 4 cups of water, add the rice and coconut, and simmer for about 20 minutes or until soft. In the last five minutes, add the ghee, cumin, salt and pepper. Stir inwell. When done, remove from heat, cover and let sit for five minutes. Delicious with any vegetable dish or dhal.

Savitri's Spicy Coconut Rice

Tridoshic
Serves: 2-3
Ingredients:
2 cups basmati rice
1 cup grated coconut
½ tsp black mustard seeds
1/8 tsp hing (asafoetida)
2-3 green chilies, chopped
¼ - ½ tsp sea salt
½ tsp fresh ground black pepper
2 Tbs ghee
6 cups water

Instructions:
Rinse the rice. Boil 6 cups of water, add the rice and simmer for about 20 minutes or until soft. Heat the ghee in a saucepan on medium heat and stirfry the mustard seeds until they pop. Next add the other spices and sauté for a minute. Now add the dry coconut and sauté about 2 minutes, or until the coconut turns golden brown. After the rice has cooked for15 minutes, add the mixture to the rice and cook them together for the last 5 minutes. When the rice will be

soft, remove from heat and cover. Let sit for 5 minutes. Great with any vegetable dish or dhal.

Sharani's Beets and Basmati Rice

Tridoshic
Serves: 3-4
Ingredients:
2 cups basmati rice
4 cups water
2 cups beets, chopped into small pieces
½ tsp fresh ground black pepper
1/8 tsp cumin pwd
1/8 coriander pwd
1 tsp sea salt or 2 tsp Braggs Liquid Amino Acids
2 Tbs ghee

Instructions:
Rinse the rice. Boil the water and add the rice. Turn heat down to low, cover and simmer for 10 minutes. Add the beets, ghee, salt and pepper and cook for another 10 minutes or until the rice is soft. Add more water if necessary. Stir occasionally to prevent sticking. Add salt to taste. Remove from heat and serve. Great with any vegetable dish or dhal.

Bolo Bolo Broccoli Basmati Rice

Tridoshic, slightly +vata
Serves: 2-3
Ingredients: 3
2 cups basmati rice
1 cup broccoli cut into small florets
¼ tsp black pepper, freshly ground
¼ tsp cumin powder

1/8 tsp turmeric powder
1/8 tsp ginger powder or ¼ tsp freshly grated ginger
2 Tbs ghee
¼ tsp sea salt or ¼- ½ tsp Braggs Liquid Amino Acids
4- 5 cups water

Instructions:
Rinse the rice. Boil 4 cups of water, add the rice and simmer about 20 minutes or until soft. In a saucepan on medium heat, sauté the broccoli in ghee for 3- 4 minutes. After a couple of minutes add the spices, salt and pepper. Mix the broccoli in the rice and cook for a few minutes. Add more water if necessary. When finished remove from heat, cover and let sit for five minutes. Serve with steamed vegetables, soup, salad or alone.

Chaitanya's Carrot Basmati Rice

Tridoshic
Serves: 3-4
Ingredients:
2 cups carrots grated
2 cup basmati rice
¼ tsp black pepper, freshly ground
¼ tsp cumin powder
2 Tbs ghee
¼ tsp sea salt or ¼- ½ tsp Braggs Liquid Amino Acids
4- 5 cups water

Instructions:
Rinse the rice. Boil 4 cups of water, add the rice and simmer for about 20 minutes or until soft. In a saucepan, heat the ghee, add the carrots and sauté for about 2 minutes. Add the salt and pepper. Mix the carrots with the rice and cook for a few minutes. Add more water if necessary. When finished remove from heat, cover and let sit for five minutes. Serve with steamed vegetables, soup, salad or alone.

Chidambaram's Cauliflower Basmati Rice

Tridoshic, slightly +vata
Serves: 3
Ingredients:
1½ cups basmati rice
1½ cups cauliflower cut into small florets
¼ tsp black pepper, freshly ground
1/8 tsp turmeric powder
2 Tbs ghee
¼ tsp sea salt
4- 5 cups water

Instructions:
Rinse the rice. Boil 4 cups of water, add the rice and simmer about 20 minutes or until soft. In a saucepan, heat the ghee, add the cauliflower and sauté for 3- 4 minutes. Add the salt and pepper. Then add the cauliflower to the rice, mix in completely and cook for a few minutes. Add more water if necessary. When finished remove from heat, cover and let sit for five minutes. Serve with steamed vegetables, soup, salad or alone.

Maha Lakshmi's Vegetable Medley Rice

Tridoshic
Serves: 4-5
Ingredients:
3 cups basmati rice
8 tomatoes, chopped
½ cup basil, chopped
½ cup celery, chopped
½ cup carrots, chopped
½ cup zucchini, chopped
½ cup bell pepper, chopped

1 onion, chopped into small pieces
3- 4 Tbs olive oil
1 large bulb garlic, minced
½ tsp sea salt or to taste
½ tsp black pepper, freshly ground or to taste
¼ tsp clove powder
¼ tsp oregano
¼ tsp cumin powder
1 Tbs cilantro, chopped
¼ tsp cayenne pepper
6 cups water

Instructions:
Rinse the rice. Boil 6 cups of water and cook the rice for about 20 minutes. Then remove from heat, cover and let sit. Heat the olive oil and sauté the vegetables and spices, except the cilantro and basil, for about 10 minutes. If needed, add a little water. Then add the basil. Add everything to the rice and simmer another 8- 10 minutes or until the rice is soft. When the rice is finished, remove from heat, add the cilantro, cover and let sit for 5 minutes.

Buddha's Bell Peppers and Rice

Tridoshic
Serves: 4
Ingredients:
2 cup basmati rice
3 small bell peppers (1 each – green, yellow and red), chopped into small pieces
1 cup red cabbage, chopped
1 yellow or white onion, chopped
1 inch fresh ginger, grated
½ tsp black pepper, freshly ground
¼ - ½ tsp sea salt or to taste

1- 2 Tbs ghee
5 cups water

Instructions:
Rinse the rice. Boil the water, add rice and simmer for about 20 minutes. In a saucepan on medium heat, heat the ghee and stirfry the onions, garlic and peppers for 3- 4 minutes. Next add the red cabbage and stirfry for 2- 3 minutes. Add the mixture, salt and pepper to the rice, and cook for another 8- 10 minutes. Add more water if necessary to avoid sticking. It is ready when the rice is soft. Remove from heat, cover and let sit five minutes. Serve with vegetables, soup or salad.

Options:
2 Tbs fresh cilantro, chopped can be added when rice is removed from the heat.
1 Tbs fresh basil, chopped and added.
For spicy rainbow rice, add 1- 2 hot chili peppers, , finely chopped. Add these with the garlic and onions in the stirfry mix.

Spanish Style Red Rice

Tridoshic
Serves: 2-3
Ingredients:
1 ½ cups basmati rice
2 large carrots, chopped into small pieces
4 Tbs white onion, chopped into small pieces
5 cloves of garlic crushed
1 medium- size bell pepper (red, yellow or green), chopped into small pieces
2 cups of tomato purée
¼ tsp sea salt or to taste
¼ tsp black pepper
¼ tsp cayenne pepper

3-4 cups of water
2- 3 Tbs cilantro, chopped
2- 3 Tbs olive oil

Optional: Adding1- 2 Tbs nutritional flakes makes this dish creamier.

Instructions:
Rinse the rice. Bring water to a boil, add the rice and simmer for about fiveminutes. Cover and let sit. Now, in a saucepan, heat the olive oil and stirfry the onions. When onions start to brown, add the garlic, tomato purée, spices, peppers and little water. Cook for about five minutes stirring constantly. Add the sauce to the rice and cook another 8- 10 minutes, or until the rice is soft. Add more water if needed to prevent sticking. When rice is done, remove from heat and mix in cilantro. Cover and let sit five minutes. If you are using nutritional flakes, add them at the end with the cilantro.

Shoba's Spicy Carrot Rice

Tridoshic
Serves: 2-3
Ingredients:
2 cups basmati rice
4- 5 cups water
1 cup carrots, grated
2-3 red hot chili peppers or 1 tsp cayenne pepper
½ tsp fresh ground black pepper
1 inch ginger, grated
1 tsp sea salt
2 Tbs ghee

Instructions:
Rinse the rice. Bring water to a boil, add the rice, reduce heat to low, and simmer for about 20 minutes. Add the carrots, ghee, chili

peppers, ginger, salt and pepper, and cook for another 10 minutes or until the rice is soft. Add a little water if necessary. Stir occasionally to prevent sticking. Add salt to taste. Remove from heat and serve. Great with any vegetable dish or dhal.

Skanda's Spicy Rice

Tridoshic
Serves: 3-4
Ingredients:
1 ½ cups basmati or jasmine rice
1½ cups tomato, chopped
½ cup dry coconut shredded or fresh grated
3 white or yellow onions, chopped
¼ tsp sea salt or to taste
1 tsp cayenne pepper
2 green chilis, chopped
½ tsp black mustard seeds
¼ cup fresh basil, chopped
3 Tbs cilantro, chopped
3 Tbs ghee
3 cups water

Instructions:
Rinse the rice. Bring 3 cups of water to a boil and simmer rice for 20 minutes. Remove from heat, cover and let sit. In a blender mix the tomatoes, coconut and basil with a little water. This should make 2 cups. Heat the ghee in a saucepan on medium heat and add the mustard seeds, onions, green chilis and spices. Cook for a few minutes until the mustard seeds pop. Then add the tomato purée. Cook for a few minutes then add to the rice and mix thoroughly. Cook tomato rice for 5 minutes or until rice is soft and fluffy. Remove from heat and mix in the cilantro and basil. Cover and let sit for 5 minutes.

Ganga Mata Green Herb Ghee Rice

Tridoshic, slightly +kapha
Serves: 2-3
Ingredients:
2 cups basmati rice
4 cups water
1 tsp fresh ground black pepper
½ cup fresh basil, chopped
¼ cup fresh dill, chopped
½ cup fresh cilantro, chopped
½ tsp sea salt
2 Tbs ghee

Instructions:
Rinse the rice. Boil the water, add the rice and simmer for 20 minutes. In the last five minutes add in the ghee, salt and pepper. Stir well. Cook until rice is soft. Remove from heat, mix in the herbs well, cover and let sit for five minutes. Great with any vegetable dish or dhal.

Pashupati's Peas and Rice

Tridoshic
Serves: 3-4
Ingredients:
2 cups green peas
¼ tsp black pepper, freshly ground
2 Tbs ghee
¼ tsp sea salt
2 cups basmati rice
4- 5 cups water

Instructions:
Rinse the rice. Boil 4 cups of water, add the rice and simmer for 20 minutes. In a saucepan, heat the ghee, add the peas and sauté for a couple of minutes. Add salt and pepper. Mix the peas into the rice and cook for a few minutes. Add more water if necessary. When finished remove from heat, cover and let sit for five minutes. Serve with steamed vegetables, soup, salad or alone.

Quinoa

Tridoshic
Serves: 1-2
Ingredients:
1 cup quinoa
3 cups water
¼- ½ tsp sea salt
1 Tbs ghee

Instructions:
Rinse the quinoa. Bring water to a boil and add the quinoa. When it boils again, reduce heat to medium and cook for about 25 minutes until grains are soft and fluffy. Mix in the salt and ghee. Great with any vegetable dish or dhal.

Quinoa Peace

Tridoshic
Serves: 1-2
Ingredients:
1 cup quinoa
1 cup green peas
3- 4 cups water
½ tsp sea salt
¼- ½ tsp black pepper

¼ tsp cumin powder
1/8 tsp turmeric powder
2 tsp ghee

Instructions:
Rinse the quinoa. Bring water to a boil and add the quinoa and peas.
When it boils again, reduce the heat to medium and cook about
15 minutes until grains are well done. Mix in the salt, pepper and
ghee. Great with any vegetable dish or dhal.

Green Quinoa Grace

Tridoshic
Serves: 2-3
Ingredients:
1 cup quinoa
4 cups water
1 cup, chopped vegetables: ¼ cup each of kale, spinach, collards
and chard (If one of these is not available, any other dark leafy green
will work.)
½ tsp cumin powder
½ tsp ginger
¼ tsp black pepper, freshly ground
1/8 tsp cardamom powder
½ tsp turmeric
¼ tsp coriander powder
¼ tsp sea salt
2- 3 Tbs ghee
2- 3 Tbs cilantro, chopped

Instructions:
Rinse the quinoa. Bring water to a boil. Meanwhile, heat the ghee
in a saucepan and stirfry the quinoa for 3- 4 minutes, stirring the
entire time. In the last 2 minutes add the spices. Now add the quinoa and vegetables to the boiling water. Bring to a boil, then reduce

to medium heat and cook for 25-30 minutes or until the quinoa is soft and fluffy. Add more salt if desired. Remove from heat, add the cilantro, cover and let sit for five minutes. Serve alone or with other vegetables or soup.

Radha Krishna Quinoa

Tridoshic
Serves: 2-3
Ingredients:
1 cup quinoa
3 cups water
½ cup asparagus, chopped
½ cup kale, chopped
½ cup collards, chopped
½ cup mustard greens, chopped
1/8 tsp ground black pepper
1/8 - ¼ tsp sea salt
1 Tbs ghee

Instructions:
Rinse the quinoa. Bring the water to a boil and simmer the quinoa for 25-30 minutes. Next, add the asparagus and cook for 5 more minutes. Add the greens and bring to a boil again. Cover, reduce heat to low and simmer for about 15- 20 minutes until quinoa is fully cooked. Remember to stir frequently to avoid sticking. Add a little more water if needed. In the last minute or two, add the ghee, salt and pepper. Remove from heat, cover and let sit for a few minutes. Serve with soup, salad, dhal, another vegetable dish or alone.

Optional: Mix in some, chopped fresh cilantro just before you let it sit for a few minutes.

Quinoa and Asparagus Arati

Tridoshic
Serves: 2-3
Ingredients:
1 cup quinoa
3 cups water
½ cup asparagus, chopped
½ cup kale, chopped
½ cup spinach, chopped
½ cup bokchoy or arugula, chopped
1/8 tsp ground black pepper
1/8 - ¼ tsp sea salt or 1 tsp Braggs Liquid Amino Acids
1 Tbs ghee

Instructions:
Rinse the quinoa. Bring the water to a boil and simmer the quinoa for about 25 minutes. Next add the asparagus and cook for 15 more minutes. Add the greens and bring to a boil again. Cover, reduce heat to low and simmer for about 10- 15 minutes until quinoa is fully cooked. Remember to stir frequently to avoid sticking. Add a little more water if needed. In the last minute or two add the ghee, salt and pepper. Remove from heat, cover and let sit for a few minutes. Serve with soup, salad, dhal, another vegetable dish or alone.

Optional: Mix in some, chopped fresh cilantro just before you let it sit for a few minutes.

You Are Creation Quinoa

Tridoshic
Serves: 2-3
Ingredients:
1½ cups quinoa
4 cups water
½ cup fresh green peas
½ cup green chard, chopped
½ cup yellow chard, chopped
½ cup red chard, chopped
1/8 tsp ground black pepper
¼ tsp cumin
¼ tsp fennel seeds
1/8 - ¼ tsp sea salt or 1 tsp Braggs Liquid Amino Acids
1 Tbs ghee

Instructions:
Rinse the quinoa. Bring the water to a boil and simmer the quinoa and fennel seeds for about 10 minutes. Next, add the green peas and cook for 10 more minutes. Add the greens and bring to a boil again. Cover, reduce heat to low and simmer for about 10- 12 minutes until quinoa is fully cooked. Remember to stir frequently to avoid sticking. Add a little more water if needed. In the last minute or two, add the ghee, salt and pepper. Remove from heat, cover and let sit for a few minutes. Serve with soup, salad, dhal, another vegetable dish or alone.

Optional: Mix in some, chopped fresh cilantro just before you let it sit for a few minutes.

Millet

Tridoshic
Serves: 1-2
Ingredients:
1 cup millet
3 cups water
¼- ½ tsp sea salt
1 Tbs ghee

Instructions:
Rinse the millet. Bring water to a boil and add the millet. When it boils again, reduce heat to medium and cook for about 35- 40 minutes until grains are soft and fluffy. Mix in the salt and ghee. Great with any vegetable dish or dhal.

Jayanti's Triple Grain Jubilee

Tridoshic
Serves: 2
Ingredients:
½ cup basmati or jasmine rice
½ cup quinoa
½ cup millet
4- 5 cups water
½ tsp black pepper, freshly ground
¼ - ½ tsp sea salt
2 tsp ghee
2 Tbs fresh lemon juice
1 Tbs basil freshly, chopped
3 Tbs cilantro, chopped
2 Tbs dill fresh, chopped
½ tsp tarragon fresh

Instructions:
Rinse the grains. Bring water to a boil and simmer the grains for about 15 minutes. Add the ghee, salt and pepper. Stir frequently. Continue cooking for 8-10 minutes longer or until the grains are soft. Add the herbs in the last 3 minutes of cooking with the exception of the cilantro. Remove from heat, add the cilantro, cover and let sit five minutes. Serve with vegetables, soup or salad.

Optional: To make saffron ghee rice, ad 1/8 tsp saffron when adding the ghee, salt and pepper.

Barley

Tridoshic
Serves: 1-2
Ingredients:
1 cup barley
3- 4 cups water
¼- ½ tsp sea salt
1 Tbs ghee

Instructions:
Rinse the barley. Bring water to a boil and add the barley. When it boils again, reduce heat to medium and cook for about 35-40 minutes until grains are soft and fluffy. Mix in the salt and ghee. Great with any vegetable dish or dhal.

Brahma's Barley and Greens

Tridoshic
Serves: 3-4
Ingredients:
2 cups barley
½ cup kale, finely chopped

½ cup collards, finely chopped
4 cups water
¼- ½ tsp sea salt or to taste or Braggs Liquid Amino Acids
½ tsp whole cumin powder
1 inch ginger, grated
1 Tbs cilantro, chopped
2 Tbs ghee

Instructions:
Bring the water to a boil, add the barley and simmer for 35- 40 minutes until soft. While barley cooks, in a saucepan on medium heat, add the ghee, ginger, cumin and greens, and sauté for a few minutes. Remove from heat and cover. When the barley is ready add the spices and greens. Mix well and cook together for a few minutes. Remove from heat, add cilantro, cover and let sit for about 10 minutes. Serve with vegetables, soup, salad or alone.

Prakriti's Barley and Peas

Tridoshic
Serves: 2-4
Ingredients:
2 cups barley
1 cup green peas
3½ cups water
¼- ½ tsp sea salt or to taste or Braggs Liquid Amino Acids
½ tsp whole cumin powder
1 inch ginger, grated
1 Tbs cilantro, chopped
2 Tbs ghee

Instructions:
Bring the water to a boil and simmer the barley for 35- 40 minutes until soft. While barley cooks, in a saucepan on medium heat, add the ghee, ginger, cumin and peas, and sauté for a few minutes.

Remove from heat and cover. When the barley is ready, add the spices and peas. Mix well and cook together for a few minutes. Remove from heat, add cilantro, cover and let sit for about 10 minutes. Serve with vegetables, soup, salad or alone.

Surya's Super Grains

Tridoshic
Serves: 2-3
Ingredients:
1 cup basmati rice
½ cup quinoa
½ cup millet
4 cups water
½ tsp black pepper, freshly ground
¼ - ½ tsp sea salt or Braggs Liquid Amino Acids
2 tsp ghee
1 Tbs cilantro, chopped

Instructions:
Rinse the grains. Bring water to a boil and cook the grains for about 20- 25 minutes or until soft. After 5 minutes of cooking the grains, add the ghee, salt and pepper. Stir frequently. The grains are finished when they are soft. Remove from heat, add the cilantro, cover and let sit five minutes. Serve with vegetables, soup or salad.

Advaita Vedanta Vegetable Quinoa Pulao

Tridoshic
Serves: 2
Ingredients:
1 cup quinoa
3 cups water

274

1 cup chopped vegetables: ¼ cup each of carrots, green peas, broccoli and cauliflower
½ tsp cumin powder
½ tsp cinnamon
¼ tsp black pepper, freshly ground
1/8 tsp clove powder
½ tsp turmeric
¼ tsp coriander powder
¼ tsp sea salt or to taste or Braggs Liquid Amino Acids
2- 3 Tbs ghee

Instructions:
Rinse the quinoa. Bring water to a boil. Meanwhile, heat the ghee in a saucepan and stirfry the quionoa for 2 minutes, stirring constantly. Add the spices and stirfry 2- 3 minutes longer. Add the quinoa and vegetables to the boiling water. Return to a boil, then reduce to medium heat and cook for about 15- 20 minutes or until the quinoa is soft and fluffy. Add more salt if desired. Remove from heat, cover and let sit for five minutes. Serve alone or with other vegetables or soup.

Parvati's Quinoa Pulao

Tridoshic
Serves: 2-3
Ingredients:
1 cup quinoa
3 cups water
1 cup, chopped vegetables: ¼ cup each of beet, tomatoes, red cabbage and eggplant
½ tsp cumin powder
½ tsp cinnamon
¼ tsp black pepper, freshly ground
1/8 tsp clove powder

½ tsp turmeric
¼ tsp coriander powder
¼ tsp sea salt or to taste
2- 3 Tbs ghee

Intructions:
Rinse the quinoa. Bring water to a boil. Meanwhile, heat the ghee in a saucepan and stirfry the quinoa for 3- 4 minutes, stirring the whole time. In the last 2 minutes add the spices. Add the quinoa and vegetables to the boiling water. Bring back to a boil, reduce to medium heat, and cook for about 20 minutes or until the quinoa is soft and fluffy. Add more salt if desired. Remove from heat, cover and let sit for five minutes. Serve alone or with vegetables or soup.

Vishuddha Veggie Quinoa

Tridoshic
Serves: 3-4
Ingredients:
1 cup quinoa
1 cup celery
1 cup carrots grated
1 cup beets, chopped into small pieces
3 cups water
¼- ½ tsp sea salt or 1 Tbs Braggs Liquid Amino Acids
¼- ½ tsp black pepper
1 tsp ghee

Instructions:
Rinse the quinoa. Bring water to a boil and add the quinoa. When it boils again reduce the heat to medium and cook for 10 minutes. Add the vegetables. Cook another 10 mintues or until grains are well done. Add a little extra water if necessary. Mix in the salt, pepper and ghee. Remove from heat, cover and let sit for five minutes. Serve with dhal or a vegetable dish.

Dhal

We are what we think.
All that we are arises with our thoughts.
With our thoughts we make the world.
Speak or act with an impure mind,
And trouble will follow you
As the wheel follows
The ox that draws the cart.
Speak or act with a pure mind,
And happiness will follow you
As your shadow, unshakeable.

— The Buddha

Kali-Flower Dhal

Tridoshic
Serves: 4-5
Ingredients:
3 cups split green mung dhal
1 small cauliflower (2 cups total) cut into small florets
½ cup tomato, finely chopped
1 pinch of hing (asafoetida)
4 Tbs ghee
2- 3 Tbs cilantro, chopped
½ Tbs ginger, freshly grated
1½ tsp cayenne pepper
1 Tbs cumin seeds
½ tsp turmeric powder
¾ cup fresh green peas
7 cups water
2 tsp salt or to taste

Instructions:

Soak dhal for at least an hour then rinse thoroughly. Boil water, add dhal and cook on medium- low until soft (about 25 minutes). Meanwhile, heat ghee in a saucepan on medium heat and add ginger, chilies and cumin. Cook until the cumin turns brown (They will brown quickly.) Add the hing (asafoetida) and cauliflower. Stirfry for 4- 5 minutes, or until slightly browned and partially cooked. Add to the dhal. Add peas and turmeric, and bring to a full boil on high heat. Reduce heat to low, partially cover and cook, stirring occasionally for another 10- 15 mintues until all is soft. Stir frequently to prevent sticking. At the last minute or two, add the salt and ghee. Remove from heat, add cilantro, cover and let sit for a few minutes.

Celestial Cilantro Dhal Fry

Tridoshic, slightly +vata
Serves: 2
Ingredients:
1 cup of yellow split dhal
½ cup green onion, chopped into small pieces.
1 green chilly, chopped
1 tomato, chopped into small pieces
¼ tsp mustard seeds
¼ tsp coriander powder
¼ tsp cumin powder
¼ tspfenugreek seeds
½ tsp of turmeric
1 tsp cayenne
½ inch grated ginger
2 Tbs of ghee
2 cups cilantro, finely chopped
¼ tsp sea salt or to taste

Instructions:
Soak dhal for at least an hour then rinse thoroughly. Cook dhal in a pressure cooker until done. Alternatively, boil in 4 cups of water for 25- 30 minutes until creamy and soft. Place cooked dhal and add ½ cup cold water in a food processor and blend. Heat ghee in a saucepan. Add herbs. When the mustard seeds start to pop, add onion, tomato and ginger. Cook until soft. Add cayenne powder and stirfry for a minute. Add to dhal mixture in a large pot and bring to boil. Simmer for 8- 10 minutes. Remove from heat and stir in the cilantro. Add salt. Cover and let sit for 5 minutes. This tastes great with basmati or cumin rice.

Devi Dhal Fry

Tridoshic, slightly +vata
Serves: 2-3
Ingredients:
1 cup yellow split dhal
½ cup green onion, chopped into small pieces
1 green chilli, chopped
1 tomato, chopped into small pieces
¼ tsp mustard seeds
¼ tsp coriander powder
¼ tsp cumin powder
¼ tsp fenugreek seeds
½ tsp of turmeric
1 tsp cayenne pepper
½ inch grated ginger
2 Tbs of ghee
¼ cup cilantro, finely chopped
½ tsp sea salt or to taste

Instructions:
Soak dhal for at least an hour then rinse thoroughly. Use 2 cups of water and cook the dhal in a pressure cooker until done. Remove dhal, add ½ cup cold water and blend. Heat ghee in a saucepan. Add herbs. When mustard seeds start to pop, add, chopped onion, tomato and ginger. Cook until soft. Add cayenne powder and stirfry for a minute. Add to dhal and bring to boil Simmer for 8- 10 minutes. Remove from heat and add cilantro and salt. This goes great with basmati or cumin rice.

Ganesh's Green Dhal

Tridoshic
Serves: 3-4
Ingredients:
1 cup spinach
1 cup kale
1 cup chard, mustard greens or collards
2 cups green split dhal
3 Tbs ghee
½ tsp cayenne pepper
½ tsp cumin powder
½ tsp coriander powder
¼ tsp turmeric powder
¼ tsp black mustard seeds
¼ tsp black pepper powder
¼ tsp sea salt or to taste
1 Tbs lemon juice
3- 4 Tbs cilantro, chopped
4- 5 cups water

Instructions:
Soak dhal for at least an hour then rinse thoroughly. Boil water, add dhal and cook on medium- low for 20- 25 minutes or until soft. Meanwhile, boil or steam the greens for about five minutes. Add the greens to the dhal when dhal is almost finished cooking. Heat ghee in a pan, add mustard seeds and cook until they pop (takes about 1 minute). Add all ingredients to the dhal except lemon juice and cilantro. Cook for another minute or two and turn off the stove. Mix in lemon juice and cilantro, cover and let sit for five minutes. Serve with rice.

Jagan Mata Makhani Dhal

Tridoshic, slightly +vata
Serves: 2
Ingredients:
½ cup red split dhal
¼ cup yellow mung dhal
¼ cup green split dhal
1 onion, chopped into small pieces
½ cup tomato , finely chopped into small pieces
2 green chilies, chopped into small pieces
¼ tsp fresh ginger, grated
2- 3 Tbs cilantro, finely chopped
½ tsp cumin seeds
¼ tsp cayenne pepper
3 Tbs ghee
1 Tbs lemon juice
Sea salt to taste

Instructions:
Soak dhal for at least an hour, then rinse thoroughly. Boil 4 cups of water and cook dhal on medium- low until soft, for about 25- 30 minutes. Add more water if necessary. Meanwhile, heat ghee in a suace pan. Add seeds. Cook for a few minutes until they pop. Add onion, ginger and green chilies. Stirfry until soft, then add tomato, cayenne and salt, and cook for a minute. Add to dhal and cook for about 5 more minutes. Remove from heat, mix in cilantro and lemon juice, cover and let sit five minutes. Serve with rice.

Mahabharata's Good Morning Mung Dhal

Tridoshic
Serves: 2-3
Ingredients:
2 cups mung dhal
4 cups water
2 Tbs coconut oil or ghee
1 tsp mustard seeds
1 dry red chili, chopped into small pieces
1 tsp ginger finely grated
2 green chili, chopped
½ tsp hing (asafoetida)
2 bay leaves
½ tsp organic raw can sugar (sucanat, turbanado)
¼ tsp sea salt or to taste
½ Tbs fresh grated coconut or 1 Tbs dry coconut flakes

Instructions:
Soak dhal for at least an hour, then rinse thoroughly. Boil water and add mung dhal. Cook on medium- low water until soft, for about 20- 25 minutes. Meanwhile, heat the coconut oil or ghee in a pan. Add the mustard seeds and the dry red chili. Stirfry until the mustard seeds pop. Add the ginger and green chili, and sauté on medium- low heat for a couple of minutes. Add the hing (asafoetida) powder and the bay leaves. Sauté briefly. Add the spices to the dhal. Stir in the sugar and salt to taste. Bring to a boil, cover and simmer for 5 minutes or until the water has been absorbed and the dhal is fully cooked (soft). If it is not fully cooked, then add some more hot water and boil. Stir in the shredded coconut and remove from the flame. Keep covered for 5 minutes before serving.

Mahesvara's Mung Bean Soup

Tridoshic
Serves: 3-4
Ingredients:
1 ½ cups split mung beans
6 cups water
1 tsp turmeric
1 tsp cumin seed
1- inch ginger, freshly grated
3 Tbs, chopped fresh cilantro
2 Tbs ghee
½ tsp sea salt
½ tsp black pepper powder

Instructions:
Soak dhal for at least an hour, then rinse thoroughly. Boil 6 cups of water, add mung beans and turmeric, and then cook on medium-low until soft. Stir occasionally. Heat the ghee in a saucepan. Add the spices to the ghee and stirfry for 1- 2 minutes. When the mung beans are soft add the spices and stir. Cook for another 5 minutes. Remove from heat and mix in the cilantro. Cover and let sit for 5 for minutes before serving.

Amala's Amazing Root Vegetable Dhal

Tridoshic
Serves: 3-4
Ingredients:
1 ½ cups mung dhal
6 cups water
½ cup, chopped carrots
¼ cup, chopped parsnips
¼ cup, chopped beets

¼ tsp turmeric powder
1 tsp cumin seed
½ tsp black mustard seed
½ tsp ginger, freshly grated
1 tsp ground coriander
¼ tsp black pepper powder
2- 3 Tbs cilantro, chopped
1 Tbs ghee
¼- ½ tsp sea salt or to taste

Instructions:
Soak dhal for at least an hour, then rinse thoroughly. Bring water to boil and add dhal. Cook 5 minutes on medium- low and add the vegetables. Stir frequently. When dhal is thoroughly soft, remove from heat. Add salt, black pepper and ginger.

While dhal is cooking, heat the ghee and add the cumin and mustard seeds. Stir until mustard seeds pop. Reduce heat, add the other spices, and stirfry for 1- 2 minutes. When dhal is finished, pour the ghee- spice mixture over it and mix together. Finally, add the cilantro and serve hot. Serve with basmati rice.

Nepal Dhal

Tridoshic
Serves: 3-4
Ingredients:
½ cup green split mung dhal
½ cup yellow split dhal
1 cup red lentil dhal
½ cup channa dhal (chickpeas)
1 onion medium size , finely chopped
1 tomato medium size , finely chopped
1 tsp green chili , finely chopped
1 tsp ginger, grated

½ tsp garlic , finely chopped
½ tsp cayenne pepper
½ tsp turmeric
¼ tsp black pepper powder
1 tsp coriander powder
½ tsp cumin powder
1/8 tsp hing (asafoetida)
4 cardamom pods
3- 4 cloves
½ tsp sea salt
3 tsp lemon juice
½ tsp mustard seeds
3 Tbs ghee
6 cups water

Instructions:

Soak all the dhals together for at least an hour then rinse thoroughly. Cook dhals in 6 cups boiling water and a pinch of salt. Cook on medium- low until soft (30- 40 minutes). Remove from heat. Add 1 cup cold water and mix in a blender. Heat ghee in deep saucepan or pot. Add mustard seeds and chilies. Heat until mustard seeds pop. Add cumin seeds. Add asafetida at the end. Add the onion and sauté until light pink or brown color. Now add chili, ginger and garlic. After 2- 3 minutes, add tomatoes. Now add the dhal mixture into it. Also, add all the dried spices into it with salt. Boil the dhal for 10- 15 minutes adding water if neccessary. When totally cooked, remove from heat. Mix in cilantro, lemon juice, and additional salt to taste. Serve with basmati or cumin rice.

Paramahansa's Palak Channa Dhal

Tridoshic, slightly +vata
Serves: 2-3
Ingredients:
2 cups spinach washed and, chopped
1 cup channa dhal (chickpeas)
2 onions, chopped
1 tsp turmeric
1 tsp cayenne pepper
2 tsp garlic, finely chopped
2 tsp ginger, freshly grated
2 small green chilies, finely chopped
½ tsp cumin powder
½ tsp coriander powder
¼ tsp black pepper powder
2 Tbs cilantro, chopped
3 bay leaves
¼ tsp sea salt or to taste
2 Tbs ghee
4 cups water

Instructions:
Soak chickpeas for at least an hour, then rinse thoroughly. Steam spinach until soft. In 4 cups boiling water, cook channa dhal with salt, pepper and turmeric powder on medium- low until soft (about 25- 30 minutes). Heat ghee in a suace pan and add cumin, chilies, ginger and garlic. Sauté for about 30 seconds. Then add the onions and stirfry until light brown. Next, add the spinach and sauté for five minutes. Add the cayenne and cooked dhal, adding water if necessary. Now add the other spices and bay leaves and cook for another 5 minutes or so until all is well cooked. Remove from heat, mix in the cilantro, and let sit for 5 minutes. Serve with basmati or cumin rice.

Ranganath's Rakta Dhal

Tridoshic, slightly +vata
Serves: 3-4
Ingredients:
2 cups red lentils
2 red onions, chopped into small pieces
1 red bell pepper , finely chopped
1 cup beets , finely chopped
2 tomatoes , finely chopped
½ tsp turmeric powder
½ tsp cayenne powder
½ tsp cumin powder
¼ tsp black pepper powder
½ tsp coriander powder
¼ tsp sea salt or to taste
2- 3 Tbs cilantro, chopped
1 Tbs fresh basil, chopped
1 tsp freshly squeezed lemon juice

Instructions:
Soak dhal for at least an hour, then rinse thoroughly. Boil 4-5 cups of water, add dhal and cook on medium- low for about 20- 25 minutes until almost soft. While the dhal is cooking, heat ghee in a pan or pot add the cumin seeds and lightly roast them. Then add the other spices to the ghee and cook for about a minute. Add the spices and all the vegetables (except the tomato, basil and cilantro) to the dhal. Cook for another 10- 5minutes until the dhal is soft. Add the tomato in the last 5 minutes. Add more water if needed. When finished, add the basil, cilantro and lemon juice. Stir, cover and let sit for 5 minutes. Serve with basmati rice.

Kripa Sagar Dhal

Tridoshic, slightly +kapha
Serves: 2-3
Ingredients:
2 cups yellow mung dhal
¼ cup each of dried dulse or agar, and arame
1 tsp ginger freshly grated
½ tsp garlic, chopped
3 green chilies
2- 3 Tbs cilantro, finely chopped
½ Tbs lemon juice
¼ tsp clove powder
¼ tsp cinnamon powder
¼ tsp turmeric powder
¼ tsp coriander powder
½ tsp cumin seeds
½ tsp mustard seeds
¼ tsp salt or to taste
2 Tbs ghee

Instructions:
Soak dhal for at least an hour, then rinse thoroughly. Soak the seaweed in 1 cup of water for 20 minutes and rinse. Boil 5 cups of water and cook the dhal on medium- low until almost soft. Chop the green chili and ginger together. Meanwhile, make a mixture of all the dry powders in ¼ cup water. Heat ghee in a pot or saucepan and add the mustard seeds. Add ginger, garlic and stir in all the spices. Allow to cook for 2- 3 minutes. Add to the dhal. Additional water may be added if necessary. Cook until the dhal is soft and add the seaweed. Cook for 3- 4 more minutes. Check taste for salt and spiciness. Add cilantro and lemon juice and stir. Cover and let sit for 5 minutes.and serve. This goes great with basmati rice and chapattis.

Shanti Niketam Dhal

Tridoshic, slightly +vata
Serves: 2-3
Ingredients:
4-5 cups water
1 ½ cups split yellow mung dhal
2 Tbs ghee
½ tsp tumeric powder
2 Tbs organic cane sugar (turbinado, sucanat etc)
½ tsp cumin powder
½ tsp coriander
¼ tsp black pepper powder
2 Tbs cilantro, chopped
A pinch (1/8 tsp) of hing (asafoetida)
¼ tsp sea salt or more if desired

Instructions:
Soak dhal for at least an hour, then rinse thoroughly. Bring water to a boil and cook dhal on medium- low for about 30 minutes. When the dhal is soft, add all of the spices and cook for another 10 to 5minutes. Remove from heat, add cilantro, cover, let sit for 5 minutes. Serve with basmati rice, jasmine rice or cumin rice.

Maha Kali Dhal (Spicy!)

Tridoshic
Serves: 3-4
Ingredients:
1 ½ cups mung beans
1 onion, chopped
1 tomato, chopped
4 hot green chilies, chopped
1- inch ginger, freshly grated

3 garlic cloves, finely chopped
½ cup green peas
½ cup carrots, chopped
1 cup spinach, chopped
¼ tsp sea salt
¼ tsp turmeric
1 tsp cayenne pepper
½ tsp mustard seeds
1 tsp cumin seeds
½ tsp coriander powder
½ tsp black pepper powder
Pinch (1/8 tsp) hing (asafoetida)

Instructions:
Soak dhal for at least an hour, then rinse thoroughly. Bring 4-5 cups of water to a boil and turn down to medium. Add the mung beans and turmeric and cook on medium- low until soft (20- 25 minutes). Boil the peas and carrots in another pot for a few minutes until they are cooked. In a stainless steel pot or frying pan, sauté the mustard seeds, cumin seeds and hing (asafoetida). Add in the onions, ginger, garlic and green chilies and stirfry for two or three minutes. Add tomatoes and stirfry for another minute or two. Add everything in with the mung beans. Add some water if the mixture is too thick. Add a little more salt if desired and cook for about 4- 5 minutes. Optional: a half cup of fresh cilantro added at the end is a nice addition.

Sashwat's Super Spinach Dhal

Tridoshic, slightly +vata
Serves: 3-4
Ingredients:
2 cup yellow mung dhal
2 cups fresh spinach , finely chopped

1 tsp ginger freshly grated
½ tsp garlic, chopped
3 green chilies
3 Tbs cilantro, finely chopped
½ Tbs lemon juice
¼ tsp clove powder
¼ tsp cinnamon powder
¼ tsp turmeric powder
¼ tsp coriander powder
½ tsp each cumin
½ tsp mustard seeds
¼ tsp sea salt or to taste
2 Tbs ghee

Instructions:

Soak dhal for at least an hour, then rinse thoroughly. Chop the green chili and ginger together. Make a mixture of all the dry powders in ¼ cup water. Heat ghee in a pot or saucepan and add the seeds. Add ginger, garlic and the mixture of powders. Cook for 2- 3 minutes. Add this to the dhal in a large pot with 8 cups of water. Additional water may be added if necessary. Cook on medium- low until the dhal is soft and then add the spinach. Cook for 3- 4 more minutes. Check taste for salt and spiciness. Add cilantro and lemon juice and stir. Cover and let sit for 5 minutes. Serve with rice.

Sweet and Sour Dhal

Tridoshic
Serves: 1-2
Ingredients:
1 ½ cup split red lentils
4 cups water
½ tsp turmeric powder
1 tsp red chili powder

1 tsp tamarind paste
1 Tbs jaggery or another raw organic cane sugar
1 tsp ghee
1 tsp cumin seeds
1 tsp mustard seeds
3 inches of ginger, finely chopped
4 small green chilies, finely chopped
¼ tsp black pepper powder
1/8 tsp hing (asafetida)
1/8 tsp sea salt or to taste
¼ cup cilantro, chopped

Instructions:
Soak lentils for at least an hour then rinse thoroughly. Boil water and add the split red lentils into it. Then add the tamarind paste, jaggery, red chili powder, turmeric powder and salt. Cook on medium- low heat for 15- 20 minutes or until the lentils is soft but not mashed. Remove from heat. Heat the ghee in another pan. Add mustard seeds and cook until they pop. Now, add the cumin seeds and other spices. Stirfry on medium heat for about 1 minute or until the cumin seeds are slightly browned. Add this to the cooked lentils and stir. Add the cilantro, green chilies and ginger. Cook covered on medium- low heat for 3- 5 minutes. You may add a little water if needed. Serve with rice.

Traditional Kerala Dhal Fry

Tridoshic, +vata
Serves: 3-4
Ingredients:
½ cup red lentils
½ cup split yellow mung dhal
¼ cup channa dhal (chickpeas)

½ tsp garam masala powder (available in most health food stores/ Indian grocery stores)

1½ cups onions, chopped

1 cup tomatoes, chopped

1 tsp turmeric powder

1 tsp red chili powder

6 Tbs ghee

½ tsp salt

3- 4 green chilies, chopped

1 tsp cumin

1 tsp mustard seed

1 tsp garlic , finely chopped

1 tsp ginger freshly grated

1 Tbs lemon juice

4- 5 Tbs cilantro, finely chopped

Instructions:

Soak dhal, lentils and chickpeas for at least an hour then rinse thoroughly. Boil 10 cups of water and cook the beans medium- low until almost soft (approximately 35 minutes). Make sure to stir frequently. Heat the ghee and sauté the onions and garlic. When the onions are a light golden color, add all the spices except the cilantro and lemon juice. Add the spiced onion mixture to the dhal and cook another 15- 20 minutes until beans are completely cooked (soft). Now add the lemon and cilantro, mix in thoroughly, remove from heat, cover and let sit for 5- 10 mintues.

Hanuman Dhal

Tridoshic

Serves: 2-3

Ingredients:

1 cup split green mung dhal

1 cup vegetables, chopped (carrots, green beans and cauliflower)

1 Tbs ghee
½ tsp black mustard seeds
½ tsp cumin seeds
1- inch ginger, freshly grated
¼ tsp turmeric powder
½ tsp chili powder
3 small, chopped green chilies
1 medium onion, chopped
¼ tsp sea salt or to taste
3- 4 Tbs, chopped cilantro

Instructions:
Soak dhal for an hour, then rinse thoroughly. Then blend with 2 cups of fresh water and the ginger, turmeric, salt and chili powder. Chop the onion and chilies. Heat the ghee and add cumin seeds and mustard seeds. When the mustard seeds start popping, add the onions and chilies and sauté for 2 minutes. Add the vegetables. Stirfry for 2 minutes and then add the dhal and stir well. Add everything to 4 cups boiling water. Keep on low flame, stirring frequently, and cook until dhal is soft. When finished, removed from heat and add cilantro. Serve with basmati rice, jasmine rice or other grain dish.

Uma's Universal Dhal

Tridoshic
Serves: 2-3
Ingredients:
2 cup green mung dhal
1 cup tomato, finely chopped
1 tsp ginger, freshly grated
½ tsp garlic, chopped
1- 2 green chilies
2- 3 Tbs cilantro, finely chopped
1 Tbs lemon juice

1 tsp dry dill
1 tsp dry tarragon
1 tsp dry basil powder
¼ tsp oregano
½ tsp cumin seeds
¼ tsp salt or to taste
2 Tbs ghee
5 cups water

Instructions:
Soak dhal for at least an hour, then rinse thoroughly. Boil 5 cups of water and cook the dhal on medium- low until almost soft. Chop the green chili and ginger and mix them together. Make a mixture of all the dry powders in 1/4 cup water. Heat ghee in a pot or saucepan and add the seeds. Add chilli, ginger, garlic and stir in all the other spices. Cook for 2- 3 minutes. Add to the dhal. Additional water may be added if necessary. Cook until the dhal is soft, then add the spinach. Cook for 3- 4 more minutes. Check taste for saltiness and spiciness. Add cilantro and lemon juice and stir. Cover and let sit for 5 minututes. Serve with rice.

Paneer, Tempeh and Tofu Dishes

Note: For all recipes, tofu, tempeh and
paneer are interchangeable.
*We must always bear in mind that we are not going
to be free, but are free already. Every idea that we
are happy or unhappy is a tremendous delusion.*

– Vivekananda

Veda's Very Broccoli and Peas Paneer

Tridoshic, slightly +kapha
Serves: 4
Ingredients:
3 cups broccoli, chopped into small florets
8 oz paneer, tempeh or tofu cut into 1- inch cubes
1 cup green peas
1 large onion, chopped
3- 4 Tbs ghee
1 tsp cumin seeds
¼ tsp coriander powder
¼ tsp turmeric powder
1/8 tsp hing (asafoetida)
¼ tsp black mustard seeds
½ tsp sea salt or to taste
¼ tsp black pepper powder
¾ tsp ginger, grated
¾ tsp garlic, chopped or minced
2- 3 green chili
1 Tbs cilantro, chopped

Instructions:
In a large stainless steel pot, heat 3 cups of water and add the ginger, garlic, green chili and broccoli. Cook for about 7- 8 minutes. Cut the paneer/tempeh/tofu into small cubes. In a saucepan or wok, heat 2 Tbs of ghee. Now, sauté the paneer/tempeh/tofu on medium heat until it is slightly golden brown, then set aside in a separate bowl. In large wok or pan, heat 2 Tbs ghee and sauté the mustard seeds, cumin seeds and, chopped onion. Sauté until the onions become slightly translucent. Now mix in salt, black pepper and spices. Finally, add the paneer/tempeh/tofu and cooked broccoli. Cook whole mixture for 8- 10 minutes. Remove from heat, add the cilantro, cover and let sit for 5 minutes. Serve with rice.

Kalidas's Cashew Paneer

Tridoshic, slightly +kapha
Serves: 2-4
Ingredients:
8 oz paneer, tempeh or tofu cut into 1- inch cubes
2 large onions, chopped
1- 3 tomatoes, chopped
1 Tbs ginger, grated
1 Tbs garlic, minced
2 green chilies
1 tsp fenugreek powder
1 tsp black mustard seeds
15 whole organic cashews
½ -1 tsp cayenne pepper
½ tsp garam masala
¼ tsp turmeric powder
4 Tbs ghcc
1 Tbs cilantro, chopped

Instructions:
In a wok or frying pan, heat 3 Tbs ghee and sauté the paneer/ tempeh/tofu and onions until light golden brown. Put the paneer/ tempeh/tofu and onions in a separate bowl. Heat 1 Tbs ghee and sauté the tomatoes and spices (except the cilantro) for 3- 4 minutes. Now add in the paneer/tempeh/tofu and cashews and cook about 5 more minutes. Remove from heat, mix in cilantro, cover and let sit 5 minutes. Serve with rice, rice noodles or grain dish.

Chili Cashew Paneer

Tridoshic
Serves: 3-4
Ingredients:
8 oz paneer, tempeh or tofu cut in 1- inch cubes
2 large onions, chopped
2 tomatoes, chopped
1 Tbs ginger, grated
1 Tbs garlic, minced
4- 5 hot green or red chilies
1 tsp fenugreek powder
1 tsp black mustard seeds
15 whole organic cashews
1 tsp cayenne pepper
½ tsp garam masala
¼ tsp sea salt
½ tsp organic cane sugar
¼ tsp turmeric powder
4 Tbs ghee
1 Tbs cilantro, chopped

Instructions:
In a wok or frying pan, heat 3 Tbs ghee and sauté the paneer, chilies and onions until light golden brown. Put this in a separate bowl. Heat 1 Tbs ghee and sauté the tomatoes and spices (except the cilantro) for 3- 4 minutes. Now add in the paneer, cashews and sugar, and cook 5 more minutes. Remove from heat, mix in cilantro, cover and let sit 5 minutes. Serve with rice, rice noodles or grain dish.

Prana's Gobi Paneer

Tridoshic, slightly +kapha
Serves: 3-4
Ingredients:
3 cups cauliflower, chopped into small florets
8 oz paneer, tempeh or tofu cut in 1- inch cubes
1 large onion, chopped
3- 4 Tbs ghee
3- 4 whole bay leaves
1 tsp cumin seeds
¼ tsp coriander powder
¼ tsp turmeric powder
1/8 tsp hing (asafoetida)
¼ tsp black mustard seeds
½ tsp sea salt or to taste
¼ tsp black pepper powder fresh ground
¾ tsp ginger, grated
¾ tsp garlic, chopped or minced
2- 3 green chilies
1 Tbs cilantro, chopped

Instructions:
Heat 3 cups of water with the ginger, garlic, green chilies and cauliflower. Cook for about 7- 8 minutes. In a saucepan or wok, heat 2 Tbs of ghee and sauté the paneer/tempeh/tofu on medium heat until slightly golden brown. Put the paneer/tempeh/tofu in a separate bowl. In a large frying pan, heat 2 Tbs ghee and sauté the mustard seeds, cumin seeds and, chopped onion until the onion becomes slightly translucent. Mix in the salt, black pepper and spices. Finally, add the paneer/tempeh/tofu and cooked cauliflower and cook 8- 10 minutes. Remove from heat, add the cilantro, cover and let sit for 5 minutes. Serve with rice.

Prema Rasamrita Paneer

Tridoshic, slightly +kapha
Serves: 3-4
Ingredients:
1 lb paneer, tempeh or tofu cut in 1- inch cubes
2- 3 green chilies, chopped
4 Tbs ghee
2 bay leaf
8- 10 black peppercorns
2 inch cinnamon stick
5 green cardamom pods
10 cloves
1 Tbs ginger, grated
1 Tbs garlic, chopped
2 cups tomato, chopped
1 Tbs red chili powder
1 tsp garam masala powder
¼ tsp sea salt or to taste
2 Tbs raw organic cane sugar
½ tsp fenugreek powder
1 cup organic whole cream (Vegans can replace with 2-3 Tbs nutritional flakes)

Optional: 1- 2 Tbs cilantro, chopped

Instructions:
Heat the ghee in a large wok or stainless steel pot. Sauté the bay leaves, peppercorns, cinnamon, green cardamoms and cloves for 2-3 minutes. Then add ginger, garlic and green chilies, and cook for 2- 3 minutes. Now add the tomato, red chili powder, garam masala powder, sea salt and 1½ cups water. Cover and cook for 10 minutes. Then add the sugar, fenugreek powder and paneer. Cook for about 8 minutes. Add fresh cream. Cook for 2- 3 minutes. Remove from heat. If following the vegan recipe, now mix in the nutritional flakes.

If using cilantro, now is the time to add it in. Cover and let sit for 5 minutes. Serve with rice, rice noodles or grain dish.

Mata Mahesvari's Mater Paneer

Tridoshic, +kapha
Serves: 3-4
Ingredients:
8 oz paneer, extra firm tofu or tempeh cut in 1- inch cubes
1½ cups green peas
½ cup yogurt (Vegans can leave out and instead add 1 heaping Tbs of nutritional flakes at the end with the cilantro)
½ cup tomatoes, chopped
½ cup white or yellow onions
2- 3 green chillies, chopped
3 tsp cilantro, chopped
2- 3 Tbs ghee (if vegan, use Earth Balance Vegan Spread or olive oil)
1 tsp ginger, grated
1 tsp garlic, minced or , finely chopped
1 tsp turmeric powder
1 tsp garam masala
1/8 tsp or a pinch of hing (asafoetida)
¼ tsp black pepper, freshly ground
¼ tsp sea salt or to taste

Instructions:
In a saucepan, stirfry the paneer/tempeh/tofu until lightly golden. In a separate pan, sauté onions and spices until onions are slightly brown. This should take 2- 3 minutes. Add the tomatoes and stirfry a few more minutes. Then add the peas and cook for 4- 5 minutes. Add the yogurt and bring to a simmer. Cook for another 5 minutes or so. Add the paneer/tempeh/tofu and cook for a few more minutes. Remove from heat and add the cilantro. Cover and let sit 5 minutes. Serve with rice or dhal.

Palak Paneer Punyam

Tridoshic, slightly +kapha
Serves: 3-4
Ingredients:
4 cups spinach
8 oz paneer, tempeh or tofu cut in 1- inch cubes
1 large onion, chopped
3- 4 Tbs ghee
3 whole bay leaves
1 tsp cumin seeds
¼ tsp black mustard seeds
¼ tsp sea salt or to taste
¼ tsp black pepper powder fresh ground
¾ tsp ginger, grated
¾ tsp garlic, chopped or minced
1- 2 green chilies
1 tsp garam masala powder

Instructions:
In a large cooking pot, heat 3 cups of water with the ginger, garlic, green chilies and spinach. Cook for about 6- 7 minutes. In a saucepan or wok, heat 2 Tbs of ghee and sauté the paneer, tempeh or tofu on medium heat until they turn, slightly golden brown. Put the paneer/tempeh/tofu in a separate bowl. Heat 2 Tbs ghee and sauté the bay leaves, mustard seeds, cumin seeds and, chopped onion. Sauté until the onions become slightly translucent. Now mix in salt, black pepper and garam masala. Finally, add the paneer/tempeh/tofu and cooked spinach and cook for 6- 7 minutes. Remove from heat, cover and let sit for 5 minutes. Serve with rice, rice noodles or grain dish.

Sahasrara Spicy Garlic Paneer

Tridoshic, slightly +kapha
Serves: 2-4
Ingredients:
½ cup garlic, crushed or chopped
8 oz paneer, tempeh or tofu cut in 1- inch cubes
1 medium onion, chopped
3- 4 Tbs ghee
½ tsp cumin powder
¼ tsp coriander powder
1 tsp cayenne pepper
¼ tsp turmeric powder
1/8 tsp hing (asafoetida)
¼ tsp black mustard seeds
½ tsp sea salt or to taste
¼ tsp black pepper powder fresh ground
¾ tsp ginger, grated
3-4 red hot chili peppers
1 Tbs cilantro, chopped

Instructions:
In a saucepan or wok, heat 2 Tbs ghee and sauté the paneer/tempeh/ tofu on medium heat until slightly golden brown. Put in a separate bowl. Heat 1- 2 Tbs ghee and sauté the garlic, ginger, chilies, mustard seeds and onions for about 5 minutes. Mix in salt, black pepper and spices. Finally, add the paneer/tempeh/tofu and cook 5 minutes. Remove from heat, add the cilantro, cover and let sit for 5 minutes. Serve with rice, rice noodles or grain dish.

Prahlad's Prema Bhakti Paneer and Peas

Tridoshic
Serves: 3
Ingredients:
1lb paneer, tofu or tempeh, cut in 1- inch cubes
4 Tbs green onions
1 cup green peas
2 tsp hot cayenne pepper or 3 green chilies, chopped
2 tsp balsamic vinegar
¼ tsp cumin powder
¼ tsp black mustard seeds
3 large cloves of garlic, minced or, chopped fine
1 tsp ginger, grated
1 Tbs cilantro, chopped
¼ tsp sea salt or to taste
¼ tsp black pepper, freshly ground
2 Tbs ghee

Instructions:
Mix together balsamic vinegar, cayenne, peas, garlic, ginger, onions, sea salt, cumin and paneer. Let this marinate for 20 minutes. Then, in a wok or saucepan, heat the ghee and mustard seeds. Add the paneer/tempeh/tofu and stirfry about 8- 10 minutes. Remove from heat, add cilantro, cover and let sit for 5 minutes. Serve with rice, rice noodles or grain dish.

Shivani's Sweet and Spicy Paneer

Tridoshic, slightly +kapha
Serves: 2-3
Ingredients:
1lb paneer, extra firm tofu or tempeh, cut in 1- inch cubes
4 Tbs green onions

1 Tbs organic cane sugar or agave
2 tsp hot cayenne pepper or 3 green chilies, chopped
1 tsp freshly squeezed lemon juice
3 cloves garlic, minced or, chopped fine
1 tsp ginger, grated
1 Tbs cilantro, chopped
¼ tsp sea salt or to taste
¼ tsp black pepper, freshly ground
2 Tbs ghee

Instructions:
Mix sugar, cayenne, lemon juice, garlic, ginger, onions, sea salt, cilantro and paneer. Marinate for 20 minutes. In a wok or saucepan, heat the ghee and add the paneer/tempeh/tofu (with the marinade). Cook for 10- 15 minutes. Remove from heat, add cilantro, cover and let sit for 15 minutes. Serve with rice, rice noodles or grain dish.

Tyagi's Trascendental Tofu

Tridoshic, slightly +kapha
Serves: 2-3
Ingredients:
1 pound extra firm tofu or tempeh cut in 1- inch cubes
4 Tbs green onions
1 cup chopped bell peppers (red, green or yellow – to make colorful use a little of each!)
2 green chilies, chopped
¼ tsp cumin powder
¼ tsp coriander powder
¼ tsp black mustard seeds
3 cloves garlic, minced or, chopped fine
1 tsp ginger, grated
1 Tbs cilantro, chopped
¼ tsp sea salt or to taste

¼ tsp black pepper, freshly ground
3 Tbs ghee

Instructions:
In a wok or saucepan heat the ghee, black mustard seeds, tofu/tempeh, peppers and garlic, and stirfry for 4- 5 minutes. Then add the other spices and cook for another 6- 7 minutes. Remove from heat and add the cilantro. Cover and let sit for 5 minutes. Serve with rice, rice noodles or grain dish.

Jagadisvari's Paneer Jubilee

Tridoshic, slightly +kapha
Serves: 2-3
Ingredients:
1 lb paneer, tempeh or tofu cut in 1- inch cubes
2 medium tomatoes, chopped into small pieces
2 bell peppers (red, yellow or green, or a combination of the three)
2 yellow or white onions
2 inches ginger, grated
3 Tbs ghee
1 tsp cumin seeds
2 red hot chilies crushed or, chopped
1- 2 green chilies, chopped
1 tsp cayenne pepper
½ tsp turmeric powder
¼ tsp sea salt or to taste
1 Tbs vinegar (red wine or balsamic)
1 tsp garam masala
3- 4 Tbs cilantro, chopped

Instructions:
Soak the paneer, tempeh or tofu in vinegar for 1- 2 hours. In a saucepan, heat 2 Tbs ghee and sauté the paneer, peppers, onions and chilies until light brown. Add 2 Tbs ghee along with the tomatoes

308

and spices (except the cilantro). Cook for 8- 10 minutes. Remove from heat, mix in cilantro, cover and let sit 5 minutes. Serve with rice, rice noodles or grain dish.

Venkatesvara's Vegetable Paneer

Tridoshic
Serves: 3-4
Ingredients:
8 oz paneer, tempeh or tofu cut in 1- inch cubes
1 cup broccoli, chopped into small florets
1 cup cauliflower, chopped into small florets
1 cup carrots, chopped into thin rounds
1 cup greens peas
1 large onion, chopped
3- 4 Tbs ghee
1 tsp cumin seeds
¼ tsp coriander powder
¼ tsp turmeric powder
1/8 tsp hing (asafoetida)
¼ tsp black mustard seeds
½ tsp sea salt or to taste
¼ tsp black pepper powder fresh ground
¾ tsp ginger, grated
¾ tsp garlic, chopped or minced
2 medium green chilies
1 Tbs cilantro, chopped

Instructions:
In a large cooking pot, heat 4 cups of water with the ginger, garlic, green chili and vegetables. Cook for 7- 8 minutes. In a saucepan or wok, heat 2 Tbs of ghee and sauté the paneer/tempeh/tofu on medium heat until slightly golden brown. Put the paneer/tempeh/tofu in a separate bowl. In a large frying pan, heat 2 Tbs ghee and

sauté the mustard seeds, cumin seeds, jalpapenos and, chopped onion. Sauté until the onions become slightly translucent. Mix in salt, black pepper and spices. Now add the paneer/tempeh/tofu and cooked vegetables. Cook for 10 minutes. Remove from heat, add the cilantro, cover and let sit for 5 minutes. Serve with rice, rice noodles or grain dish.

Chutneys

Practice seeing the good in others. With a change of attitude you will be able to see Goodness everywhere you look. Imagine that each person is sent to you by God, and you will be able to be kind and loving to everyone.

— Amma

Rama's Ruby Red Beet Chutney

Tridoshic
Serves: 2-3
Ingredients:
1 cup beets grated
½ cup urad dhal (soak 1- 2 hours before hand)
½ cup shredded coconut
3- 4 red chilies
2- 3 curry leaves
1 small tamarind
1 tsp garlic, chopped
¼ tsp sea salt
¼ tsp black pepper
1-2 Tbs ghee

Instructions:

Heat the ghee and stirfry the urad dhal until it is golden brown. Add the curry leaves, red chilies and garlic, and sauté a few minutes. Next, add the beets and sauté until cooked (3- 4 minutes). Now, add the coconut and sauté for 1- 2 minutes. Let it cool and then mix in a blender with tamarind, sea salt and black pepper. Chutney will be nice and thick. Serve with rice, rice noodles or grain dish.

Shankari's Cilantro Chutney

Tridoshic
Serves: 2-3
Ingredients:
1 cup cilantro
½ cup water
1½ Tbs shredded, unsweetened coconut
1½ Tbs roasted cashews
1 tsp cumin seeds

½ tsp salt
½ inch ginger, grated
1 large clove garlic, chopped
1 green chili pepper, chopped

Instructions:
Combine all ingredients in a blender or food processor and mix for
1- 2 minutes. Serve with curries, rice, dhal or a main dish.

Satya's Super Coconut Chutney

Tridoshic, slightly +kapha
Serves: 2-4
Ingredients:
The meat of one fresh coconut thinly, chopped
3 large cloves of garlic, chopped
2 medium onions (green, white or yellow), chopped
3- 4 fresh mint leaves
¼ tsp sea salt or to taste
1 Tbs ghee
¼ tsp mustard seeds
¼ tsp cumin seeds
A few curry leaves

Instructions:
In a blender or food processor, mix the coconut into a paste. Add
into the coconut, the onion, garlic, salt and mint leaves, and blend
into a smooth paste. Cover and refrigerate. Before serving, heat the
ghee in a saucepan, and sauté first the mustard seeds, then add the
cumin seeds, then finally add the curry leaves. Mix into the chutney
and serve.

Mahisasura Mardini Mint Chutney

Tridoshic
Serves: 3-4
Ingredients:
1 cup fresh mint
½ cup water
1½ Tbs shredded, unsweetened coconut
1 Tbs roasted cashews
1 tsp cumin seeds
½ tsp sea salt
¼ inch ginger, grated
1 large clove garlic, chopped
1 green chili pepper, chopped

Instructions:
Combine all ingredients in a blender or food processor and mix for 1- 2 minutes. Serve with curries, rice, dhal or any main dish.

Tat Tvam Asi Tomato Chutney

Tridoshic
Serves: 3-4
Ingredients:
2 Tbs ghee
1- 2 whole dried red chilies
1 tsp cumin seeds
1- inch stick of cinnamon
2 cups tomatoes well, chopped
3 Tbs organic cane sugar
½ tsp sea salt

Instructions:
Heat the ghee in a large saucepan on medium heat. Add the chilies, cumin seeds and cinnamon stick, and sauté a few minutes until the

cumin seeds turn brown. Now, add the tomatoes, sugar and salt, and sauté for 10- 5minutes until the chutney is relatively dry. It can be served warm, room temperature or chilled.

Tattva Mayi Tomato Mint Chutney

Tridoshic, slightly +pitta
Serves: 3-4
Ingredients:
2 Tbs ghee
¼ cup fresh mint, chopped
1- 2 whole dried red chilies
1 tsp cumin seeds
1- inch whole stick of cinnamon
2 cups tomatoes well, chopped
3 Tbs organic cane sugar
½ tsp sea salt
¼ tsp black pepper fine powder

Instructions:
Heat the ghee in a large saucepan on medium heat. Add the chilies, cumin seeds and cinnamon stick, and sauté a few minutes until the cumin seeds turn brown. Now, add the tomatoes, sugar and salt, and sauté for 10 minutes. Add the mint and sauté for about 5 more minutes or until the chutney is somewhat dry. It can be served warm, room temperature or chilled.

Beverages

My child, never lose courage. Never lose your trust in God or in life. Always be optimistic, no matter what situations you find yourself in. It's very important to be optimistic. Pessimism is a form of darkness, a form of ignorance that prevents God's light from entering into your life. Pessimism is like a curse, an illusory curse created by the illusory mind. Life is filled with God's light, but only by being optimistic will you experience that light.

– Amma

Creamy Chai Delight

Tridoshic
Serves 1-2
Ingredients:
2 cups of water
5 whole cloves
1/16 tsp cinnamon powder
1/8 tsp cardamom powder
1/16 fine ground black pepper powder
½ inch grated ginger or 1 tsp ginger juice
1 heaping tsp organic black tea
2 cups raw organic cow milk (If vegan use almond, hemp, rice milk, etc.)
2 heaping tsp raw organic cane sugar or other sweetner

Instructions:
Bring water to a boil and cook the spices for 2- 3 minutes. Reduce heat and add the black tea and let it cook for 2- 3 more minutes. Add the milk and cook until it is almost boiling. Remove from heat, strain out the tea, add sweetner and enjoy. Vata types should use 3 cups milk to one part water. Pitta types should use equal milk and water. Kapha types can use 3 cups water and 1 part milk. Kapha types may also want to use less sugar or even stevia. If you are sensitive to caffeine, leave out the black tea and skip step 2.

Vishwa's Vanilla Chai

Tridoshic
Serves 1-2
Ingredients:
2 cups of water
1 Tbs organic vanilla extract or 1 heaping tsp vanilla powder
1/16 tsp cinnamon powder

1/8 tsp cardamom powder
½ inch grated ginger or 1 tsp ginger juice
1 heaping tsp organic black tea
2 cups raw organic cow milk. (If vegan use almond, hemp, rice milk, etc)
2 heaping tsps raw organic cane sugar or raw blue agave nectar

Instructions:
Bring water to a boil and cook the spices in it for 2- 3 minutes. Reduce heat, add the black tea and let it cook for 2- 3 more minutes. Add the milk and heat until it is almost boiling. Remove from heat, strain, add vanilla and sweetner and enjoy.
If you are sensitive to caffeine, you can leave out the black tea and skip step 2.

Mount Meru Magical Masala Tea

Tridoshic, slightly +pitta
Ingredients:
½ tsp black pepper powder
½ tsp cardamom powder
½ tsp cinnamon powder
¼ tsp clove powder
1 tsp ginger powder

Instructions:
Mix all the spices together. You can make a large quantity and save it in a glass container. Put ¼ tsp in a cup. Add 8- 12 oz boiling water. Let steep a few minutes and sweeten. If you want to make this a milk masala tea, use equal parts milk (raw cow's milk, hemp, almond or rice) and water; bring just to a boil and pour over spices.

Raw Almond Chai Vijaya

Tridoshic, +kapha
Serves 1
Ingredients:
7- 10 almonds (soaked overnight in a cup of water and then peeled to remove skin)
12 oz of hemp, rice or almond milk
¼ tsp ginger powder
¼ tsp cardamom powder
1/8 tsp cinnamon powder
1/8 tsp black pepper powder finely ground
Pinch of clove powder
1 tsp vanilla extract (optional)
½ tsp honey or organic raw cane sugar (optional)

Instructions:
Combine ingredients in a blender and blend on high for 1- 2 minutes. In the wintertime, add more black pepper and ginger.

Achyut's Almond Date Divinity

Tridoshic, +kapha
Serves 1
Ingredients:
4 almonds (soaked overnight in a cup of water and then peeled to remove skin)
3 dates (Medjool work best) remove seeds
12 oz of hemp, rice or almond milk
¼ tsp ginger powder
¼ tsp cardamom powder
1/8 tsp cinnamon powder
1/8 tsp black pepper powder finely ground
½ tsp organic vanilla extract

1 pinch of clove powder

Instructions:
Combine ingredients in a blender and blend on high for 1- 2 minutes. In the wintertime, add more black pepper and ginger.

Dhanvantari's Date Delicacy

Tridoshic, +kapha
Serves 1
Ingredients:
4- 5 dates (Medjool work best) remove seeds
12 oz of hemp, rice or almond milk
¼ tsp ginger powder
¼ tsp cardamom powder
1/8 tsp cinnamon powder
1/8 tsp black pepper powder finely ground
a pinch of clove powder
¼- ½ tsp organic vanilla extract

Instructions:
Combine ingredients in a blender and mix on high for 1- 2 minutes. In the wintertime, add more black pepper and ginger.

Aum Guru Mata's Ojas Tonic

Tridoshic, +kapha
Serves 1
Ingredients:
10 almonds (soaked overnight and peeled)
3 dates (Medjool work best) with seed removed
8- 12 oz water

Instructions:
Combine ingredients and blend on high for 1- 2 minutes.

He Amba's Herbal Ojas Tonic

Tridoshic, +kapha
Serves 1
Ingredients:
10 almonds (soaked overnight in a cup of water and then peeled to remove skin)
3 dates (Medjool work best) with seeds removed
¼ tsp kapikacchu powder
¼ tsp ashwagandha powder
¼ tsp shatavari powder
¼ tsp maca powder
1 tsp organic vanilla extract
Add extra honey or agave if desired (½- 1 tsp)
12 oz of water

Instructions:
Combine ingredients in a blender and mix on high for 1- 2 minutes.

Sudhamani's Shakti Ojas Tonic

Tridoshic, +kapha
Serves 1
Ingredients:
10 almonds (soaked overnight and peeled)
3 dates (Medjool work best) with seed removed
4- 5 saffron stems
¼ tsp organic vanilla extract
8- 12 oz water

Instructions:
Combine ingredients in a blender and mix on high for 1- 2 minutes.

Tandava Turmeric Milk

Tridoshic
Serves 1
Ingredients:
10 oz raw cow/goat milk, or almond, hemp or rice milk
½ tsp turmeric powder
½ tsp organic raw honey or agave

Instructions:
Add turmeric and milk to a stainless steel pot and bring almost to a boil. Remove from heat. Let it cool for a couple of minutes. Add sweetner. Enjoy.

Gangadhara's Turmeric Ginger Milk

Tridoshic
Serves 1
Ingredients:
12 oz raw cow/goat milk, or almond, hemp or rice milk
½ tsp turmeric powder
½ tsp ginger powder
½- 1 tsp organic raw honey or agave

Instructions
Add spices and milk to a stainless steel pot and bring almost to a boil. Remove from heat. Let it cool for a couple of minutes and add sweetener.

Maha Deva Turmeric Chai

Tridoshic
Serves 1
Ingredients:
12 oz raw cow/goat milk, or almond, hemp, or rice milk

½ tsp turmeric powder
¼ tsp ginger powder
¼ tsp cinnamon powder
1/8 tsp cardamom powder
1/8 tsp clove
1/8 black pepper powder finely ground
½- 1 tsp organic raw honey or agave

Instructions:
Add spicess and milk in a stainless steel saucepan and bring almost to a boil. Remove from heat. Let cool a couple of minutes and add sweetener.

Light of Creation Chai Lassi

Tridoshic
Serves: 1-2
Ingredients:
2/3 cup fresh, organic yogurt
1¼ cups water
¼ tsp ginger powder
¼ tsp ground black pepper
¼ tsp ground cardamom powder
1/8 tsp cinnamon powder
Pinch of clove powder
1 heaping tsp of organic cane sugar (sucanat, turbinado, etc) or honey or agave

Instructions:
In a blender mix all ingredients together for about a minute and enjoy.

Note: If you want this to be a caffeinated chai lassi, use cold black tea instead of water.

Rasya's Cardamom Rose Lassi

Tridoshic
Serves: 1-2
Ingredients:
½ cup fresh, organic yogurt
1¼ cups water
¼ tsp pinch ground cardamom
1 Tbs food grade pure rose water
¼- ½ tsp raw organic cane sugar (sucanat, turbinado, etc) or honey

Instructions:
In a blender mix all ingredients together for about a minute. Strain and enjoy.

Note: If using honey, add it after you pour the lassi into a glass, and stir briskly with a spoon.

Decadent Dakini Chocolate Lassi

Tridoshic, slightly +kapha
Serves: 1-2
Ingredients:
2/3 cup fresh, organic yogurt
1 1/4 cups water
1 heaping Tbs organic cocoa powder
1 tsp organic cane sugar (sucanat, turbinado, etc) or honey

Instructions:
In a blender mix all ingredients together for about a minute. Enjoy.

Cooling Mint Cilantro Lassi

Tridoshic, slightly +kapha
Serves: 1-2
Ingredients:
2/3 cup fresh yogurt
1¼ cups water
½ tsp ginger, freshly grated or ¼ tsp powder
1 Tbs, chopped fresh cilantro
2- 3 fresh mint leaves
¼ tsp cardamom powder
1/8 tsp freshly ground black pepper
1/8 tsp sea salt or Himayalan salt (pinch) to taste

Instructions:
Combine all the ingredients in a blender and mix on high for about 2 minutes. You may strain if you like.
Option 2: Instead of salt, use honey or organic cane sugar (1/4 tsp or so)

Energizing Lassi

Tridoshic
Serves 2
Ingredients:
1½ cups fresh yogurt
2½ cups water
1 heaping tsp maca powder
1 tsp heaping kapikacchu powder (mucuna puriens)
1/8 tsp cinnamon powder
1/8 tsp cardamom powder
1/8 tsp ginger powder
1/8 tsp black pepper powder
1 Tbs organic vanilla extract

1 tsp organic cane sugar (sucanat, turbinado, etc), honey, agave or a pinch of stevia

For those who like it spicy, add a pinch of cayenne pepper and more ginger.

Instructions:

In a blender mix all ingredients together for about a minute. Enjoy.

Maha Rani Tulasi Lassi

Tridoshic

Serves 1-2

Ingredients:

2/3 cup fresh, organic yogurt

1¼ cups water

4 fresh tulasi (holy basil) leaves or 1/8 tsp tulasi powder

1/8 tsp ginger powder

1 small pinch ground black pepper

1 small pinch ground cardamom powder

½ tsp of organic cane sugar (sucanat, turbinado, etc), honey or agave

Instructions:

In a blender, mix all ingredients together for about a minute. Enjoy.

Rasalila Rosehip Lassi

Tridoshic

Serves 1-2

Ingredients:

3/4 cups fresh, organic yogurt

1¼ cup water

1 tsp organic cane sugar (turbinado, sucanat, etc), honey or agave

3- 4 whole rosehips

¼ tsp ground cardamom powder

¼ tsp ginger powder

Instructions:
In a blender mix all the ingredients together for about a minute. Strain and enjoy.

Sweet Surrender Lassi

Tridoshic, slightly + kapha
Serves 1-2
Ingredients:
2/3 cup fresh, organic yogurt
1¼ cups water
1 tsp of organic cane sugar (sucanat, turbinado, etc), honey or agave

Instructions:
Blend ingredients together for a minute or vigorously stir with a spoon. Enjoy.

Vimala Vanilla Lassi

Tridoshic, slightly +kapha
Serves 1-2
Ingredients:
2/3 cup fresh, organic yogurt
1¼ cups water
1 heaping Tbs organic vanilla powder or 2 tsp organic vanilla extract
1 tsp organic cane sugar (sucanat, turbinado, etc) or honey

Instructions:
Blend all ingredients together for about 2 minutes. Enjoy.

Gandharva Ginger Juice

Tridoshic
Serves 1
Ingredients:
2 oz freshly juiced ginger
8 oz water
¼- ½ tsp honey

Instructions:
Put ingredients in a blender and mix for 20 seconds, or stir together in a cup with a spoon.

Jai Ambe Ginger Lemon Juice

Tridoshic, slightly +pitta
Serves 1
Ingredients:
2 oz fresh ginger juice
1 oz freshly squeezed lemon juice
10 oz water
¼- ½ tsp honey

Instructions:
Put ingredients in a blender and mix for 1 minute.

Manipura Ginger Mint

Tridoshic, slightly +pitta
Serves 1
Ingredients:
1 Tbs fresh mint leaves
½ tsp dry ginger or ¼ tsp ginger, freshly grated
¼ tsp finely ground black pepper
12 oz water

¼ tsp honey

Instructions:
Put ingredients in a blender and mix for 1 minute.

Mantrini's Gingerlicious Mint

Tridoshic
Serves 1
Ingredients:
2- 3 oz freshly juiced ginger
8- 10 oz water
1 tsp fresh mint leaves
¼- ½ tsp honey or agave

Instructions:
Put ingredients in a blender and mix for 1 minute.

Indra's Island Paradise

Tridoshic, slightly +pitta
Serves 1
Ingredients:
1 oz freshly squeezed lemon or sweet lime
2 oz fresh pineapple juice
2 oz fresh ginger juice
8 oz water
1 tsp fresh mint leaves
¼ tsp honey

Instructions:
Put all ingredients in a blender and mix for 1 minute.

Lalita's Lemon Ginger Honey Mint

Tridoshic
Serves 1
Ingredients:
2 Tbs freshly squeezed lemon or sweet lime
2 oz fresh ginger juice
8- 10 oz water
1 tsp fresh mint leaves
¼ tsp honey

Instructions:
Put all ingredients in a blender and mix for 1 minute.

Atma Vidya's Refresh and Awake

Tridoshic
Serves 1
Ingredients:
2 Tbs freshly squeezed lemon or sweet lime
2 oz fresh pineapple juice
2 oz pomegranate juice
2 oz fresh ginger juice
6 oz water
1 tsp fresh mint leaves
1/8 tsp cayenne pepper
¼ tsp honey

Instructions:
Put all ingredients in a blender and mix for 1 minute.

Aum Namo Tulasi Maha Rani Mint Delight

Tridoshic
Serves 1
Ingredients:
½ tsp dried tulasi leaves or 4- 5 fresh leaves
1 tsp fresh mint leaves
½ tsp dry ginger or ¼ tsp ginger, freshly grated
¼ tsp finely ground black pepper
12 oz water
¼ tsp honey

Instructions:
Put all ingredients in a blender and mix for 1 minute.

Amritanandamayi's Amazing Alchemy

Tridoshic
Serves 1
Ingredients:
1 Tbs fresh mint leaves
½ tsp ginger, freshly grated
4 oz fresh pineapple juice
8 oz water
¼-1/2 tsp honey

Instructions:
Put all ingredients in a blender and mix for 30 seconds.

Vrndavana Tulsi Mint Delight

Tridoshic
Serves 1
Ingredients:
½ tsp dried tulasi leaves or 4- 5 fresh leaves

1 Tbs fresh mint leaves
1 cup water
¼ tsp honey

Instructions:
Put everythingin a blender and mix for 1 minute.

Arjuna's Apple Mint Cooler

Tridoshic
Serves 1
Ingredients:
8 oz freshly squeezed apple juice
1 Tbs fresh mint leaves
½ tsp honey

Instructions:
Combine the ingredients in a blender and mix for 1 minute.

Aghora Apple Ginger Lemon Mint

Tridoshic
Serves 1
Ingredients:
8 oz freshly squeezed apple juice
2 oz freshly squeezed lemon juice
1 Tbs fresh mint leaves
1 Tbs fresh ginger juice

Instructions:
Combine the ingredients in a blender and mix for 1 minute.

Ramana's Red Delicious

Tridoshic
Serves 1
Ingredients:
5 oz freshly squeezed apple juice
3 oz freshly squeezed red grape juice
1 Tbs fresh ginger juice

Gaia's Green Goddess Juice

Tridoshic
Serves 1
Ingredients:
2 Tbs mint leaves
1 Tbs cilantro leaves
1 tsp ginger juice or ¼ tsp powder
¼- ½ tsp honey or agave
Pinch or more of cayenne pepper
1 tsp spirulina powder
8 oz water or apple juice

Instructions:
Put all the ingredients in a blender and mix for 1 minute.

Ma Amritesvari's Morning Sunrise

Tridoshic
Serves 1
Ingredients:
4 oz orange juice
4 oz pineapple juice
1 tsp ginger juice or 1/8 tsp ginger powder
1 Tbs lemon juice

Optional: mix in 1 tsp spirulina powder

Hrim Kali's Hawaiian Heaven

Tridoshic
Serves 1
Ingredients:
4 oz freshly squeezed orange juice
4 oz freshly squeezed pineapple juice
¼ cup freshly, chopped mango
¼ cup freshly, chopped papaya

Instructions:
Put in blender and mix for 1 minute. Additional supplements like spirulina or open cell chlorella can be added.

Bhaktavatsala's Blue Hawaiian

Tridoshic
Serves 1
Ingredients:
4 oz fresh coconut water
4 oz freshly squeezed pineapple juice
½ cup blueberries
¼ cup mango

Instructions:
Combine the ingredients in a blender and mix for 1 minute.

Nischala's Nectar of Immortality

Tridoshic
Serves 1
Ingredients:
5 oz fresh coconut water

5 oz freshly squeezed pineapple juice
¼ cup blueberries
¼ cup freshly cut mango
¼ cup freshly cut papaya
1 Tbs freshly squeezed lime juice

Instructions:
Combine the ingredients in a blender and mix for 1 minute.

Karunamayi sneha arunodayam nana
Saranagati ninte charanalaye
Amritesvari annapurnnesvari ente
Hrdayam ni, nan cheyta pujaphalam

O' compassionate Mother, You are the awakener of love.
I surrender at Your sacred feet. Immortal Goddess,
Goddess of nourishment, please grant me the
Bliss of worshipping You within my heart.

– Karunamayi Sneha Arunodayam, Bhajanamritam Vol. IV

Glossary

Agni- the digestive fire

Alterative- a substance that alters the blood; blood cleanser

Ama- toxins, undigested food

Amenorrhea- the absence of menstruation

Analgesic- pain relieving substance

Anthelmintic- a substance that kills worms

Antibiotic- a substance that kills bacteria

Antipruritic- a substance that stops itching

Antipyretic- a substance that reduces fever

Antispasmodic- a substance that relieves muscular contraction and spasms

Aperient- a substance that is a mild laxative

Aphrodisiac- a substance that strengthens the reproductive system

Astringent- a substance that causes cellular contraction, dries discharge and reduces leakage

Carminative- a substance that alleviates gas, bloating, and digestive spasms

Demulcent- a soft and mucilaginous substance that protects the mucous membranes

Diaphoretic- a substance that promotes sweating

Diuretic- a substance that promotes urination

Dysmenorrhoea- menstruation with pain

Emetic- a substance that promotes vomiting

Emmenagogue- a substance that promotes menstruation and the circulation of blood into the uterus

Expectorant- a substance that promotes coughing and the removal of phlegm from the lungs

Febrifuge- a substance that reduces fever

Hemostatic- a substance that stops bleeding

Laxative- a substance that promotes bowel movements

Lithotriptic- a substance that dissolves gallstones, kidney and bladder stones

Menorrhagia- excessive menstrual flow

Nervine- a substance that nourishes and relaxes the nervous system

Prabhava- the unique action of a substance

Rajas- the quality responsible for activity, movement, energy

Rasa- the taste of a substance

Rejuvenative- a substance that strengthens, tonfies and nourishes the whole body

Sattva- the quality of purity, light, compassion, peace

Sedative- a substance that tranquilizes the nervous system

Stimulant- a substance that increase circulation, metabolism and organ function

Tamas- the quality of dullness, darkness, inertia

Vasodilator- a substance that relaxes the blood vessels

Vipaka- the post- digestive effect of a substance

Virya- the energetics of a substance

Vulnerary- a substance that helps to heal a wound

Bibliography

Atreya. *Ayurvedic Healing for Women*. New Delhi, India: Motilal Banarsidas, Pvt. Ltd., 2000.

Babu, Dr. Madham Shetty Suresh. *Yoga Ratnakara, Vol. I*. Varanasi, India: Chowkhamba Sanskrit Series, 2005.

Barnard, Neal, M.D. "Doctor in the House." *PETA's Animal Times* Fall 2004: 7.

Barnard, Neal, M.D. *The Power of Your Plate*. Summertown, TN: Book Publishing Co., 1990.

Cole, Sebastian. Ayurvedic Medicine: The Principles of Traditional Practice. Elsevier, Ltd., 2006.

Dash, Vaidya Bhagwan and Sharma, R.K. *Caraka Samhita, Vol. I-VII*. Varanasi, India: Chowkhamba Sanskrit Series, 2005.

Devi, Sri Mata Amritanandamayi. The Awakening of Universal Motherhood: An Address Given by Sri Mata Amritanandamayi Devi at the Global Peace Initiative of Women Religious and Spiritual Leaders at Palais des Nations, Geneva, October 7th, 2002. Amritapuri, India: Mata Amritanandamayi Mission Trust, 2003.

Devi, Sri Mata Amritanandamayi. *For My Children: The Teachings of Her Holiness Sri Mata Amritanandamayi Devi*. Amritapuri, India: Mata Amritanandamayi Mission Trust, 1995.

Devi, Sri Mata Amritanandamayi. *Immortal Light: Advice to Householders*. Amritapuri, India: Mata Amritanandamayi Mission Trust, 2006.

Devi, Sri Mata Amritanandamayi. Living in Harmony: An Address Given by Sri Mata Amritanandamayi Devi at the Millennium World Peace Summit of Religious and Spiritual Leaders at The United Nations General Assembly, August 29th, 2000. Amritapuri, India: Mata Amritanandamayi Mission Trust, 2005.

Devi, Sri Mata Amritanandamayi. May Peace and Happiness Prevail: Keynote Address by Sri Mata Amritanandamayi Devi during the Closing Plenary Session of The Parliament of World's Religions in Barcelona, Spain, on July 13th, 2004.

Amritapuri, India: Mata Amritanandamayi Mission Trust, 2004.

Devi, Sri Mata Amritanandamayi. May Your Hearts Blossom: An Address by Sri Mata Amritanandamayi Devi at the Parliament of the World's Religions, Chicago, September 1993. Amritapuri, India: Mata Amritanandamayi Mission Trust, 2005.

Devi, Sri Mata Amritanandamayi. Unity is Peace: An Address by Sri Mata Amritanandamayi Devi at the Interfaith Celebration in Honor of the 50th Anniversary of The United Nations on October 21st, 1995, at the Cathedral of St. John the Divine, New York. Amritapuri, India: Mata Amritanandamayi Mission Trust, 1996.

Frawley, Dr. David. *Ayurveda and the Mind.* Twin Lakes, WI: Lotus Press, 1997.

Frawley, Dr. David. *Ayurvedic Healing: A Comprehensive Guide.* Salt Lake City, UT: Passage Press, 1989.

Frawley, Dr. David. *Yoga and Ayurveda: Self- Healing and Self- Realization.* Twin Lakes, WI: Lotus Press, 1999.

Frawley, Dr. David and Lad, Dr. Vasant. *The Yoga of Herbs.* Santa Fe, NM: Lotus Press, 1986.

Gerras, Charles. *The Complete Book of Vitamins.* Emmaus, PA: Rodhale Press, 1977.

Joshi, Binod Kumar, Joshi, Geeta, and Sah, Ram Lal. *Vedic Health Care System: Clinical Practice of Sushrutokta Marma Chikitsa and Siravedhan.* New Delhi, India: New Age Books, 2002.

Joshi, Sunil. Ayurvedic Panchakarma: The Science of Healing and Rejuvenation. Twin Lakes, WI: Lotus Press, 1997.

Lad, Dr. Vasant. *Ayurveda: The Science of Self- Healing.* Twin Lakes, WI: Lotus Press, 1984.

Lad, Dr. Vasant. *Textbook of Ayurveda, Vol. I: Fundamental Principles.* Albuquerque, NM: The Ayurvedic Press, 2002.

Lad, Dr. Vasant. Textbook of Ayurveda, Vol. II: A Complete Guide to Clinical Assessment. Albuquerque, NM: The Ayurvedic Press, 2006.

Lanou, Amy. "Healthy Eating for Life for Children." *Physicians' Committee for Responsible Medicine.* New York: John Wiley and Sons, 2002: 49.

Lappe, Frances Moore. *Diet for a Small Planet.* New York, NY: Ballantine Books, 1975.

Manoj, Dr. T. *Ayurveda.* Trivandrum, India: Aims Health Publications, 2000.

Menon, C.V. Narayana, comp. *The Thousand Names of the Divine Mother: Sri Lalita Sahasranama.* Amritapuri, Kerala, India: Mata Amritanandamayi Mission Trust, 2004.

Miller, Dr. Light. *Ayurvedic Remedies.* Twin Lakes, WI: Lotus Press, 1999.

Murthy, Prof. K.R.Srikantha. *Vagbhata's Astanga Hrdayam.* Varanasi, India: Chowkhamba Krishnadas Academy, 2004.

"The Natural Resources Defense Council 25 Year Report." New York, NY: Natural Resources Defense Council.

Paranjpe, Dr. Prakash. *Ayurvedic Medicine: The Living Tradition.* New Delhi, India: Chaukhamba Sanskrit Pratishthan, 2003.

Paranjpe, Dr. Prakash. Indian Medicinal Plants: Forgotten Healers: A Guide to Ayurvedic Herbal Medicine. New Delhi, India: Chaukhamba Sanskrit Pratishthan, 2001.

Pitchford, Paul. *Healing with Whole Foods.* Berkeley, CA: North Atlantic Books, 2002.

Puri, Swami Amritaswarupananda. *From Amma's Heart: Conversations with Sri Mata Amritanandamayi Devi.* Amritapuri, India: Mata Amritanandamayi Mission Trust, 2005.

Puri, Swami Amritaswarupananda, trans. *Man and Nature.* Amritapuri, India: Mata Amritanandamayi Mission Trust, 2005.

Ranade, Dr. Subhash. *Natural Healing Through Ayurveda.* New Delhi, India: Motilal Banarsidas Pvt. Ltd., 1999.

Reinfeld, Mark and Rinaldi, Bo. *Vegan Fusion.* Kapa'a, HI: Thousand Petals Publishing, 2005.

Robbins, John. *The Food Revolution.* Boston, MA: Conari Press, 2001.

Saraswati, Swami Satyananda. *Kali Puja.* New Delhi, India: Devi Mandir Publications, 1996.

Shastri, V.V.Subramanaya. *Tridosha Theory: A Study on the Fundamental Principles of Ayurveda.* Malappuram Dist. Kerala, India: Kottakkal Arya Vaidya Sala Publications Dept., 2000.

Subramuniyaswami, Satguru Sivaya. *How to Win an Argument with a Meat Eater.* Kauai, HI: Himayalan Academy Publications, 2000.

Svoboda, Robert E. *Ayurveda: Life, Health and Longevity.* India: Penguin Books, 1992.

Svoboda, Robert E. *Prakriti: Your Ayurvedic Constitution.* Twin Lakes, MI: Lotus Press, 1999.

Tirtha, Swami Sada Shiva. *The Ayurvedic Encyclopedia.* New Delhi, India: Health Harmony, 2006.

Tiwari, Maya. *Ayurveda Secrets of Healing.* Twin Lakes, WI: Lotus Press, 1995.

"Vegetarian Diets." *Journal of the American Dietetic Association.* Association and Dietitians of Canada, June 2003: 748- 765.

Winter, Ruth. *A Consumer's Dictionary of Food Additives.* New York, NY: Crown Publishers, Inc., 1989, 1984, 1978.

Yogananda, Paramahansa. God Talks with Arjuna: The Bhagavad Gita: The Royal Science of God Realization, Vol. I and II. Dakshineshwar, Kolkata, India: Yogada Satsanga Society of India, 2005.

Website references

American Vegetarian. "Spiritual Basis." 1998 http://www2.acorn.net/doc/avspirit.doc> (Aug. 2000)

American Vegetarian. "Quotable Quotes." January 28, 1998 http://www.acorn.net/av/avquotes.html> (Aug. 2000)

Associated Press. "E. Coli in up to Half of U.S. Cattle." February 29, 2000 http://www.msnbc.com/news/376128.asp?cp1=1 (July 2000)

People for the Ethical Treatment of Animals. "Jesus was a Vegetarian." 2000 http://www.jesusveg.com> (Aug. 2000)

Union of Concerned Scientists. "World Scientists' Warning to Humanity." 1992 ucs@igc.apc.org

Vegan Outreach. "The Transformation of Animals into Food." 2000 http://www.veganoutreach.org/wv/wv2.html (Aug. 2000)

www.ingramcontent.com/pod-product-compliance
Lightning Source LLC
Chambersburg PA
CBHW051413090426
42737CB00014B/2638